D1604336

SATAN & SALEM

25.

1692

The deposition of Ann putnam who testifieth and saith that on the 8th of may
at euening I saw the apperishtion of mr George Burroughs who greviously
tortored me and urged me to writ in his book which I refused then he tould
me that his two first wiues would appere to me presantly and tell me a grat many
lyes but I should not beleue them: then Immediatly appeared to me the forme
of two women in winding sheats and napkins about their heads: at which I was
gratly affrighted: and they turned their faces towards mr Burroughs and
loked very red and angrey and tould him that he had been a cruell man
to them: and that their blood did crie for vengance against him: and also
tould him that they should be cloathed with white robes in heaven when he
should be cast into hell: and Immediatly he vanished away: and as soon as he
was gon the two women turned their faces towards me and looked as pail as
a white wall: and tould me that they wore mr Burroughs two first wiues
and that he had murthered them: and one tould me that she was his first wife
and he stabed hir under the left arme and put a peace of sealing wax on the
wound and she pulled aside the winding sheat and shewed me the place: and
also tould me that she was in the house where mr parish now liues whit it was don
and the other tould me that mr Burroughs and that wife which he hath now
kiled hir in the vessell as she was coming to se hir friends becaus they would haue one another: and they both charged me
that I should tell these things to the majestraits before mr Burroughs face: and if
he did not own them they did not know but that they should appere
their: this morning also mr Lawson and his daughter Ann appeared to me
whom I knew: and tould me that mr Burroughs murthered them: this morning
also apper to me another woman in a winding sheat and tould me that she was
good man fullers first wife and mr Burroughs kiled hir: because there was sum
differance between hir husband and him: also on the 9th may duering the time
of his examination he did most greviously torment and afflect mary walcott
mercy lewes Elex Hubburd and Abigail williams by pinching pricking and choaking them
                                                            Jurat in Curia
we whose names are under writen being present with ann putnam at the
times aboue mentioned: saw hir tortered and hard hir refuse to writ in the
book also hard hir declare what is aboue writen: what she said she saw
and hard from the apperishtion of mr George and from them which acc
for murthering of them

ann putnam: owned this hir testimony to be the
truth upon hir oath before the Jariars of Inquest
this: 3d: of agust 92

Edward putnam
Robert Morrell
Thomos putnam

Satan & Salem

The Witch-Hunt Crisis of 1692

BENJAMIN C. RAY

UNIVERSITY OF VIRGINIA PRESS

Charlottesville and London

University of Virginia Press

© 2015 by the Rector and Visitors of the University of Virginia

Printed in the United States of America on acid-free paper

First published 2015

9 8 7 6 5 4 3 2 1

Library of Congress Cataloging-in-Publication Data

Ray, Benjamin C., 1940–

    Satan and Salem : the witch-hunt crisis of 1692 / Benjamin C. Ray.

    pages cm

    Includes bibliographical references and index.

    ISBN 978-0-8139-3707-6 (cloth : alk. paper) — ISBN 978-0-8139-3708-3 (e-book)

    1. Witch hunting—Massachusetts—Salem—History—17th century. 2. Witchcraft—
Massachusetts—Salem—History. I. Title.

    BF1575.R28 2015

    133.4'3097445—dc23

                                                                2014036306

Frontispiece: Deposition of Ann Putnam Jr. v. George Burroughs, May 8, 1692. (From
the records of the Court of Oyer and Terminer, 1692, property of the Supreme Judicial
Court, Division of Archives and Records Preservation; on deposit at the Peabody
Essex Museum, Salem, Mass.)

To the memory of Joshua Rea, Sarah Rea,

Daniel Rea, and Hepzibah Rea of Salem Village,

signers of the petition for Rebecca Nurse,

May 1692

CONTENTS

ACKNOWLEDGMENTS

It is a pleasure to acknowledge the generosity of several academic colleagues and directors of archives whose assistance has made this book possible. I was fortunate to be able to collaborate with Bernard Rosenthal, who joined me in securing a grant from the National Endowment for the Humanities to produce both a digital archive of the court records, the Salem Witch Trials Documentary Archive (salem.lib.virginia.edu), and a new print edition, *Records of the Salem Witch-Hunt* (*RSWH*), which was published in 2009. Both the new edition, with its accurate transcriptions, introductory essays, and critical notes, and the Salem Witch Trials Documentary Archive, with its extensive primary resources, maps, and digital tools, have been foundational for the writing of the book. I have benefited, too, from two landmark books by colleagues in the field, Bernard Rosenthal's *Salem Story* (1993) and Mary Beth Norton's *In the Devil's Snare* (2002), whose collaborative work and scholarly standards are models of research in this area. Marilynne K. Roach, author of the valuable "Biographical Notes" section of the *RSWH,* has been a helpful colleague in responding to many questions about historical details, both large and small.

Also indispensible has been the assistance of the directors and librarians at several major archives. In 1999, during the early days of archival digitization, directors of archives in Boston and Salem welcomed me to digitize their well-cared-for manuscript collections. William Fowler, former President of the Massachusetts Historical Society, and Peter Drummey, Librarian, supported the scanning of the Society's collection of witch trials court records, which was done with the assistance of Nancy Heywood, Digital Projects Coordinator. Roberta Zhongi, former Keeper of Rare Books and Manuscripts, Boston Public Library, permitted me to digitize the library's collection of court records. Daniel Monroe, Director of the Peabody Essex Museum, and William LaMoy, former Director of the Phillips Library, authorized digitization of many of the library's holdings of court records, with the help of Jane Axelrod and her staff. Over the years, I have returned several times to digitize court records in the Massachusetts Archives, under the helpful supervision of Michael Comeau, Martha Clark, and Elizabeth Bouvier. I also wish to thank Richard Trask, Director of the Danvers Archival Collection, for giving me constant access to the Danvers collection and for his insights into the history of Salem Village. Richard D'Abate, former Director of the Maine Historical Society, and Nicholas Noyes, Curator, have also permitted me to digitize their holdings.

The online Salem Witch Trials Documentary Archive, on whose sources this book depends, was the creation of the University of Virginia's Institute of Advanced Technology, then under supervision its founding director John Unsworth. David Seaman, founding Director of the Electronic Text Center, supervised the creation of the initial website of the court records. Unsworth oversaw the building of the larger Documentary Archive by the institute's capable staff, supervised by Worthy Martin and Daniel Pitti. The Documentary Archive's search tools for the court records have proven to be essential. Michael Furlough, former Director of the University of Virginia Library's Geostat Center, also supervised the creation of the digital maps of Salem Village, Andover, and Salem Town, and Chris Gist of the Scholar's Lab created valuable maps of the Gallows Hill area. The University of Virginia's Special Collections Library digitized its copies of the volumes by Increase Mather, Cotton Mather, and Robert Calef. The Beverly Historical Society kindly permitted the digitization of its rare copy of John Hale's *Modest Enquiry*. The Documentary Archive has now migrated to the Scholar's Lab, University of Virginia Library, under the directorship of Bethany Nowviskie, and Wayne Graham, Head of Research and Development, has continued to improve the Archive's functionality.

Many graduate students have also assisted in the creation of the Archive. Kent McConnell was the Project Director, and Andrea Dickins, Mendy Gladden, Colleen Guilford, Guy Aiken, and Joseph Stuart have done many hours of XML tagging, as well as my neighbor Jane Whitehill Rotch.

I also learned a great deal while preparing historical materials for two documentaries, National Geographic Channel's *Salem Witch Trials Conspiracy* and the Essex Heritage Commission's *Salem Witch-Hunt,* and especially from Executive Producer and Director Tom Phillips, and the production team at Wide-Eyed Entertainment.

My two editors at the University of Virginia Press, Richard Holway and Mark Mones, have done a splendid job of shepherding the manuscript through to print publication and the e-book version. I have benefitted significantly from the initial editing suggestions by David Griffin and later by Linda Rhoades, formerly editor of the *New England Quarterly,* and from

Susan Murray; every author should be so fortunate to have such expert guidance. I am enormously grateful to Professors David Hall and Richard Latner for their careful reading of a draft manuscript and for giving me detailed critical suggestions that have helped to strengthen the book's factual base and its interpretations. Needless to say, I take full responsibility for any problems that remain.

Finally, I owe a debt of gratitude to Dr. Anthony and Christine Patton of Danvers, Massachusetts, for the many days of generous hospitality in their home during years of research visits to Danvers, Salem, and Boston; their friendship and encouragement have constantly inspired my work.

INTRODUCTION
STAINS UPON
OUR LAND

I am afraid that ages will not wear off that reproach and those
stains which these things will leave behind them upon our land.
—*Thomas Brattle*

The notorious Salem witchcraft episode of 1692 is different from any other witch-hunt in New England. More
extreme in every respect, it lasted longer, jailed more suspects, condemned and executed more people, and ranged
over more territory. Soon afterward it was repudiated by
the government as a colossal mistake. The seven months
of prosecutions and executions resulted in 152 arrests, 54
confessions, 28 convictions, 19 executions (by hanging),
and 5 deaths—including that of an infant—due to poor
jail conditions. A seventy-year-old man was crushed to
death with stones; and a Puritan minister was convicted
and hanged as a witch. In the end, twenty-five communities and hundreds of people became involved. The names
of more than 1,400 people appear in the court records,
ranging from accusers, accused, and the family members
of each group to ministers, magistrates, constables, jury
members, jail keepers, and even the blacksmiths who
made the shackles for the accused. For New England,
the toll of arrests and executions and community involvement was breathtaking.

After seven months of relentless witch-hunting, from
March through mid-September 1692, the Boston ministers, the governor, and other leaders realized that the
runaway witch trials court in Salem was threatening to
undermine the stability of the whole Massachusetts Bay
Province. In October 1692, after the Salem court had temporarily recessed following a series of nineteen deadly tri-

als, Thomas Brattle, Boston's distinguished mathematician and the treasurer of Harvard College, took up his pen and spoke his conscience. His now celebrated "Letter," which Brattle circulated among his friends in the Boston legislature when there was an opportunity to take up the question of closing down the special Salem court, was bold and unrelenting. Brattle's criticism, expressed in terms of Enlightenment rationalism, was directed not only at the court's irregular procedures and the taking of innocent life but at the larger question of New England's cherished civil liberties: "if the Devil will be heard against us, and his testimony taken, to the seizing and apprehending of us, our liberty vanishes, and we are fools if we boast of our liberty."[1]

Writing at the same time, the governor of Massachusetts, Sir William Phips, was even more direct. He told his overseers in London that he was compelled to stop the trials because of the devastation of so many lives and because the rampant and illegal seizure of the property of those executed had "threatened this Province with destruccion." No wonder that the governor, whose administration was responsible for initiating the trials, quickly repudiated the whole affair as a great "delusion of the Devil." Also unprecedented in New England were the apologies and monetary restitutions that eventually followed.[2]

Today, it is tempting to suppose that the Salem witch-hunt was the inevitable result of a few simple factors: hysterical girls, gullible judges, and fanatic ministers. But nothing about this complex and widespread series of events was inevitable or simplistic.

Historians have repeatedly asked why Salem's witch-hunt became so widespread, lasted so long, and spiraled so dangerously out of control. Paul Boyer and Stephen Nissenbaum, who wrestled with this question in their landmark book *Salem Possessed,* pointed out that the excesses of the Salem witch-hunt were caused by "something deeper than the kind of chronic, petty squabbles between near neighbors which seem to have been at the root of earlier and far less severe witchcraft episodes in New England."[3] In New England, as in Europe, inexplicable misfortunes, such as the sudden and undiagnosable death of a family member or a prized farm animal, were often attributed to demonic acts—that is, witchcraft—committed by malicious neighbors. But in New England, witchcraft proceedings were relatively rare; they usually involved accusations against only two or three people on any one occasion, and they were confined to a single community. Puritan New Englanders were no less fearful of witches than were the Catholics and

Protestants in Europe, where witch-hunts flourished. But between the mid-1660s and the 1690s, New England ministers and magistrates had kept the lid on the popular willingness to blame personal misfortunes on conflicts with one's neighbors.

The Salem episode began modestly enough. Four afflicted young girls in Salem Village accused three socially marginal women of practicing witchcraft. On their own, these numbers were not exceptional. Soon, however, four more Villagers were accused, and several adults became afflicted. In three weeks, the number of afflicted accusers increased from four to ten. Within six weeks, the accusations quadrupled, and targeted people well outside Salem Village. The Salem authorities were clearly no longer dealing with the usual conflicts that had prompted earlier, smaller witch-hunts.

For historians, the candidates for the "something" that caused the Salem witch-hunt range widely from political uncertainty in Massachusetts at the end of the seventeenth century, to increasingly secular influences upon a religiously conservative society, and, more recently, to the Indian raids along the Maine frontier. None of these key factor interpretations, however, has been taken in itself as satisfactory.

Scholars have recently pointed out that although Massachusetts had been lacking a governor and a charter and a fully operative legal system for some years before the accusations started in March 1692, it was well known by January 1692 that both a new governor and new charter were on the way from London. In the interim, the legal system was functioning well enough for the jails to become filled with witchcraft suspects before the new governor and charter arrived in May 1692.[4] Whatever political uncertainty and lack of higher courts there may have been since 1689, governmental order was operating well enough, and it was on the verge of being fully restored when the outbreak occurred. Moreover, by contemporary standards, the witch-hunt in Salem Village was unremarkable at first, hardly the crisis it became two months later, when the new governor arrived in Boston.

Nor, as Boyer and Nissenbaum proposed in *Salem Possessed,* was Salem Village geographically divided between religiously conservative agrarian accusers in the western part of the Village and their secular and commercially minded victims in the east.[5] An up-to-date map of the accusations in Salem Village (see page 189) does not bear out a geographic and economic division. Such an interpretation also reduces the episode to an easy-to-understand product of modernization—a clash between premodern and modern mentalities. This approach fails to take into account particular decisions and motives of individuals and groups at the various levels of society as well as a number of particular circumstances that contributed to the crisis.

Mary Beth Norton rightly points to the concurrence between the Second Indian War (also known as King William's War) of 1688–97 and the witchcraft accusations in Salem in 1692, two disparate events that were both viewed as the devil's attempt to undermine New England. Norton also indicates that the Salem leaders, magistrates John Hathorne and Jonathan Corwin, who were members of the Governor's Council, ordered the withdrawal of the militia force garrisoned at Fort Royal in Falmouth (now Portland), Maine, thus leaving the northern frontier undefended and open to the supposedly devil-inspired Indian attacks of the 1690s. She proposes that the magistrates' sense of guilt for that fateful decision induced them to zealously prosecute Satan's witches at home, thereby compensating for their failure to resist Satan's forces to the north.[6]

But court records barely mention the Indian war, and only a few accusers of the dozens involved had been caught up in the Second Indian War of 1688 or the earlier King Philip's War of 1675–78. What persuaded the Salem magistrates to zealously prosecute suspected witches was not the Indian attacks on the frontier but the leaders of the local community closer to home: the minister of Salem Village, the influential parents of the afflicted girls, the Village doctor, and several ministers of neighboring communities.

Current in the popular literature is the simplistic theory that the Salem Village girls' afflictions were caused by a biomedical illness of some kind. The court records, however, indicate that the young accusers were alert in the courtroom and did not display symptoms of any medical or mental impairment, such as ergot poisoning or meningitis.[7] That the accusers fell into fits on cue from the magistrates and regained their composure immediately upon performing the so-called "touch test" by touching a defendant in the courtroom (touching a witch supposedly drew off the witch's evil power from the afflicted person) disproves any biomedical explanation of their actions.

On the other side, a few historians have maintained that, from the outset, the accusers intentionally faked their afflictions.[8] In the courtroom, the young accusers were made to confront their alleged tormentors, and they responded as the magistrates expected. Their behavior was conventional, akin to that described in numerous period accounts of witchcraft afflictions. Traumatized by face-to-face encounters with what they believed to be witches wielding demonic powers, the "afflicted" became frightened and played the role that was required of them. In time, they embellished their "fits" with pins stuck in their arms and hands, blood flowing from their lips, and by convulsing and falling down. Whether or not their conduct was always self-conscious and calculated or genuinely traumatized cannot be determined from the court records and contemporary accounts, which furnish evidence for both points of view.

Although no single factor fully explains the dangerous excesses of the Salem trials, a common thread runs through the whole series of events. It is the claim initiated by the four girls in Salem Village that their Christian faith was the target of Satan's attack. This repeated charge is unique to the Salem crisis. The witches were "tormenting" them, the girls insisted, to make them "sign the Devil's book" and join the devil's company as witches themselves. This claim was taken up and amplified by other accusers and by confessed witches as well. Thereafter, accusers and confessors reported seeing specters ("shapes" and "appearances") of witches gathering for worship in the pasture next to the Salem Village minister's house. Satan was trying to subvert the ministry of the new pastor, Reverend Samuel Parris, and turn Salem Village into "the first seat of Satan's Tyranny," as the previous minister declared when he visited the Village, thus confirming Parris's ominous preaching about the devil attacking the Village church. Fear continued to stimulate the young accusers' imaginations. Soon, two dozen witches' specters, then forty, were seen in the Village. In the following months, confessed witches enlarged the scope of the plot: three hundred witches were allegedly seen in Salem Village, and it was said that Satan's aim was to "abolish all the Churches in the land." It was not just the church in Salem Village but New England's foundational institution that was under attack.

The dynamics between the church and the rest of the community of which it was a part are therefore central to understanding what initially happened in Salem Village. The Reverend Parris was a controversial and polarizing figure who became the center of conflict. Even before the first witchcraft accusation had been made, the new minister was preaching inflammatory sermons charging that the devil was trying to "pull down" his church. His warnings about the devil acting against his ministry seemed to explain what was happening, at least to most church members. Parris prepared many depositions against the accused, and the magistrates selected him to record a number of the court's preliminary hearings. After the trials were over, his opponents in Salem Village called him "the beginner and procurer" of the crisis and eventually forced him to leave. Historians have debated the significance of Samuel Parris's involvement, but today his role in the build-up to the witch-hunt is considered crucial.

Still, although Parris's sermons warning of a satanic attack on the Salem Village church seem to have been influential at the outset of the witch-hunt, they did not alone cause or solely sustain the event. Many personal motives, institutional procedures, and unique circumstances were involved. One of the primary aims of the present book is to show that, far from being precipitated by a single key person or circumstance, the Salem crisis was the result of a perfect storm of factors that culminated in a grand moral catastrophe in the still-young English colony of Massachusetts. The Salem witch trials are best studied, then, not as a crime needing to be solved so that blame can be properly ascribed but—as the historical records so richly portray—as a multivalent societal tragedy involving a number of critical factors and several major characters, each with a share of responsibility. Thus, it is essential that we understand the religious and sociocultural context as well as the diverse historical contingencies and individual actions that came together in Essex County in 1692.

Close attention to the court records, for example, clarifies the role of Tituba, the Indian slave of Samuel Parris. For decades, historians have blamed her for triggering the witchcraft accusations when she supposedly performed acts of fortune-telling before the two girls in the Parris household. Neither the court records nor any other contemporary account mentions such rituals. What the records do reveal is how magistrate John Hathorne's interrogation shaped Tituba's confession around the standard Puritan notion of a contract with the devil and the concept of "signing the devil's book." The young afflicted accusers picked up this idea, and it became a common theme among the tormented accusers and those who confessed. Contemporary sources also reveal that Samuel Parris may have forced Tituba to confess before the magistrates. Tituba not only confessed and confirmed the presence of two witchcraft suspects in the Village; she also offered her own original claim: a wider satanic threat, emanating from Boston, was afoot in the Village, and there were more witches waiting in darkness. Thus the witch-hunt began.

In addition to Samuel Parris, Thomas Putnam actively supported the

Salem Village accusers. The court records show that Putnam was the most prolific writer of depositions, mainly on behalf of his daughter Ann Putnam and the five other afflicted Village girls whose courtroom torments and testimony were vital throughout the trials. Putnam also worked closely with the Salem magistrates, who were deeply committed to prosecuting the alleged witches.

The witch trials, however, were not simply a local Salem affair. After the first three months of preliminary hearings and after the establishment of the new government in Boston, the decision to move forward with indictments and trials was made at the highest level, by the governor and his Council in Boston. Nine members of the Governor's Council served as judges on a special Court of Oyer and Terminer ("To Hear and Determine") that adjudicated the witchcraft cases. For three months, witchcraft suspects had filled the local jails, and after the new governor arrived, something had to be done.

Given the scope and complexity of the Salem witch trials, we return to our original question of how they exploded seemingly beyond control. Why did the Salem magistrates, the local ministers, and the Boston government reverse thirty years of judicial restraint in resolving complaints about witchcraft and let the Salem trials get out of hand? The purpose of this book is to explore this question. Salem's distinctiveness lies not in its initial accusations, but in their escalation throughout twenty-five different communities in Essex County until, as the governor realized, the social order was severely threatened.

Previous witch-hunts in New England had remained effectively quarantined within the boundaries of their originating communities. In Salem, the number of accusations accelerated so rapidly that it comes as no surprise that the court records reveal the absence of standard legal constraints from the beginning, and that the girls' dramatic behavior both inside and outside the courtroom had a strong impact on their society, far beyond any previous experience of witchcraft.

A tipping point occurred in mid-April, six weeks into the legal process, with a spate of new accusations followed by new confessions that legitimated the court's mounting prosecutions. In the midst of this acceleration of the legal process, the Reverend George Burroughs, a former minister of Salem Village, came under fire. It was claimed that Burroughs had turned to the dark side and was wreaking revenge on Salem Village, which had previously dismissed him from its pulpit. His specter was seen leading many others in satanic masses next to Samuel Parris's house. The sensational story of a Puritan minister as Satan's high priest attacking the Village began to spread at the same time as the escalation of the accusations by the reckless court. The convergence of these two factors propelled the Salem witch trials into the runaway debacle that they became.

Only recently have historians taken up the question of why the town of Andover, Salem Village's western neighbor, became the locus of the witch-hunt's extensive second phase, which accounted for a third of all the witch-craft accusations. Confessions of guilt became the norm in Andover, further legitimating the legal proceedings and driving the witch trials recklessly forward. Eventually, Andover's absurdly high number of confessions, forty all told, raised questions about the court's procedure, which in turn contributed to the court's eventual closure.

The Salem trials were also exceptional because so much of the courtroom activity focused on the performances of afflictions by a group of six girls and young women from Salem Village, aged between eleven and twenty years old. The court gave extraordinary legal power to these young accusers, who became the prosecution's star witnesses. For seven long months, they were repeatedly called upon to perform their afflictions in court as evidence, thus making the accusations by themselves and by others appear valid in the view of the judges and juries, although most of the later accusations originated from individuals outside the Village whom the girls did not know. Only the "afflicted," as they were called, could see and feel the torments of witches' specters and thus provide "eyewitness" evidence before the magistrates and jury that the court considered objective.

The young afflicted females from Salem Village and later the afflicted women from nearby Andover were given center stage in the Salem courtroom in a stunning reversal of the usual gender roles. Accusers in New England witchcraft cases were mostly adult men. Never before had girls and young unmarried women, who were normally socially and legally powerless—to be "seen and not heard"—in New England's patriarchal society, been given such religious and legal prominence by their parents, ministers, and magistrates. Only when Boston's critics eventually discredited the young Village accusers and their spectral evidence in court did the prosecutions stop.

One of the most significant questions about the Salem trials concerns the court's privileging of so-called spectral evidence, which only the afflicted could see and feel. Such dubious evidence had rarely been used in previous New England witch trials. In Salem, however, almost all the indictments carried the sole charge that the young accusers were "tortured, afflicted, pined, consumed, and wasted" by the invisible specters of the alleged witches, who were said to have tried to force their afflicted victims to sign the devil's book. All of the defendants who were convicted were sent to the gallows on the basis of indictments specifying spectral affliction alone, despite the cautionary advice of Boston's leading ministers about the reliability of such evidence.

A remarkable number of court records of the Salem trials survive today, nearly 950. Most are located in archives in Salem and Boston. These records document the legal proceedings in surprising detail. The bulk of the records that were used in the 1692 proceedings tell the story of the long and complicated legal process.

Thanks to the recent efforts of a team of scholars, that collection of records is now available in a newly edited and expanded edition. *Records of the Salem Witch-Hunt* (Bernard Rosenthal, general editor) was published in 2009. It includes seventy newly collected documents that did not appear in the last compilation, *The Salem Witchcraft Papers,* published in 1977. *Records of the Salem Witch-Hunt* also improves upon former compilations by arranging documents in chronological order. In addition, it includes scholarly notes and extensive introductory essays that explain the legal process and the unique linguistic terms that were employed.

By setting forth the chronology and detailing what happened during the legal proceedings, the new edition goes a long way toward helping us understand more about how the witch-hunt played out over time. It also identifies who was writing the hundreds of documents, most of which involve multiple hands, thus helping scholars identify the key leaders who were driving the legal process forward. Such information is invaluable. Transcriptions of nearly all of the records are online at the Salem Witch Trials Documentary Archive (http://salem.lib.virginia.edu/). The Salem Archive's transcriptions, based on a revised and expanded version of the *Salem Witchcraft Papers,* are searchable by name and date and for any word or phrase, and they are linked to digital images of most of the original manuscripts. This book's citations refer both to the online transcriptions of the court records of the newly edited *Salem Witchcraft Papers* and to the same records in *Records of the Salem Witch-Hunt.*

The court records, however, reveal only part of the story. The rest lies in other, related sources that document what happened outside the courtroom in the months and years before, during, and after the trials. These sources are also available in digital form at the online Salem Archive, and the present work will make full use of them. Two indispensable sources are "The Salem Village Record Book," written by the Village clerk, and the "Church Record Book Belonging to Salem Village," written by Samuel Parris and later by the Reverend Joseph Green. The two books chronicle the social, religious, and economic transactions and conflicts in Salem Village that occurred before, during, and after the arrival of the Reverend Samuel Parris. Another essential source is *The Sermon Notebook of Samuel Parris,* a collection that contains Parris's sermons. It includes the inflammatory sermons he preached leading up to the first accusations and thereafter. Parris's sermons transformed Salem Village's mounting opposition to him into a cosmic battle between God and Satan, creating a highly charged atmosphere in which fears of witchcraft and accusations flourished.

A few eyewitness accounts were also published. The Reverend Deodat Lawson, Salem Village's former minister, wrote the first, soon after the initial accusations and examinations. Published in Boston under the title *A Brief and True Narrative,* it offers a sympathetic account of the Village accusers and their afflictions during the first weeks of the outbreak. An equally revealing account from the opposite perspective is that of Thomas Brattle, who attended some of the proceedings. His privately circulated "Letter," written in early October 1692, is bitingly sarcastic in tone and was designed to expose the magistrates' gullibility, the court's injustice, and the accusers' delusions. Another skeptic's account is Robert Calef's *More Wonders of the Invisible World,* published in 1700, eight years after the end of the witch trials. Calef was a Boston merchant who took an interest in the trials and wrote a critical account based on his own observations and reports from others. The Reverend John Hale of Beverly, an initial supporter of the trials, also wrote an account after realizing that the trials were in error. His book, *A Modest Enquiry into the Nature of Witchcraft,* published in 1697, presents valuable information about the beginning of the girls' afflictions and the legal process. These firsthand descriptions and interpretations of the trials are indispensible sources for any student of the Salem witch-hunt, and they are available in digital form in the online Salem Archive.

The trials were brought to a close in October 1692, after the Reverend Increase Mather, president of Harvard College and Boston's most prominent minister, released a lengthy treatise entitled *Cases of Conscience Concerning Evil Spirits*. Endorsed by Boston's leading ministers, Mather's authoritative book, although late in coming, invalidated spectral evidence and the so-called "touch test" used in the courtroom. Specters, Mather wrote, could take the shape of an innocent person; hence all the testimony about specters tormenting the "afflicted" could no longer be used against the accused. Mather followed up in early October by writing a report that described the coercion used to obtain false confessions that cast doubt upon the use of confessions as evidence of witchcraft. Shortly thereafter the governor closed the special Court of Oyer and Terminer.

In an atmosphere of skepticism and criticism, the governor and the chief magistrate, William Stoughton, attempted to give the Salem trials official legitimation. They commissioned Cotton Mather, Increase Mather's son and an influential Boston minister, to write a full-blown defense. Titled *Wonders of the Invisible World,* Cotton Mather's vindication of the special court's proceedings was rushed into print in October 1692.

It is also important to consider the series of government actions, from the initial eagerness to justify the trials in 1692 to the eventual repudiation of them several years later. It would take years before the government would grant financial restitution to the families of the condemned and executed and clear their names, the last of which were exonerated and cleared from the Massachusetts record only in 2001. That the government eventually acknowledged its mistakes and recognized the devastating effects of the trials on the families of the condemned and executed is a revealing story that is rarely told.

Today's visitors to Salem know that people were executed there for witchcraft in 1692. They may come away without knowing that the nineteen people convicted and executed on Gallows Hill were not in fact worshipping the devil and casting spells, and that they were later declared innocent. Because of the continuing lack of clarity about the innocence or guilt of Salem's "witches," the belief that there was witchcraft in Salem persists today.[9]

The City of Salem in fact trades on the tragedy of 1692 and has long been known as Witch City, with its multiple tourist shops and witch "museums" that tell the story of the witch trials in sensational and generally inaccurate ways. In Salem, the witch trials have become the subject of an entertainment industry—a full-blown exploitation of the tragedy. Various "museum" attractions transform the horror of the witch trials into a fantasy world that offers visitors the opportunity to "reexperience" the events of 1692 in haunted house–like settings. While most so-called witch museums and ghost tours give a nod to the innocence of the accused, they still focus on the ghoulish aspects of the trials (real or imagined). Salem's several witch museums display diorama scenes of screaming and snarling accusers, helpless and cowering defendants, and human bodies hanging from tree limbs. Without these tourist venues, much of the economic vitality of downtown Salem, long abandoned by department stores and retail shops for the nearby shopping mall, would suffer. The festive banners on Salem's lampposts, the emblems on its fire trucks, the shoulder patches on its police officers' uniforms, and even the local newspaper logo all display, as a kind of city emblem, the image of a jaunty-looking witch wearing a pointy hat and flying on a broomstick. The local high school athletic teams also call themselves the "Salem Witches." A statue of the actress Elizabeth Montgomery of the 1960s TV comedy *Bewitched,* shown sitting on a broomstick in her role as the witch Samantha Stephens, stands on the corner of one of Salem's major intersections as a lighthearted depreciation of the horrors of the witch-hunt. A block away is the "Witch House," the former home of Jonathan Corwin, one of the judges on the Court of Oyer and Terminer. The house is owned by the City of Salem and is open to visitors. The Witch House and the National Park Service's Visitor Center are the two tourist venues where the story of the witch-hunt is accurately told.

Tourism in Witch City reaches its peak during Salem's monthlong October attraction called "Haunted Happenings," which culminates in a Halloween parade. The presence of a sizable Wicca community in Salem supports the perception that Salem once harbored real practicing witches who worshipped alternative spirits and cast magic spells, although there is no historical connection between the modern Wicca movement and the Puritans accused of witchcraft in Salem.

The present book is organized chronologically and thematically around central personalities and events of the Salem witch trials, and it makes use of the latest research. The book's ample citations contain links to the extensive collection of relevant documents, source texts, images, and maps that are part of the Salem Witch Trials Documentary Archive (http://

salem.lib.virginia.edu/). With direct access to the primary-source materials via links to web pages in the Salem Archive, the reader can grasp the full documentary contexts of selected citations and quotations.

History is an interpretative enterprise and not just a collection of documents. Answers to historical questions depend on the vantage point the historian takes in relation to the various sources. Every historian will place different emphasis upon the role of key individuals and certain sociopolitical circumstances, and every historian writes with an eye to present-day relevance. Crafting plausible interpretations while not overreaching the sources is the historian's balancing act. The present account aims to maintain a balance between the two and, with links to digitized materials, to offer readers the opportunity to test its interpretations. As the reader will discover, contingencies and ambiguities abound in the historical record. This book, then, not only concerns the history of the Salem witch trials but also lays bare some of the challenges of writing that history. It focuses on how the witch trials unfolded and less on the question of why, which is more limiting and often results in a simplistic verdict of a single cause. The Salem witch trials are not a "cold case" to be solved but a tragedy to be investigated in all its complexity of who, what, where, when, and how.

It is a supreme irony that the Massachusetts Puritans, who fled persecution in England, turned into persecutors in their own adopted land. But the Salem tragedy resonates at a deeper moral level than this historical paradox. Salem's victims, who faced death rather than confess to a lie, have left an indelible mark on American moral consciousness. Salem's acts of heroism and villainy, as well as its moral challenges, appear today quite familiar. Indeed, Arthur Miller's *The Crucible* has made its way into countless high school English literature classes, retelling the tale of the Salem witch trials as an allegory for an America under government repression during the Senator Joe McCarthy era at the time of the Red Scare in the 1950s. In the previous century Nathaniel Hawthorne, feeling anguish at his great-great-grandfather's role as a zealous judge in the witch trials, saw the Salem tragedy as a cautionary tale about humanity's dangerous tendency to fixate on the possibility of evil in the minds of others. Both Hawthorne and Miller saw Salem as a worthy lesson for future generations.

All of those executed in Salem were innocent victims, and some—Rebecca Nurse and the Reverend George Burroughs—have been called

New England's first Christian martyrs. They could have escaped their fate by falsely confessing to being witches in order to save themselves. But they did not, so important to them was their moral conscience and their belief in their innocence before God, despite the prejudices of the court. It is this pathos and humanity, as well as the injustice of the trials and the failure of community, that has carried the story down through three centuries as one of the most vivid moral narratives in the makeup of America's historical imagination.

The story of Salem is the locus classicus of America's concept of the witch-hunt, a sociopolitical phenomenon that periodically erupts at both the local and national level in our society. Thomas Brattle wrote in 1692 that the "ages will not wear off that reproach and those stains which these things will leave behind them upon our land."[10] Later generations of writers have taken Brattle's "reproach" and turned it into an enduring lesson about the ever-present possibilities of religious fanaticism, social prejudice, and governmental persecution of the innocent.

SAMUEL PARRIS AND
THE NEW COVENANT

Christ having begun a new work, it is the main drift of
the Devil to pull it all down.
— *Reverend Samuel Parris, January 1691/2*

This poor village . . . the first seat of Satans Tyranny . . .
the Rendezvous of Devils.
— *Reverend Deodat Lawson, March 1692*

The seaport town of Salem was settled in 1626, and Salem
Village, then called Salem Farms, lay within its boundaries, about five to eight miles inland from the Town center. The distance between Salem Farms and the Town
made the required weekly attendance at the Town's only
church, the First Church, arduous at times, especially in
the winter months. It was equally difficult for the Village
men to travel frequently to Salem for militia training. In
the 1670s and 1680s, Salem Town had granted independent town status to the neighboring villages of Wenham,
Manchester, Beverly, and Marblehead, which were originally part of Salem Town, and authorized them to build
their own churches, choose their own ministers, and levy
their own taxes. Salem Farms, for its part, also wanted to
gain township status and achieve its independence from
the Town's taxes, which accounted for a significant portion of the Town's tax base.

In 1672, the Town granted the Farms the status of a
parish, naming it Salem Village, but would not grant it independence as a fully fledged self-governing town. Salem

gave the Village the right to build its own meetinghouse and appoint a minister, which was the first step toward gaining independence. Salem Village was also allowed to establish its own militia training ground. Members of the Village's wealthy Putnam and Porter families often served as representatives to Salem's governing board of selectmen. Several of the Village's leading men also served as officers in the Salem militia and attained high social standing. But for the time being, Salem Village was still required to pay taxes to Salem and remained subject to the Town's religious and administrative authority, unable to resolve all its internal disputes.

The Town did, however, grant the Village the right to collect taxes from its inhabitants to pay the salary of their minister. Significantly, all the inhabitants of the Village were required to pay the taxes, whether or not they were members of the church. This meant that Village preachers had to satisfy the religious interests of the majority of the Village inhabitants, which proved difficult from the beginning.

During the next seventeen years, three ministers came and went in Salem Village, as factions within the community contested each one in turn. If the ministers had been ordained, they might have enjoyed more security, but the Salem Town authorities would not permit it, this being one of the steps leading to township status. The Village ministers were not ordained and could not administer the sacraments of baptism and the Lord's Supper, which had to be obtained through membership in the First Church in Salem Town.

The Village's conflicts over its ministers could be rancorous, and in each case one faction or another forced the minister out by refusing to collect the taxes required for his salary. In 1682, Jeremiah Watts described the strife within the Village in a letter to the Reverend George Burroughs, who was then serving as its minister. Watts complained that "brother is against brother and neighbors against neighbors, all quarreling and smiting one another." Watts lamented that the Village's incessant bickering kept the people from uniting behind the common cause of gaining independence from the Town. For Watts, the role of the minister involved not only preaching from the pulpit but also uniting the community in spiritual peace. That peace was eluding Salem Village, which for Watts meant that "this is the time of the Antichrist's reign," when religious differences turned into bitterness and division. Watts's remarks would prove to be prophetic.[1]

A year after Watts wrote his letter, the large and influential Putnam family succeeded in ousting Burroughs from the ministry. The Village then hired the Reverend Deodat Lawson, who lasted only five years. By this time, Salem Town had decided to grant the Village the right to ordain its own minister and establish a fully covenanted church. But some in the Village disapproved of Lawson, and the Town authorities also regarded him as an unsuitable candidate. Lawson was therefore dismissed, and the search for a new minister began. In Puritan Massachusetts, there was only one church per settlement, unless it was a large town, and it had to be a Puritan church.

The reason for the disagreement over Lawson does not appear in the records. But Lawson's later friendship with his successor, the Reverend Samuel Parris, and the fact that the same group of Village men who objected to Lawson would later object to Parris suggest that the dispute concerned church polity and the Village's sense of identity.[2] The position of an ordained minister was considered a lifetime post, and whoever filled it would not only serve as the Village's spiritual guide but also become an influential voice in its affairs. After Lawson's departure, a small delegation traveled to Boston to meet with Samuel Parris about his becoming the Village's first ordained minister.

Samuel Parris was born in London in 1653. His father, Thomas Parris, was a plantation owner in Barbados, and Samuel spent part of his youth there. He attended Harvard College in the early 1670s. But when his father died, he had to leave Harvard before obtaining a degree so he could manage his father's estate in Barbados, which he had inherited. Within a few years, however, a declining economy in Barbados forced him to sell his properties, including most of his slaves, at a loss. He returned to Boston and used the proceeds to set himself up as a merchant. During this time he became a member of Boston's First Church, where his uncle, the Reverend John Oxenbridge, was the minister.[3]

Parris did not prosper as a merchant, and so he decided to try his hand at the ministry. In the summer of 1688, as an affiliate of Boston's First Church, he began to serve as a part-time preacher in the frontier settlement of Stow, Massachusetts. It was at this time that a delegation of elders from Salem Village sought him out.

Their choice is curious. During this period, there was a surplus of Harvard graduates looking for parishes, and some had advanced theological degrees. With so many well-qualified candidates in the field, Parris's qualifications seem meager by comparison. Parris had received the requisite clerical education at Harvard, but he had not graduated and had only a few months of part-time experience in the ministry. Perhaps the other potential candidates thought it wise to avoid Salem Village because of its reputation for conflict over its ministers. In any case, the Salem Village record book indicates that Parris was the only person the elders approached.

In the 1680s and 1690s, clerical change was in the air. The pastors of the original settlers were retiring or dying off, and congregations were hiring replacements. Second-generation churches and ministers were diverging from older ecclesiastical forms. Debates about church polity, ministers' salaries, and living arrangements were echoing throughout New England.[4]

It is possible that the elders were attracted to Parris because of his association with Boston's First Church. The First Church was well known for its opposition to the popular Halfway Covenant, a liberal policy instituted in 1662. It was a policy which opened church membership and the sacrament of baptism to more people, a policy that Parris and his allies in Salem Village would also oppose.

The Village elders' negotiations with Parris over his appointment proved difficult and extended over several months. Like other second-generation ministers, Parris wanted a higher salary than his predecessors, and he insisted upon ownership of the Village parsonage. The last delegation to meet with Parris was a group of younger men who were intent on closing the deal but whose authority to negotiate was uncertain. Without having the Village's full endorsement on all points, especially granting him ownership of the Village parsonage, Parris accepted the invitation to become Salem Village's first ordained minister, and his demands for the parsonage and higher salary were granted to him. The men who made these arrangements were members of the large and influential Putnam family of Salem Village or close friends of the Putnams.[5]

When Parris arrived, there were twenty-five Village residents who had become members in full communion of the First Church in Salem Town. They would become the founders of the new Village church, now for the first time in seventeen years authorized to offer baptism and the Lord's Supper.

In preparation for Parris's ordination in November 1689, the First Church in Salem formally released its twenty-five Village residents, so that "they might be a Church of themselves for themselves and their children" in the Village.[6] Almost half of this group were members of the Putnam family.[7] Fourteen other residents were full members of other neighboring churches but, having settled in Salem Village, attended church there because it was nearby. The majority of the adults in Salem Village were not members of any church or were only halfway members.

Salem's three magistrates—Bartholomew Gedney, John Hathorne, and Jonathan Corwin—attended Parris's ordination as representatives of the Town's civil authority. The three men were also assistants to the General Court in Boston and thus influential members of the Bay Colony's central government. Parris's ordination therefore had powerful political backing. The Reverend Nicholas Noyes, the assistant minister of First Church in Salem, ordained Parris as the Village's new minister, and the Reverend John Hale of Beverly and the Reverend Samuel Phillips of nearby Rowley also "imposed hands."[8] Thus the new church was established in Salem Village "by consent with the Approbation of the Magistrates and the neighbor ministers."[9]

According to the historian Harry Stout, the young men educated at Harvard in the 1680s and 1690s were encouraged to be community leaders as the "watchmen and prophets of their generation"[10] In a time of declining religious fervor, Parris arrived in Salem Village with an evangelical mission to expand and enliven the new church. Like other young ministers of his day, Parris was a sacramentalist. The sacraments were the core of the church's mission, and he intended to make the sacrament of the Lord's Supper the cornerstone of church membership.[11] His emphasis on the sacraments in his sermons, especially the importance of the Lord's Supper, stemmed from his desire to engender a lively sense of God's presence in the people's lives. In his ordination sermon in November 1689, Parris accused the Village residents of living for years in "an Egyptian-like disgrace" and for being "out of visible & Sacramental communion with God in his Ordinances," that is, the Lord's Supper and baptism.[12]

Although Parris's opening sermon was a standard Puritan jeremiad describing God's displeasure and urging renewed faith,[13] his claim that his pastorate would remove "God's reproach" from the Village might have stirred some resentment in his congregation. Everyone knew that Salem Town had blocked the Village from having an ordained minister authorized to deliver the sacraments, which it had long wanted. Parris tempered his criticism by declaring that his arrival meant that the community "had found favour in God's eyes" and could finally benefit from "seals of the covenant," the sacraments of baptism and communion. He also insisted that "you are to pay me that Reverence which is due to an Embassadour of Christ Jesus."[14] Despite

Parris's apparent self-assurance about his new position, the Village's fractious behavior toward its previous ministers must have given him pause over his ability to control it.

Parris was impatient to grow his small congregation of twenty-five founding members, and he issued a strong warning to those who refrained from becoming members in full communion. Avoiding the sacraments, Parris said, would be "offensive to God." "The contempt of the sacraments is damnable and destructive," he stressed. "Therefore, you cannot hereafter live without partaking of the ordinances, but you will of necessity heighten your sins by such neglects or omissions." Like his uncle John Oxenbridge at the First Church in Boston, Parris spoke of founding a "pure" church, consisting only of members in full communion—known as God's Holy Elect or visible saints—and able to partake of the sacraments under his spiritual authority. Parris distinguished between the "clean" full members of his church and the "unclean" nonmembers: "I am to make a difference between ye clean & unclean," he announced, "so as to labour to cleanse and purge the one, & confirm & strengthen the other." He would recruit the "unclean" by emphasizing their separateness and promoting the benefits of full communion by which they would obtain the sacraments.[15]

Parris, however, was fighting against the more liberalizing religious currents of his time. Most churches in New England had experienced a decline in full membership and sought to maintain the size of their congregations by embracing the practice of "extended baptism" or halfway membership. This policy did not require a person to stand up before the congregation and give a "relation" of God's grace in their lives. The "halfway" solution allowed baptized members to meet privately with the minister and pledge to "own the covenant" of the church's teachings. As halfway members, they were permitted to baptize their children, but they could not partake of the Lord's Supper or vote in church affairs.

During this period, it was popularly believed that baptism, not the Lord's Supper, was the most important sacrament. Baptism was considered necessary for salvation and sufficient for a family to maintain the much-desired continuity in the covenant. Thus, in 1662, the Halfway Covenant was created so that baptized parents who were not full members could have their children obtain the all-important sacrament of baptism. For a child to die without having been baptized was deemed a "sad intimation" of God's anger. Parents, especially expectant mothers and mothers of newborns, were eager to become halfway members so their children could be "within the protective shelter of God's blessing."[16]

A month after he arrived in Salem Village, Parris announced the procedures for achieving full church membership. People who presented themselves were to relate before the congregation "the Faith and Repentance, wrought in their souls." They were to do this "in their own tongues, & mouths,"[17] and there had to be "some testimony from the Brethren" to endorse an individual's admission to membership. With the passing of the founding generation, however, most New Englanders had lost their religious confidence and so could not, in good conscience, make a public confession that God's grace was guiding their lives.

Two months after announcing the requirements for church membership, Parris and the church brethren decided to restrict access to baptism to full members only, that is, as Parris put it, to "covenant professing believers & their infant seed."[18] Parris and the leaders of the church thereby rejected the Halfway Covenant, which by the 1690s had been adopted by two-thirds of the congregations in Massachusetts, including the mother church in Salem Town, as well as several of Salem Village's neighboring parishes.[19]

Parris's conservatism was risky, as he certainly knew from his uncle's experience. When John Oxenbridge shunned the Halfway Covenant at Boston's First Church in the early 1670s, a large body of his congregation broke away to found the more liberal Third Church. The two congregations continued to quarrel, and in 1671 Oxenbridge warned that if they persisted in quarreling, "Satan and his instruments" might "blow up . . . real division among us, or the repute or report of it," and they would regret these disputes.[20]

But change was in the air, and after the 1660s, disputes within churches increased for a variety of social, economic, and religious reasons. Like Oxenbridge, Parris was not a man to avoid conflict. He and his uncle both believed in a "pure church" made up exclusively of professing members who were in full communion, the Elect or saints, as opposed to a mixed congregation of full and halfway members.[21] Because the majority of adults in Salem Village were not members of any church or were only halfway members, most were now prevented from having their children baptized unless they submitted to a public confession of faith and became full members.

At first, though, Parris's evangelical methods worked. Between January 1690 and January 1691, twenty-seven people joined the Village church, a gratifying sign of the success of Parris's persuasive exhortation from the pulpit. With the influx of new members, mostly women of childbearing age, the full covenant membership more than doubled in size, and Parris began baptizing the new members' children.[22] But that promising trend was soon to change. In the seven months after January 1691, only seven Villagers joined the church. After August 1691, no one was admitted as a full member for nearly two years, and baptisms fell off dramatically.

As early as December 1689, only a month after Parris had been ordained, his opponents took decisive action. Thirty-eight Village men, none of them church members, withheld their tax payments for the minister's salary. Parris did not in fact receive full payment of his salary for the first two years of his tenure.[23] Parris's rejection of the Halfway Covenant in February 1690 coincided with the increased opposition to his ministry. Perhaps, as the editors of Parris's sermons suggest, Parris's decision to limit church membership was intended to block his adversaries, thus denying them the halfway status that would enable them to obtain baptism for their offspring.[24]

In response to this opposition, Parris preached a sermon containing a thinly veiled allusion to himself as being in the same position as Christ betrayed by Judas. "Wicked men," he declared, "will give 30 pieces of silver to be rid of Christ: they would not give half so much for his gracious presence & holy sermons . . . for the maintenance of the pure Religion." In the summer of 1691, as the anti-Parris contingent grew, the minister's sermons took on an increasingly militant tone. "Put on the whole armour of God, that ye may be able to stand against the wiles of the devil," Parris instructed. "Christ furnisheth the believer with skill, strength, Courage, Weapons, & all military accomplishments for Victory." Thus did Parris portray the opposition to his ministry as part of the grand cosmic struggle between the forces of good and evil, God and Satan.[25] A frustrated and angry Parris railed against Village holdouts: "If you are ashamed to own Christ now, to profess him before the World . . . hereafter Christ will be shamed of you."[26]

For the first two years, Parris preached a series of communion sermons on the theme of the "wounded and bruised" Christ. Although he based his sermons on the work of the Puritan theologian William Ames, he disregarded Ames's liberalism. Ames claimed that Christ's suffering was the means of redemption, whereas Parris maintained that Christ's sufferings were caused by "our transgressions" and "our iniquities." He portrayed Christ's agonies in graphic detail: "Look upon him as one that you have pierced & wounded by your sins." He drove home the point that refusing to become a full member of the church and partake of the sacraments was among the most egregious of sins and added to Christ's sufferings.[27]

Parris directed his invective at the Village's large number of unchurched residents, whom the Puritans called the "reprobate." As a matter of policy, they were required to attend church services along with church members. But as custom dictated, they were also required to leave the meetinghouse during the monthly communion services after the scripture readings and preaching. From the beginning, Parris tried to shame this large group before they departed, urging them to stay behind and scolding them for departing: "[W]ill you . . . hide your faces from him as if he were not worth beholding? Oh such of you as are going away from this most lively Ordinance, instead of staying and beholding Christ in communion."[28] Parris would later refer to church members as the "godly" and to nonmembers as the "wicked" and "vile," terms far stronger than the standard Calvinist vocabulary of "unregenerate" and "reprobate." The residents of Salem Village had not previously experienced this kind of overt religious humiliation and ostracism.

Unrelenting in his campaign to engender evangelical fervor, Parris was insensitive to the feelings of the majority, who for seventeen years had been denied the sacraments in their own Village church. He fashioned his sermons pointedly to demarcate the "precious" from "the wicked and unconverted." In so doing, he hoped to prod more of the nonmembers into the covenant and at the same time to castigate those who did not join.

Again drawing a parallel between himself and the abandoned Christ at the time of his Passion, Parris would declare that "all of them [Jesus's disciples] forsook him," making a pointed reference to the majority of Salem Villagers who did not partake of the Lord's Supper. To the saints gathered around the meetinghouse communion table, on the other hand, Parris declared that the Lord's Supper was a means of obtaining God's grace: "It is true Christ is not here in his flesh: but it's as true Christ is here with all his benefits spiritually to all believers as here is bread." Parris boldly proclaimed his own central role: "I have chosen you out of the World. . . . I have separated you from the World. . . . Why it is by Preaching of the word, that a church is born & propagated."[29]

Parris seems to have been motivated by an evangelical piety, learned from his experience of the First Church in Boston, and as Richard Latner suggests, he wanted to renew and purify religion in Salem Village. Led by its conservative minister, the Village church set itself on a course opposite that of the church in Salem Town, which in a more tolerant and inclusive spirit had long before adopted the Halfway Covenant, thus enlarging and broadening its congregation.[30]

In October 1691, at a Village meeting, the reprobate staged a political coup. Five men were elected to form a new tax-rate committee, but unlike the previous two tax-rate committees, none of those voted into office was a church member.[31] The Village meeting was not, of course, a church meeting, and the subject of church polity, particularly that of church membership, could not be raised. But it could deal with this matter indirectly in terms of the minister's salary and property, things the Village as a whole could vote on that would impact the minister and his new policies. The members of the new committee questioned the amount of Parris's salary, and the meeting voted not to levy the taxes to pay for it. The committee also questioned Parris's ownership of the parsonage, which they asserted was Village property, and the meeting expressed uncertainty about the original title to it. Thus, instead of stirring up an evangelical revival, Parris managed to revive the Village's former factionalism. The majority of those attending the meeting were now eager to drive Parris from his post.[32]

At this time, approximately 140 adults, or 70 percent of the mature population, were not full members of the Salem Village church. And most would not have been well disposed toward Parris, who had restricted the means for obtaining baptism for their children. Parris had chosen to associate himself with the influential Putnam families, most of whom were full church members. The Putnams had been involved in the Village leadership and the affairs of the ministry for decades, and they had weathered previous conflicts that were common to Salem Village. Never before, however, had a minister resisted the will of the people and refused to leave. As Boyer and Nissenbaum indicate, "by late 1691 . . . the village had reached the point of total institutional polarization: the church speaking for one group, the Village Committee for another."[33]

Parris's sermons reflected his anger over the unwillingness of more people to join the covenant. To be sure, at this time in the Bay Colony only a minority of people within any Puritan community were full members of a church covenant. But as Larry Gragg has pointed out, the two-year stagnation in membership at the Salem Village church indicates that public opinion had turned against Parris.

In December 1692, Parris's supporters petitioned the county court to enforce the collection of the tax for Parris's salary. The petition described the situation that had developed during 1691, when his salary was cut off. It mentioned the growing influence of "a few" who had "drawn away others" and persuaded even those sympathetic to Parris to "absent themselves" from Village meetings or refrain from casting their votes. Indeed, hardly any meetings were held in the Village during 1691, and so the issue of Parris's unpaid salary remained unaddressed. The meetinghouse was falling into disrepair. Some people were failing to attend church services or meet with him, Parris's record book documents. Enthusiasm was clearly waning, which Parris interpreted as a "slight and neglect" that "did not a little trouble me."[34]

The battle lines were drawn, and Parris fought back. Allusions to Satan were common in Puritan preaching, but as Village opposition mounted, Parris became convinced that the devil was the root cause of the Village's controversy, and his preaching conveyed that message. The editors of Parris's sermons point out that "the Satanic theme dominates his sermons during the four months immediately preceding the witchcraft accusations."[35] Parris had translated local opposition to his ministry into a demonic attack on the Village church, part of a cosmic battle between Satan and Christ.

In early January 1692, Parris declared most explicitly that "Christ having begun a new work, it is the main drift of the Devil to pull it all down."[36] Christ's "new work" was the new Village congregation, under Parris's leadership, and Parris cast his opponents as the devil's minions, who sought to destroy the church in their efforts to get rid of him.

Then the devil struck against the minister in his own home. Given Parris's centrality to the quarrel and the fact that the church elders' emergency meetings were being held in his house, it is not surprising that the two young children in his household would be the first to be emotionally affected by the disturbing events surrounding them. In mid-January 1692,[37] according to the reckoning of his Indian slave Tituba, Parris's nine-year-old daughter, Betty, and eleven-year-old niece, Abigail Williams, began to act strangely. They crawled under chairs, gestured bizarrely, and made "ridiculous speeches."[38] The girls' behavior raised suspicions that they were bewitched.

According to the Reverend John Hale, who wrote an eyewitness account,

Parris initially called in "some Worthy Gentlemen from Salem," namely the Salem magistrates Hathorne, Gedney, and Corwin. He also summoned some "Neighbour Ministers," most likely Hale and Noyes, to observe the afflicted girls in his house. The magistrates and ministers, Hale recorded, "had enquired diligently into the Sufferings of the Afflicted, concluded they were preternatural, and feared the hand of Satan was in them."[39]

Although it is not mentioned in Hale's account, the question with which the ministers and magistrates had to reckon was whether the afflicted girls were directly possessed by the devil himself or were bewitched by acts of witchcraft, that is, by someone making use of the devil's power. In the case of diabolic possession, the girls themselves would be held accountable for attracting the devil to themselves; if witchcraft were involved, the blame would lie with individuals in the Village who had used witchcraft to cause their afflictions. In either case, extensive use of prayer, spiritual counseling, fasting, and Bible readings were the prescribed treatment.

In this regard, Parris appears to have initially followed the example of Cotton Mather. Hale tells us that Mather's recent publication *Memorable Providences* described his handling of the bewitched Goodwin children in Boston in 1688 and was widely known. Mather and another individual had brought two of the afflicted Goodwin girls to their homes, where they were kept under close observation and subjected to extensive prayer and counseling until their torments ceased. Hale also notes that the local magistrates and ministers advised Parris to pursue such a path: he "should sit still and wait upon the Providence of God to see what time might discover."[40]

In the Goodwin case, a physician was eventually called to diagnose the cause of the children's torments, and he pronounced them bewitched. Hale reports that Parris did likewise: he summoned several physicians to examine the children, and they concluded the children's fits were preternatural and the "hand of Satan" was involved. After several weeks, when, according to Hale, the children "still . . . grew worse," Parris called in another physician, whom local tradition says was Dr. William Griggs. Griggs declared, apparently definitively, that the children were under "the evil hand." The best estimate for the date of Griggs's diagnosis is mid-February 1692.[41]

Dr. Griggs, who had recently moved from Gloucester to a home near Salem Village, was one of the few doctors in the vicinity. It is also likely that Parris knew him from his days at Boston's First Church, where Griggs's wife, Rachel, was a member and where their children had been baptized.[42] Parris would later list Griggs as a church member in Salem Village, perhaps because of his full membership in some other church before moving to the Village community. During the 1670s and 1680s, Griggs had served on several grand juries in Essex County, which were supervised by some of the same magistrates who would conduct the Salem trials. Griggs was therefore known to the Salem magistrates, and they would have trusted his judgment.

It has also been suggested that Griggs made the witchcraft diagnosis in order to gain Parris's favor in the Salem Village community, where he was eager to establish his medical practice. Whatever Griggs's motives may have been, it was one of the prerogatives of the medical profession to diagnose witchcraft in cases of unknown illnesses. Indeed, the Salem court records mention several other doctors who made the same diagnosis about individuals whose symptoms seemed medically unknown and untreatable.[43]

About a month after the two girls in Parris's house became stricken, Thomas Putnam's twelve-year-old daughter, Ann, and Dr. Griggs's seventeen-year-old niece, Elizabeth Hubbard, also became afflicted in the same manner as Parris's daughter and niece. Hale does not say precisely at what point Parris called in Griggs for a diagnosis. But afterward, according to Hale, "the neighbours quickly took up [Griggs's diagnosis] and concluded they [the girls] were bewitched."[44] Mather had noted in *Memorable Providences* that a physician's diagnosis in Boston legitimated the arrest and examination of the washerwoman Goodwife Ann Glover, who was then tried and executed. Hale tells us that the Salem magistrates used Mather's account of the Glover case as one of their legal guides.

If Parris's dark preaching about Satan's machinations in the Village had influenced the girls in his household, their repeated afflictions had a reciprocal effect on his preaching. Parris redoubled his pulpit offensive against Village opposition. In mid-February 1692, he charged that "for our slighting of Christ Jesus, God is angry and sending forth destroyers." God was punishing the Village for its dispute over its minister by sending forth his demons to influence his foes and afflict the girls. Still, Parris encouraged his listeners not "to be offended at the present low condition of the Church in the midst of its enemies."[45]

In a sermon, delivered just two weeks before his daughter and niece voiced their first accusations, Parris told his congregation that "assistants of Satan" were at work in Salem Village. These words would have constituted a formal charge of witchcraft had they been directed toward a particular individual. Sometime in mid-February, then, Parris's suspicions were confirmed by Dr. Griggs's diagnosis. Soon thereafter, Mary Sibley, a neighbor of Parris's and a new church member, secretly told Parris's slave John Indian to make a "witch cake" from the children's urine and rye meal. It would be fed to a dog and burned in a fire, with the result that the children would be able to name their tormentors.[46]

Parris would later say that it was John Indian who made the witch cake, but Tituba, according to Hale's account, admitted to having a hand in it. Parris then denounced the witch-cake procedure before his congregation as a "Diabolical means." For him it was a turning point in the whole affair; and he declared that "by this means . . . the Devil hath been raised." For the first time, the girls were able to name their tormentors, whose "apparitions" they saw. The witch-cake test was an occult procedure, which Parris decried as "going to the Devil for help against the Devil." But it confirmed for Parris and his congregation that witchcraft was at work, and it led to the first accusations of February 29.[47]

After several weeks of treatment by prayer and fasting had failed, Parris now shifted to an aggressive posture. He blamed Mary Sibley before the assembled church members for "raising" the devil. He presented this interpretation after five accusations and examinations had taken place, saying that the devil's "rage is vehement and terrible, and when he shall be silenced, the Lord only knows." In this way, Parris distanced himself from any direct involvement, even though the afflictions had started in his own household; and he implied that there was more demonic turmoil to come.

During the previous months, Parris's foreboding sermons had created the perfect climate in which fears of witchcraft could flourish. He reinforced that climate by making a public spectacle of the girls' disturbing behavior. To quote Hale again:

There were two or three private Fasts at the Ministers House, one of which was kept by sundry Neighbour Ministers, and after this, another in Publick at the Village, and several days afterwards of publick Humiliation, during these molestations, not only there, but in other Congregations for them. And one General Fast by Order of the General Court, observed throughout the Bay Province to seek the Lord that he would rebuke Satan.[48]

Sunday after Sunday, Parris had framed the escalating struggle over his ministry as a demonic attack on his church. The Village girls also performed their afflictions during worship services, as the previous Village minister, Reverend Deodat Lawson, saw for himself when he visited.[49] Thus, as Larry Gragg points out, it appears that Parris eventually decided not to continue with the isolation therapy described by Cotton Mather in the case of two of the Goodwin children until their afflictions stopped. In his diary, Mather says that at the beginning of the outbreak in Salem Village he offered to take all six of the afflicted girls, to "see whether . . . *Prayer* and *Fasting* would not put an end unto these heavy Trials," but his offer was declined.[50] Had Parris and the families of the girls agreed to do this, it seems obvious that the afflictions would have stopped and the authorities would have been given time to reconsider further legal action.

Indeed, if Parris had wanted to calm down the excitement, he might have sent Abigail Williams away from the turmoil, as he had his daughter Betty, whom he placed with Stephen Sewall, a relative of his wife's, in Salem Town. He not only kept Abigail at home but wrote ten depositions on her behalf. As we shall see, Abigail was also instrumental in ramping up the number of witches reported to be gathering in the Village outside Parris's house. What, then, was Parris's motive for keeping Abigail at home and endorsing her accusations? We shall never know, of course, but it would appear that her accusations were useful to him, even though she was underage, and he wanted to keep her at home to manage her activity as one of the "afflicted" girls for purposes of prosecution.

Given the Village's continued exposure to the afflicted girls, there is little wonder that members of Parris's congregation would attribute the children's disturbing behavior to the presence of the devil's agents—witches—in the Village. Was Parris using the display of the girls' afflictions to win more church members, as the editors of his sermons suggest?[51] This is a tempting speculation, but it is unsupported by the evidence. Church membership remained stagnant, and Parris's opponents would continue to refuse to pay his salary.

––––––––––

Who was it that the girls first blamed for their torments? The initial complaints and arrest warrants, dated February 29, named Sarah Good, Sarah Osborne, and Tituba in that order. Good's arrest warrant was written out separately from the two others, whose warrants were combined, and she was the first to be examined. If this sequence and the evidence of the examinations is a clue, then thirty-eight-year-old Sarah Good may have been the first to have been accused and thus the first to trigger the accusations. Good, in fact, was the only one to have confronted Parris directly at his house in a face-to-face encounter in what was understood to be a threatening manner, which was, perhaps, observed by the two girls. The examination record explains how it happened.

Sarah Good, her husband, William Good, a weaver, and their five-year-old daughter, Dorothy, were impoverished residents of Salem Village, living in rented rooms. Sarah Good's examination indicates that she had a reputation for begging and grumbling when she went away from people's houses. The records refer to Good's turning away from Parris's house and muttering indistinguishable words after Parris had given her something for her child.[52] Neighborly charity was a moral norm in Puritan society, and refusal to comply with a neighbor's request for food, or to give it grudgingly, was a common context for witchcraft accusations. If a misfortune befell the family of the person who declined a neighbor's request or granted it reluctantly, he or she sometimes suspected that the individual turned away was seeking revenge by secret acts of witchcraft; if cross words were spoken or an angry look given, they could be interpreted as casting a spell. John Hale's account put it succinctly: "If after anger between neighbors mischief followed, this oft bred suspicion of witchcraft in the matter."[53]

Thus magistrate Hathorne asked Sarah Good, "why did you go away muttering from Mr. Paris house[?]" Good denied that her words caused any ill effect, saying she did "noe harme" to the children and "never did noe harme to mr parr[is]."[54] Hathorne persisted with this line of questioning: "what is it that you say when you goe muttering away from persons houses[?]" She answered that she was reciting a psalm and stumbled her way through some verses. In summarizing the case against her, Attorney General Thomas Newton wrote: "S[arah] G[ood]: mumbled when she went away from Mr Parriss & the Children after hurt."[55] Newton's notation about Good's mumbling upon leaving Parris's doorway and the girls being "hurt" immediately afterward comes close to answering the question about who initially was perceived to have caused the afflictions of the girls in the Parris household.

Perhaps the girls had been standing at the doorway when Parris opened it, and they may have overheard what they believed to have been a curse as

Good muttered some words as she departed. In any case Parris must have related the incident to the magistrates so they would question her about it and use it against her. Whether the girls' fears about Good's mumbling (and possibly uttering a curse) provoked their afflictions or whether Parris represented it to the magistrates as the cause is unknown. But Good's apparition may have been the first that the girls identified, hence she became the first to be examined.

The magistrates turned next to the middle-aged Sarah Osborne.[56] Everyone in the Village knew that Osborne had turned her back on the church and had not attended for more than a year. She and her husband were also embroiled in a bitter inheritance dispute with the Putnam family.[57] In response to Hathorne's interrogation, Osborne denied any knowledge of evil spirits or the devil and denied causing the girls' torments. When the magistrates told her that Good had identified her as the person hurting the children, she responded, "I do not know that the devil goes about in my likeness to doe any hurt." In making this defense, she was the first person to explicitly challenge the magistrates' key assumption that spectral evidence—the seeing of a suspect's "shape" or "likeness"—was proof that the suspect was guilty. As Osborne implied, the devil might take her likeness and use it to hurt someone, but she herself could be entirely innocent. Osborne's objection was not original; others would make the same defense, and the Boston ministers would also raise it as an objection. It would eventually emerge as the key criticism of the trials.

Hathorne then told the girls "to see if they did know her" on the basis of the specter that they claimed to have seen. They immediately identified her as one of the women causing their torments and accused her of being a witch. Osborne was asked to explain what she meant when she had been heard to say that she was "more like to be bewitched then that she was a witch." She said that she had once been frightened at night by "a thing like an Indian all black" that bewitched her and pulled her out of bed. Someone in the audience called out that Osborne had said that "shee would never believe that lying spirit any more." Questioned about the "lying spirit," she said that it had told her not to attend church. Hathorne responded by accusing Osborne of yielding to "the devil." Apparently interpreting her long absence from church as deliberate compliance with the devil's orders, and therefore evidence that she was an enemy of the church, Hathorne ordered her to be held for trial. Later, Thomas Putnam wrote a deposition on behalf of his twelve-year-old daughter, Ann, claiming that she was first tormented by Osborne on February 25.[58]

The third defendant, Tituba, Parris's Indian slave, was examined immediately after Osborne. She confirmed that both Good and Osborne were witches and, more alarmingly, revealed that there were more witches to be found. As we shall see, Parris may have beaten Tituba to make her confess to witchcraft and name others. The court records show that her convincing confession propelled the legal process forward, far beyond what Parris or the magistrates may have imagined.

2

TITUBA'S CONFESSION

Titibe what evil spirit have you familiarity with?
— *Magistrate John Hathorne, March 1, 1692*

For more than a century, historians and popular writers have been intrigued by Samuel Parris's enslaved Indian, Tituba. Tituba has, until recently, been cast as a voodoo-practicing Caribbean-Indian slave (or African American or African slave) whose fortune-telling séances frightened the two young girls in Parris's home, prompting them to accuse her and others of witchcraft, thus precipitating the witch trials. Despite its enduring currency, scholars have recently dismissed this interpretation of Tituba as the "dark Eve" who lured Satan to Salem Village. No evidence to support it has been found in the seventeenth-century sources; rather, it springs from the imaginations of nineteenth-century historians and storytellers. Later writers also changed Tituba's ethnicity from Indian in the court records (mentioned consistently twenty-six times) to half-Indian, half–African American, to, in Arthur Miller's play *The Crucible,* fully African American.[1] The best historical evidence suggests that Tituba was originally from the Caribbean. Parris appears to have brought her with him, together with her husband, John Indian, from Barbados to Boston and then to Salem Village.[2]

Tituba was the third person to be examined after Sarah Good and Sarah Osborne, all on the same day, March 1. She confessed to bewitching the afflicted girls of

Parris's household and convinced the magistrates that Good and Osborne were witches. But she did not stop there. Under the pressure of Hathorne's questioning, Tituba divulged that there were more witches abroad, as many as nine, all recruited by the devil, "some in Boston & Some here." Their purpose, she indicated, was to attack the minister's children and the children of Thomas Putnam and Dr. Griggs. With this shocking news of a sizable plot against God's faithful, the witch-hunt began.[3]

Tituba announced that the devil himself, whom she described as a spectral figure dressed in black—which accusers subsequently called the "black man"—was leading the attack against the Village. In the weeks and months to come, the young Salem Village accusers and later confessors seized and elaborated upon Tituba's testimony about "signing the devil's book" and joining with Satan's other witches. Soon, Satan's purported assault was rumored to involve not just the Village church but all the churches in the province—the very heart and soul of Puritan society. A close analysis of Tituba's confession also reveals the largely unrecognized role that the magistrate John Hathorne played in shaping the basic content of her testimony.

Tituba's alarming tale of a grand demonic conspiracy, directly orchestrated by Satan and secretly unfolding in the minister's own home, exceeded the bounds of earlier, local witchcraft episodes and transformed the girls' torments from ordinary cases of witchcraft into a cosmic struggle between Satan and the church, thus giving the situation a high level of urgency. Satan was behind it, and Good and Osborne were described by Tituba as taking orders directly from him and joining in the wider plot. The ministry was Satan's primary target, as Parris had long been declaring from the pulpit. Tituba's testimony about Satan's arrival in the Village to recruit witches and attack the minister's family made Salem's story unique in the annals of New England witchcraft, and it was immediately convincing.

———————

When Tituba entered the Salem Village meetinghouse and stood before the magistrates immediately after Good's and Osborne's examinations, she would have known that her codefendants had been ordered to jail for trial.[4] According to John Hale, the magistrates had previously questioned her about the making of a "witch cake" to discover the identity of the witches afflicting the two girls in Parris's house.[5] Hale says that Tituba admitted to carrying out the procedure with her husband, John Indian. She denied, however, that she was a witch, and she was not charged.

Once the legal process started, though, Betty Parris and Abigail Williams—the two girls in Parris's household, joined by Ann Putnam Jr. and Elizabeth Hubbard, accused her of causing "spectral torments," and thus she found herself standing in court before the magistrates.

Strong circumstantial evidence suggests that Tituba's cooperation in court was in fact coerced by her master. The Boston merchant Robert Calef, who later published a detailed exposé of the Salem trials, reported that Tituba had said that Parris beat her prior to her examination and that her confession in court was the result of this abuse. Calef's account does not specify whether he spoke to Tituba himself or whether his report was based on hearsay.[6] Hale, too, related that a physical examination of Tituba at the time revealed "marks of the Devils wounding of her,"[7] which suggests that she may have borne visible bruises. In summarizing the evidence against Sarah Good, Attorney General Thomas Newton noted that Tituba's leg appeared "pinched," additional confirmation that she may have been recently bruised.[8]

The court record also reveals that Hathorne knew that, prior to her examination, Parris had wanted Tituba to tell him about her involvement with the girls' bewitchment. During her first examination, Tituba declared that "when hir master hath asked hir about these things she Sayth thay [the witches] will nott lett hir Tell."[9] Thus, it appears likely that Parris wanted a confession from Tituba and that she refused; he may have beaten her to force her to confess the next day in court. At any rate, such a scenario is the most plausible explanation for her compliance before the magistrates. Tituba did what her master forced her to do.

On the day Tituba was examined, Parris received a copy of the Reverend William Perkins's legal manual on the prosecution of witchcraft, inscribed on that date (March 1) by Robert Sanderson, who had been a deacon of the First Church in Boston when Parris was a member there.[10] According to Perkins's guidelines, if a confessed witch named other people as witches, that testimony was solid evidence that they should be arrested and examined. Parris's timely acquisition of Perkins's witch-hunting manual, when taken in conjunction with other evidence, suggests his keen interest in assisting the prosecution. Moreover, it further supports the likelihood that Parris forced Tituba to confess, for her confession would offer legally potent "eyewitness" evidence of a confessed witch against Good and Osborne, thus confirming the girls' accusations and driving the legal process forward.

Sarah Good had already said that Sarah Osborne was a witch, but her accusation was an act of self-defense and lacked any legal standing. Tituba's testimony, because she had already confessed, was more effective. Attorney General Newton made note of several points in Tituba's testimony that he intended to use against Good at her trial, which indicates that Tituba's confession was taken to be valid evidence.[11] Moreover, if Parris had informed the magistrates in advance that Tituba would confess, it made sense for them to schedule her examination after Good's and Osborne's, since her testimony would provide firsthand evidence to refute their denials.

Tituba's testimony about a wider satanic conspiracy, which was instigated by outsiders and aimed against the minister's household, appears to have been her own invention. It was explosive and consistent with her master's warnings from the pulpit. Her statement may also have been a strategic move to deflect attention from herself and establish herself as a valued informant. Altogether, the magistrates interrogated Tituba on five separate occasions, first in court and thereafter in jail, an indication that she was regarded as a highly significant source.[12]

There are three surviving records of Tituba's initial examination on March 1, 1692, each written by a different hand. One writer was Joseph Putnam of Salem Village, who was not an experienced note taker. His account, the shortest of the three, omits important information but is useful insofar as it basically corroborates the two other accounts.[13] One of the others was written by Ezekiel Cheever, also of Salem Village, who recorded several other examinations. The third and most detailed was written by the Salem magistrate Jonathan Corwin. Cheever's and Corwin's accounts, undoubtedly constructed on the basis of extensive notes, are in substantial agreement, although their wording is not identical.[14] Tituba was examined again on the following day, after she had been jailed, and this examination was also recorded by Corwin. These four accounts comprise what is generally referred to as Tituba's "confession."[15]

From the beginning, the records show that Hathorne did not challenge Tituba's responses as he did those of Good and Osborne, but instead pressed her for details. Tituba complied by answering his questions, sometimes with initial denials and momentary hesitations. Following Hathorne's prompts, she told a tale of a well-organized plot against the two children in Parris's household and two other girls in the homes of church members Thomas Putnam and Dr. William Griggs.

Tituba also invented a leader for the plot, a specter who, she said, looked "like a man" dressed in "black clothes," who came to Parris's house, accompanied by two unidentified female specters from Boston. All were invisible to everyone except Tituba. Tituba named Good and Osborne as the two other witches whose specters were present in Parris's house together with the others, and they had "hurt" Abigail Williams and Betty Parris. The court records reveal that Hathorne, Osborne, Tituba, and Abigail Williams were the first to use the words "likeness," "shape," and "appearance," in reference to a person's specter, during the legal proceedings. Thereafter, evidence of defendants' likenesses or specters would become the defining feature of the Salem proceedings. When Hathorne asked, "who doe you see who it is that torments these children now," Tituba responded, "yes it is [Sarah] Good, Good shee hurts them in her own shape."[16]

Under Hathorne's interrogation, Tituba related that she had first encountered the shapes of a man and his two female companions in the lean-to chamber at the rear of Parris's house. They had come from Boston, she explained, and the devil forced her to serve him, threatening to cut off her head if she did not and urging her to "hurt" the children: "[Some]one like a man Just as I was going to sleep Came to me, this was when the Children were first hurt, he sayed he would kill the children & she would never be well, and he Sayed if I would not serve him he would doe Soe to me."[17]

Hathorne wanted to know how she had tormented the girls and asked if she was familiar with demonic animal spirits. Answering in the affirmative, she described several such spirits, a cat, a black dog, and a yellow bird. Tituba also said that she had traveled in spectral form to Dr. Griggs's house to torment his niece Elizabeth Hubbard, and then went to Thomas Putnam's, where Good and Osborne "make me hurt the Child," Ann Putnam Jr. "How did you goe? whatt doe you Ride upon?" Hathorne inquired. Tituba knew the appropriate answer and told about flying through the air to Boston and back to Salem Village on a pole, a device common in European witchcraft lore. The record indicates that Hathorne knew that Parris had already tried to make Tituba confess, and Hathorne therefore asked her what she had told her master. She said that she refused to tell him anything because "they" (Good and Osborne) would cut off her head.[18]

Hathorne urged Tituba to provide more details about the devil's appearance. "He goes in black clothes a tal man, with white hair I think," she responded. The young accusers would later refer to this figure as "the black man," another conventional element in English folklore. Sometimes, Tituba said, he also took the shape of a black dog or a black hog.

Near the end of the first examination, Hathorne posed a revealing question, "Did not you hurt Mr. Currin's child?" The child in question was the nine-year-old son of the magistrate Jonathan Corwin.[19] Corwin's son (named George after his grandfather) was presumably suffering from a strange illness, the word "hurt" suggesting witchcraft, and Corwin had likely told Hathorne about it. Tituba seemed unsurprised by the inquiry and denied any involvement. She accused Good and Osborne of "hurting" the boy, thus confirming the court's suspicions that he was in fact bewitched. There is no record of Corwin's response, but Tituba's confirmation of his son's bewitchment would undoubtedly have strengthened his commitment to the witch-hunt.

When the girls began to exhibit their fits once again, Tituba identified their tormentor as Sarah Good. Asked to identify the other witches who had accompanied the black man, Tituba refused, saying, "they [the specters of Good and Osborne] blinded hir & would nott lett hir see." Thus the first examination ended with Tituba claiming to be a victim, along with the girls.[20]

Hathorne interrogated Tituba the next day (March 2) in the Salem prison. He began with a question that he had not asked before, about the devil's covenant. This question was central to the Puritan understanding of witchcraft as a compact with the devil, from whom a witch obtained her powers. "What covenant did you make with ye man that Came to you? What did he tell you?" Tituba answered that "he Tell me he god, & I must believe him and Serve him Six years & he would give me many fine things." The encounter had taken place "about Six Weeks [ago] & a little more, Friday night before Abigail [Williams] was ill"—that is, when Abigail began exhibiting afflicted behavior. The 1692 calendar indicates that this date would have been a few days after Friday, January 15.[21] Two weeks before, Parris had preached a sermon about the devil wanting to "pull down" his newly established congregation in the village. A month later he spoke about God's anger at "our slighting of Christ Jesus" causing him to "send forth destroyers," that is, devils and witches.[22]

Pursuing the topic of the devil's compact, Hathorne asked whether the devil had said anything about writing on paper: "What did he Say you must do? Did he Say you must Write any thing? Did he ofer you any paper?" The information he was attempting to extract was whether Tituba had signed a covenant with the devil. Apparently she did not understand what he meant, and she responded that the devil had offered her some "fine things." Later on, she commented that "the man" came to her with a book. Hathorne then asked more directly, "Did not he make you write your Name?" At this point, Tituba grasped his meaning and knew exactly what to say: "I made a marke in ye book & made itt wth red like Bloud." Tituba chose her words carefully: she had not signed the devil's book in her own blood but "with red like blood," thus she had fooled the devil and, technically, protected herself. Stalling for time, she promised the devil that she would sign his book again later, that time in blood.

It is important to recognize that Hathorne, not Tituba, introduced the notion of signing the devil's book into her testimony. That illusory procedure was modeled on the Puritan practice of making a covenant with God, which people signified when they became church members and their names were entered into the church record book. Henceforth, that concept, which was known but had never gained prominence in New England, would become the dominant theme of Salem's witch-hunt.

Hathorne continued, "Did you see any other marks in the book?" Tituba said she saw "a gret many" including those of Good and Osborne, along with several others. Wanting to know the scope of the threat, Hathorne asked how many signatures or marks she saw. "Nine," she replied. "Did he tell you where the nine lived?" Hathorne asked. "Yes, some in Boston & Some Here in this Towne," she said, "but he would not tell me who they were." Tituba thus placed Good's and Osborne's acts of bewitchment within her own construct of a wider framework of the devil's scheme to subvert the Village and its minister.[23]

The record of her testimony clearly demonstrates that Tituba's confession was a collaborative creation. Eager to portray herself as the innocent victim of a demonic plot, she made up her story as she went along, striving to provide acceptable answers to Hathorne's leading questions. During her interrogation, Hathorne provided the standard Puritan witchcraft checklist, and Tituba obliged by filling in the details. In addition to signing the devil's book, Hathorne's inquiry addressed other Puritan witchcraft concepts, such as demonic animal spirits, witches' specters, the appearance of the devil, and witches riding on poles—all central to the prosecution of witches as defined in Perkins's manual and other witchcraft handbooks.

_____

From that point forward, with Tituba safely in jail, the young Village accusers took on the larger, more aggressive role of identifying additional suspects. They reported seeing witches' specters attacking other members of the community and witches gathering in the village, first outside the meetinghouse, then in the field next to Parris's house. They consistently testified that the devil and his witches tortured them to make them sign his book and join the devil's congregation. Prior to Tituba's examination, the young girls had indicated only that Good and Osborne had tormented them in spectral form; afterward, they added the detail about the devil's book, which gave their afflictions meaning and put themselves squarely in the role of victims of Satan's larger plot. Each time, the girls said that they painfully resisted signing or even touching the book. Tituba's story thus became the girls' story, and they became Salem Village's principal witch-finders.

That story was also consistent with Parris's threatening sermons about the devil trying to "pull down" his church. We will never know whether Parris's dark warnings inspired Tituba's tale of a satanic plot, but the similarities could not have gone unnoticed among members of the Village congregation.[24]

Following her examination, Parris and Thomas Putnam submitted depositions that supported Tituba's testimony. They explained that the girls' fits had stopped when Tituba began to confess, thus confirming that she was telling the truth, the assumption being that her confession had freed her from the devil's powers to torment. Parris, who was present at Tituba's examination, supported her claim that Good and Osborne had afflicted her during her confession. The endorsements of Tituba's confession by Parris and Putnam, the parents of three of the four afflicted girls, undoubtedly gave her confession a solid backing in the Village community as well as in the court. Attorney General Newton also noted that Tituba was "taken dumb" at times during her testimony, which was seen as evidence against Good and thus as evidence in support of Tituba's truthfulness.

Years later, John Hale, who had initially believed in the court's efforts, wrote that Tituba's confession played a pivotal role at the beginning of the proceedings. He concluded that "the success of Tituba's confession encouraged those in Authority to examine others who were suspected, and the event was, that [later] more confessed. . . . And thus was this matter driven on." Hale's explanation attests to how effectively Tituba performed the part of an innocent victim and reliable informer.[25] Thereafter, magistrates would try to force every defendant to confess and give evidence against other suspects, as Tituba had done. Tituba was compliant and consistent in her testimony, Hale notes; she was always in agreement with the accusers, and she showed that she suffered like them and was suitably repentant. Subsequent confessors would do the same.

Three weeks after the accusations began, the Salem magistrates invited the Reverend Deodat Lawson, Parris's predecessor in Salem Village, to visit, and Parris offered him the pulpit so he could preach to the Village congregation. Lawson later revealed that he was particularly interested in going to the Village because he had been told that the deaths of his wife and daughter, which had occurred three years earlier when he was serving as the Village minister, had been caused by "the Malicious Operations of the Infernal Powers." Lawson's sermon, delivered on Thursday, March 24, confirmed and expanded on the notion that the devil was plotting against the church, establishing, as he put it, "the first seat of Satans Tyranny . . . against the souls of many in this place." Indeed, Lawson maintained that the Village was "where he attempts to set up his Kingdom, in Opposition to Christ's Kingdom." Lawson also expressed what must have been obvious to all: Satan was targeting the "Covenant People of God," that is, the daughters (and later wives) of Village church members. "Surely his design is, that CHRISTS Kingdom may be divided against itself." But God had sent "the Fire of his Holy displeasure, to put out some Fires of Contention, that have been amongst you," undoubtedly a reference to the conflict in the Village over Parris.[26]

Lawson's sermon was a typical Puritan jeremiad. Christians should try to defeat Satan by turning closer to God through prayer, fasting, and repentance. While Lawson also emphasized legal action against the "instruments in these horrid operations," he placed emphasis upon reconciliation to God. This providential understanding of witchcraft—that is, that God intended it as an impetus to his people to correct their errant ways—was a moderate view for it explained people's misfortunes within a moral sphere in which they had some power over their fates, not as a cosmic battle beyond their control between the forces of good and evil.

One prominent Puritan theologian who advocated the moderate approach was Richard Bernard, whose *Guide to Grand-Jury Men* cautioned against accepting spectral evidence. For Bernard, as for Lawson, witchcraft was ultimately God's providential use of the devil to punish people for their sins so they would turn closer to God. Thus Bernard titled one of his chapters "God's hand is first to be considered in all crosses, whatsoever the means be, and whosoever the instruments." Bernard advised that the appropriate response to witchcraft was a thorough "searching of our ways . . . to the acknowledgement of our sins, and to confess God to be just: and so humble our selves in fasting and prayer, leaving our ill courses, and labouring to be reformed, and so remove Gods hand."[27] Lawson developed this same theme in his sermon. "The people of this place . . . [are] under the Fearful judgment of GOD." God alone had singled out this place, "this poor Village for the first seat of Satans Tyranny." For Lawson, the remedy was twofold: First was "Prayer[,] the most proper Antidote against the old Serpent's Venemous Operations." So, "Multitudes of Prayers should go up to God; for suitable Grace and Strength to defend us." Second was justice. Lawson addressed the magistrates who were in attendance: "Do all that in you Lyes, to check and Rebuke Satan . . . to discover his Instruments in these Horrid Operations."[28]

Three days after Lawson preached to the Village church, Samuel Parris took to the pulpit. He chose not to follow Lawson's moderate lead but went on the attack. He took his sermon theme from Jesus's words aimed at Judas, "Have not I chosen you twelve, and one of you is the Devil?" He offered no solution to the frightening prospect of Satan's continuing to assault "Christ's little church." With church members Martha Cory and Rebecca Nurse now accused and remanded to jail for trial, along with Good, Osborne, and Tituba, he implied that no one was above suspicion. "Lord knows," said Parris, "how many devils there are in [t]his church, & who they are." Such individuals, he warned, should "forbear to come to the Lords Table, lest Satan enter more powerfully in you."[29]

He went on to speculate about how many witches there might be in his congregation: "Why so, Christ knows how many Devils [are] among us: wither one or ten, or 20 & also who they are." Parris was pointing out that even among the Elect of his congregation, whom he had worked so hard to recruit, there might be some of Satan's agents, possibly as many as twenty, nearly half of the number of church members! At the end of his sermon, Parris listed in a perfunctory way the types of sins, such as lying, slandering, envy, drunkenness, and pride, that can "make us Devils." Parris had already tried several weeks of prayer with no result. He could offer no other solution, only the warning that Christ knows "who these Devils are among us," as a spur to the witch-hunt that had just begun.[30]

Parris had effectively magnified Tituba's fabricated notion of a satanic conspiracy, which was now enlarged into a full-blown apocalyptic narrative of satanic attacks against Salem Village at large, not only against its former and present ministers but the congregation itself. "We are either Saints, or Devils," Parris informed his congregation; "The scripture gives us no medium."[31] Thus Parris polarized his community into two camps: godly church members, and the ungodly remainder, some of whom might even be members of the church. He recklessly raised suspicions against his opponents, some of whom, such as the Nurse family, were full members of the church.

Around this time, Parris took his young daughter Betty from Salem Village and placed her in the home of Salem resident Stephen Sewall. Betty's fits eventually subsided, and she disappears from the court records.

In the end, Tituba was never brought to trial by the Court of Oyer and Terminer. In May 1693, the newly established Superior Court of Judicature formally indicted her, along with dozens of other witchcraft defendants still in prison. She was acquitted of the charge of "covenanting with the Devil." The word *Ignoramus*, written on the back of Tituba's indictment, records the grand jury's verdict. It means, literally, "we have no knowledge of it"; that is, the jury found the evidence of her once momentous confession about a witchcraft conspiracy against Salem Village unconvincing.[32] Her case was therefore dismissed.

According to Calef's account, after the trials were over Samuel Parris told Tituba that he would not pay her jail fees and take her back unless she would "stand to" her original confession. But Tituba was no fool. Her self-composure and tactical wisdom under interrogation enabled her to survive the Salem maelstrom. She owed nothing to her manipulative master, who had caused her to suffer. Tituba remained in jail for several more months until sometime in December 1693, when she was sold to an individual who paid her jail fees. According to the Salem jail keeper's account, Tituba was held in jail for a total of twenty-two months, longer than any of the Salem defendants.[33]

THE VILLAGE GIRLS WHO
CRIED "WITCH!"

3

Presently they were all tormented.
— *March 1, 1692*

They are in their Fits tempted to be Witches . . .
and are tortured, because they will not yield.
— *Deodat Lawson*

The most curious, and perhaps the most studied, aspect of the Salem witch-hunt episode is the courtroom behavior of the "afflicted girls." Month after month, six females, aged eleven to twenty, held center stage in a remarkable public spectacle, one that had deadly consequences. In sociological terms, the girls' public performances of their afflictions upended their real-life status. Young females in Puritan society were to be seen and not heard, as Mary Beth Norton notes, and, if heard, certainly not sought after and listened to.

The core group of Salem Village witchcraft accusers included eleven-year-old Abigail Williams, the niece of Samuel Parris, who lived in his home. Twelve-year-old Ann Putnam Jr. and seventeen-year-old Mary Walcott were cousins and members of the Putnam family. Three others—seventeen-year-old Mercy Lewis, seventeen-year-old Elizabeth Hubbard, twenty-year-old Mary Warren—were maidservants. Living at a distance from their families, and thus deprived of their economic and emotional support, the maidservants ranked near the bottom of the social hierarchy, and their prospects for an advantageous marriage were negligible. Firmly under the control of the adults who employed them and whose purposes they served, the maidservants were extraordinarily vulnerable. Abigail Williams was not a servant but apparently a family relation who was sent away from home to live with a higher-status family to improve her social prospects. Abigail was quite firmly under the authority of her host family and her uncle Samuel Parris.

Historians' interpretations of what triggered and sustained the girls' behaviors have varied widely. Were they merely pawns in the hands of adult authority figures? Were they suffering from a then-unknown biomedical illness or a deep psychological trauma? Were they not fully aware of the murderous ramifications of their actions? Did they intentionally collaborate among themselves and fake their "fits"? All of these explanations and various combinations of them are represented in the literature about the Salem witch trials. Often unconsidered, however, are the ways in which contemporary participants and eyewitness observers viewed the young accusers.

Modern interpretations will always be of interest, but the wide range of seventeenth-century interpretations enables us to understand how the girls' behavior was understood at the time and how attitudes toward them changed over time. These interpretations are not too different from those that are currently proposed.

Throughout the seven long months of hearings and trials, the afflicted girls and women of Salem Village captivated onlookers and juries in dozens of courtroom dramas, first in the Salem Village meetinghouse and later in the court sessions in public houses in Salem Town. The court's star witnesses, on whom the Court of Oyer and Terminer relied from beginning to end, became notorious in Essex County as expert witch-finders. Their testimony and behavior in court remained the touchstone for magistrates, judges, and jurors, at both examinations and trials, and their names appear on nearly all the indictments. Granting such prominence to the young "afflicted," as they were often called, was extremely rare in New England.

As rumors and allegations fed to Salem Village the names of people in other communities who were suspected by their neighbors, the young accusers became afflicted, complaints were filed, and arrests made. When the crisis spread to Andover in mid-July, the core group of Village accusers was supplemented by five young Andover "afflicted," girls aged twelve through nineteen, and a few adults whose testimony was used to validate charges in Andover and neighboring communities.

By late August, however, the young accusers' reputations had begun to diminish, even as Chief Magistrate William Stoughton stepped up the use of their testimony, rushing more cases to trial and ordering more executions in anticipation of the court's recess in mid-September. During the peak of the trials, from late August to mid-September, the Village girls and young women, including those from Andover, were instrumental in the execution of thirteen people, and they appeared in the Salem court multiple times per week. By early September, however, the Boston ministers had discounted the evidentiary value of the girls' afflictions, and a month later the governor prepared to shut down the court at the end of its fourth session. The afflicted girls had become an embarrassment to the legal system. The contemporary Boston critic Thomas Brattle would call their claim to be able to see specters with their eyes firmly shut "nonsensical." The afflicted accusers would eventually be regarded as "deluded" and "possessed" by the devil. Years later, as the government moved to compensate victims' families for the injustices done to them, it would come to the same conclusion, denouncing the principal accusers as "profligate and vicious."

It is important to emphasize, however, that from the beginning, the afflicted girls and young women of Salem Village were never in control of their own fates. Their families and the authorities, both ministers and magistrates, stage-managed the girls' actions at every step of the way, and the young accusers did their best to behave as was expected of them. They fought hard against every defendant, apparently reanimating their original traumas of demonic attack in the presence of the magistrates and the accused who stood before them. One of the magistrates' most crucial decisions was to gather the accusers together in the courtroom and have them perform their afflictions before the accused, the magistrates, and crowds of onlookers rather than simply describe their torments in private sessions. As time went on, the young accusers warmed to their part and played it with increasingly dramatic flair and deadly consequences. Nothing on this scale had been seen before in New England—a theater of demonic malevolence for everyone to observe and gossip about, reprised in almost weekly court sessions.

Questions about the reliability of such evidence as well as suspicions of fraud and delusion were raised soon enough by defiant defendants and critical observers alike. At first, however, neither the adults observing nor the girls themselves could say what was troubling them. Their erratic behavior was obviously disturbing, but in the beginning the girls did not, or could not, identify the cause of their suffering. The authorities' initial approach was diagnostic. Had the devil taken possession of the girls, in which case they might be charged with attracting him, or were they being targeted by neighbors who were in league with the devil? In either event, the symptoms might be indistinguishable. Other diagnoses were also possible. The girls could be "dissembling" or "counterfeiting," or they could be "distracted," that is, mentally unbalanced.

The surviving eyewitness sources contain no clinical or entirely neutral description of the girls' initial behavior, although the report of John Hale, the only observer to write an eyewitness account of the girls' initial afflictions, comes close. Hale begins by noting that the two girls in Parris's house, nine-year-old Betty Parris and eleven-year-old Abigail Williams, were "sadly Afflicted of they knew not what Distempers." The last phrase leaves the door open. Were they suffering from demonic possession or bewitchment? Hale goes on to recount that the witch-cake procedure, administered by Tituba, enabled the girls to "see" their tormentors. Thus Hale, like others, chose to interpret the girls' condition as bewitchment.

Hale's description continues by introducing the notion of "invisible agents" and discounts any known medical causes: "These Children were bitten and pinched by invisible agents; their arms, necks, and backs turned this way and that way, and returned back again, so as it was impossible for them to do of themselves, and beyond the power of any Epileptick Fits, or natural Disease to effect." Hale continues: "Sometimes they were taken dumb, their mouths stopped, their throats choked, their limbs wracked and tormented so as might move an heart of stone, to sympathize with them, with bowels of compassion for them."[1] Robert Calef, relying on secondhand reports, portrayed the girls as "getting into Holes, and creeping under Chairs and Stools, and to use sundry odd Postures and Antick Gestures, uttering foolish, ridiculous Speeches, which neither they themselves nor any others could make sense of."[2]

Hale also pointed out that the girls' behavior closely resembled that of the four bewitched Goodwin children in Boston, aged four to thirteen. Historians agree that the Goodwin case, described in detail by Cotton Mather in his popular pamphlet *Memorable Providences,* provided the model for the behavior of the children in Parris's house and a guide to its interpretation. "Sometimes they would be Deaf, sometimes Dumb, and sometimes Blind," wrote Mather, "and often, all this at once. One while their Tongues would be drawn down their Throats . . . Jaws went out of joint. . . . They would at times ly in a benummed condition and be drawn together as those that are ty'd Neck and Heels. . . . They would make most pitteous out-cries, that they were cut with Knives, and struck with Blows that they could not bear. . . . [Y]ea, their Heads would be twisted almost round."[3]

Like the Goodwin children, the Salem girls were enacting stereotypical "afflicted" behavior. At first they were unable to indicate its cause, and it had to be diagnosed for them. Were they waiting for the community's diagnosis, which would be authoritative and provide a remedy? Parris initially followed Cotton Mather's procedure in the Goodwin case—fasting and prayer—and he took young Betty away from the chaos in order to recover, as Mather did with one of the afflicted Goodwin children. But Parris also exhibited the girls to the community and enlisted neighboring ministers to help with prayers in their own churches. In Salem Village, as in the Goodwin case, a physician was eventually called, and it was he who diagnosed witchcraft. From that moment, the authorities believed they were dealing with demonic powers—witches.

Soon after Dr. Griggs made his diagnosis, the matter was taken out of Parris's hands when the girls began to identify their tormentors. The girls must have known the purpose of the witch-cake procedure carried out by John Indian and Tituba because afterward, as Parris explained, they immediately began seeing "apparitions" and naming those who bewitched them.[4]

The third girl to be afflicted was twelve-year-old Ann Putnam Jr., daughter of Thomas and Ann Putnam, both church members. The legal process came a little later on when, as Hale noted, there were "persons who were of age to be witnesses." The first "person of age" (more than fourteen years old) to be named as a victim and a witness was seventeen-year-old Elizabeth Hubbard. She was the grandniece of Dr. Griggs's wife, Rachel Hubbard Griggs, and was an indentured maidservant in the home of Dr. Griggs, who, like the Putnams, was a Village church member. Elizabeth's claim of bewitchment, along with that of Ann Putnam Jr., thus brought the church squarely into view. For the devil to attack a family's children or its maidservant was to attack the family itself, and it was generally the father, as head of the household, who made the witchcraft complaint.

If the devil was afflicting the two girls in Parris's house as a way of attacking him, young Ann Putnam, as the daughter of Parris's most ardent supporter, may have felt vulnerable as well. The large, extended Putnam family was also the backbone of the Village congregation. Ann was the niece of one of the church deacons, Edward Putnam. She was also the niece of Mary Sibley, the church member who had instigated the witch-cake procedure, and the niece of the former deacon Jonathan Walcott. Another of Sibley's nieces was seventeen-year-old Mary Walcott, who would soon join the group of afflicted. Thomas Putnam wrote his daughter's initial deposition, and he would go on to produce dozens more on her behalf as well as that of other Village accusers and provide them for the grand jury.

Twelve-year-old Ann was the eldest of six children. Three years before, she had watched her six-month-old sister, Sarah, die in a disturbing manner that she later described as being "whipped" to death.[5] Her sister's death throes must have been distressing to observe, and Ann would later accuse John Willard of Salem Village of killing her sister by means of witchcraft. Like the other afflicted girls, Ann responded in court when prompted by the magistrates and performed her torments during the examinations of Good, Osborne, and Tituba. During Tituba's interrogation, she cried out that the previous night the specters of Good and Osborne tried to make "hir Cutt of hir own head."[6]

Witches, the court records reveal, are said to hate those who discover them. Elizabeth Hubbard was the grandniece and maidservant in the home of Dr. Griggs. If the witches were to retaliate against her great-uncle for exposing them, then Elizabeth had reason to fear that they might target her.[7] Indeed, the day before Tituba's examination, Hubbard had apparently said that a demonic wolf spirit had been sent to attack her as she was leaving the house of John and Elizabeth Procter. Confirming Hubbard's statement, Tituba claimed that Sarah Good had "set a wolfe upon her to afflict her."[8]

Up to this point, the four girls had accused three socially marginal women, each a likely suspect in her own way. Good had seemed to utter a curse at Parris after begging food at his house; Osborne had refused to attend church in obedience to a demonic spirit; and Tituba had admitted to carrying out the occult witch-cake procedure that Parris condemned as diabolical. The girls were called into court together as witnesses and performed their torments on cue from the judges. When Sarah Good was being examined, "Hathorne desired the children all of them to looke upon her [Good], and see, if this were the person that hurt them and so they all did looke upon her and said this was one of the persons that did torment them. presently they were all tormented."[9]

The procedures the magistrates instituted in Salem were not customary in New England courts. Usually the accusers were adults, and usually the evidence was observable, called *maleficium,* such as a serious illness or physical injury, not temporary torments by invisible specters. The judges also complied with the request of the Village "neighbors" to bring the girls into the courtroom as a group, instead of making them testify separately in accord with well-known legal guidelines.

Given the special circumstances in which they found themselves, the magistrates took their precedent from the Goodwin case. There, too, the young accusers were brought into court and "fell into sad fits before the whole Assembly."[10] The magistrates had also arranged for the defendant in the case, Goodwife Ann Glover, to manipulate rag dolls that were found in her house. The dolls, or poppets, as they were called, supposedly represented the children, and as Glover twisted the dolls, the children immediately "fell into fits," thus providing evidence of her guilt. The Salem magistrates constructed a similar scenario. Gathering the girls and defendants together in a packed courtroom and then provoking an encounter that prompted the accusers to perform their fits, often in response to the defendants' movements, the judges developed a procedure for displaying evidence. In English courts, evidence of acts of witchcraft required two eyewitnesses, and this was the girls' role, to testify to the unobservable and to make the effect of unseen forces visible in the courtroom.

During the preliminary examinations, the courtroom became not only the venue in which the justices could consider the evidence of the girls' behavior but a public stage where the girls enacted their roles before "so many hundred people." From time to time, members of the crowd interjected their recriminations against the accused, which the court recorders duly noted; occasionally the noise of the crowd was so loud that the recorders doubted whether they heard all that was said. The defendants, held stiffly by constables grasping each arm, were immobilized,[11] while the accusers were all activity, emotion, and suffering. The court records indicate that all attention was directed to them. Their pitiful screams and contortions gave them credibility, while the defendants, appearing to be uncooperative in the face of harsh questioning, lost all moral integrity in the eyes of the court.

Initially, as the examination records indicate, the four young accusers acted only in response to the magistrates' directions: they identified the defendants as their tormentors and performed their afflictions as evidence. Two weeks later, emboldened by more courtroom drama in which they were cast as the star performers, the girls began taking the initiative. When the former Village minister Reverend Deodat Lawson arrived in mid-March, seventeen-year-old Mary Walcott made sure he took note of her as a witchcraft victim. Mary—cousin of Ann Putnam and daughter of Jonathan Walcott, a deacon during Lawson's tenure, and niece of Mary Sibley, the woman who urged John Indian to make the witch cake—soon became one of the most active accusers. During the next six months, she would be involved in twenty-eight witchcraft cases.

Walcott's house was just down the road from Ingersoll's tavern, where Lawson was staying. Mary greeted him as soon as he arrived. "As she stood by the [tavern] door," Lawson reported, "[she] was bitten, so that she cried out of her Wrist, and looking on it with a Candle, we saw apparently the marks of Teeth both upper and lower set, on each side of her wrist." Biting her own wrist was an audacious move. She appears to have wanted to test Lawson to see if he would endorse the girls' spectral claims—in this case the "evidence" that a witch's specter had bitten her wrist. Lawson used a candle to illuminate the injury as darkness fell, and his account suggests that he was only too willing to be convinced.[12]

That evening, Lawson went next door to visit Parris's home. For the visitor's benefit, Abigail Williams initiated a violent demonstration of bewitched behavior. She ran around the great room saying "Whish! Whish! Whish!" as if she were flying, just as the Goodwin children had done, and she cried out that Rebecca Nurse was trying to make her sign the devil's book.[13] She ran into the fireplace, attempting to avoid Nurse's specter, and started wildly to throw firebrands into the room to defend herself, putting the whole household at risk.[14]

In church the next day, the girls showed Lawson, who was invited to preach, that Satan could use them to disrupt the service and humiliate the minister before the congregation. As the service began, Walcott, Williams, Putnam, and Hubbard all performed their fits. Lawson admitted that it "did something interrupt me in my First Prayer; being so unusual." Then Abigail did something even more astonishing. From the balcony, where children sat, she ordered Lawson, "Now stand up, and Name your [sermon]

Text." Lawson complied, reading a quotation from the prophet Zachariah 3:2: "And the Lord said unto Satan, The Lord rebuke thee, O Satan." The biblical quotation did not silence Satan, who was obviously speaking through the two girls. Hearing the biblical verse, Williams boldly shot back, "It is a long text."[15]

Later, at the start of the afternoon service, Williams again confronted Lawson and expressed her disapproval of his text: "I know no Doctrine you had, If you did name one, I have forgot it." In challenging Lawson, Williams spoke as someone under the power of the devil who could not tolerate hearing religious teaching, the same behavior Cotton Mather had described in the Goodwin case. At one point, Williams boldly interrupted the sermon, saying that she saw the specter of Martha Cory, a church member who was almost certainly present in the congregation, upon an overhead beam allowing a yellow bird, a witch's familiar spirit, to suck between her fingers. This was a shocking public accusation in the midst of a worship service. The yellow bird was a spirit animal first mentioned by Tituba as belonging to Sarah Good. Ann Putnam then spoke out from the balcony, saying that the yellow bird was now sitting on Lawson's hat, which was hanging on a peg next to the pulpit in full view, which indicated that the demonic spirit had no fear of a Puritan clergyman.

In Puritan New England, children and teenagers were taught strict obedience to adults and to fear God's judgment. A young person rebuking a minister to his face was unheard of except in rare cases of demoniacs, that is, people who were possessed by the devil. Speaking as though they were under Satan's influence was a risky step for Walcott, Williams, and Ann Putnam because they could be subjected to interrogation about their relationship with the devil. Were they possessed as well as bewitched, and thus, perhaps, willing agents voicing the devil's demands? Their demonstration, however, was convincing, and by this time they were regarded as the innocent victims of Satan's power. The congregation was undoubtedly stunned by such a striking confirmation of the devil's activity in the community, boldly attacking children as well as a married woman during the worship service. Lawson's sermon delivered later that week pointed out the obvious: Satan was besieging Salem Village's "Covenant People of God."[16]

What came next was equally remarkable. The four girls were summoned to court as witnesses at two more examinations: those of elderly Martha Cory and of seventy-one-year-old Rebecca Nurse. At the first examination, the girls answered the usual questions about Cory's appearance afflicting them. Then, twisting their bodies into painful contortions, they began to imitate Cory's physical movements in exaggerated ways to demonstrate that she was bewitching them with her demonic powers. According to Lawson's account, "The afflicted persons asked her [Cory] why she did not go to the company of Witches which were before the Meeting house mustering? Did she not hear the Drum beat?"[17]

The claim that a group of witches' specters had gathered outside the church, mustering like a company of militia (about twenty in number) and threatening the legal proceedings within, was something altogether new—a clear affirmation of the girls' effectiveness as witch-finders. They were capable of seeing not only the specters of witches who were afflicting themselves but also other specters who had come to the Village to threaten and disrupt the witch-hunt. This claim was a daring step and carried forward Tituba's initial testimony that there were more witches yet to be discovered—indeed a whole company of them.

At Cory's examination, seventeen-year-old Mercy Lewis, the maidservant in the household of Thomas Putnam, joined the young accusers. A refugee from Falmouth (now Portland), Maine, which had been destroyed by Indian attacks in 1676, Lewis and her family had recently moved to Salem. She undoubtedly had seen the horror of those attacks on members of her family and had possibly witnessed the killing of her grandparents. As Mary Beth Norton has pointed out, Mercy Lewis may have seen Satan's raising up witches in Salem Village as part and parcel of his causing Indian attacks against communities in the Maine frontier from which she and her family had fled.[18] During the course of the episode, Lewis was involved in the accusations against a total of twenty-four people. Thomas Putnam prepared most of her depositions.

Piety, Martha Cory assumed, would serve as her protection. She protested to the magistrates, "I am a Gospel-woman, & do you think I can have to do with witchcraft too?" Two years before, she had made a profession of faith before the congregation and had been accepted into the Village covenant. How could she now be suspected of witchcraft, especially on the basis of the claims by four young girls as well as one clearly hysterical Ann Putnam Sr.?

When Ann Putnam Jr. claimed to be tormented by Martha Cory, Edward Putnam, a deacon in the church, and Ezekiel Cheever went to Cory's house to question her. Cory told them that she was already aware that people were "talking of me," and she guessed that someone had leveled an accusation against her. Did the accuser say what she was wearing? she asked, seeking proof that the accuser had correctly identified her. Her question surprised the two men because just before they left to visit Cory, they had asked Ann to describe the clothes Cory's specter was wearing. Ann cleverly replied that she did not know because Cory had blinded her. Given her inquiry, Putnam and Cheever concluded that Cory had "showed us a pretty trick," which reinforced their suspicions. At her examination, they reported that Cory had insisted that there were no witches in Salem Village, except for the three that had been accused.[19]

Indeed, at her examination she twice rebuked the judges, saying, "we must not believe these distracted children." By "distracted" she meant that her young accusers were mentally unstable, and she believed the justices were gullible. Reading between the lines of Cory's examination and the text of Putnam and Cheever's account suggests that Cory may have previously mentioned to others her doubts about the girls' emotional stability as well as the magistrates' judgment, and thus attracted the girls' attention. The girls' accusation of Cory would be their first retaliatory strike against an individual who cast doubt upon their legitimacy. The magistrates retorted, "You charge these children with distraction: it is a note of distraction when persons vary in a minute, but these fix upon you, this is not the manner of distraction."[20]

The magistrates were correct. The girls were closely following Hathorne's lead at every moment, as the record clearly demonstrates. In the midst of Hathorne's badgering, the recorder noted that the "Children [said] there is a man whispering in her [Cory's] ear," a reference to Tituba's "black man." Immediately Hathorne interrupted his line of questioning and demanded, "What did he [the black man] say?" When Cory refused to answer, the girls began to act out their torments. They imitated in exaggerated ways every movement the nervous Martha Cory made. When she bit her lower lip or squeezed her hands, the girls did the same and screamed out in pain. Hathorne seized upon their behavior to denounce Cory's claim that the girls were mentally impaired: "Do not you see these children & women are rational & sober as their neighbours?"[21]

Hathorne's observation, along with the obvious fact that the girls were not suffering any long-lasting mental or physical impairment, as is clear from the court records, would later be used to cast doubt on the girls' credibility and the magistrates' judgment. Thomas Brattle, who witnessed the court's activity, noted that "Many of these afflicted persons, who have scores of strange fitts in a day, yet in the intervals of time are hale and hearty, robust and lusty, as tho' nothing had afflicted them." As Brattle implied, the girls were not suffering from any demonic infirmity because their symptoms were not constant but intermittent and clearly within their control.[22]

The records do not indicate why Cory became the girls' target, but a likely reason was her outspoken criticism of the girls and the magistrates.[23] When Putnam and Cheever visited her home, Cory had told them that the magistrates were "blind" and that she would "open their eyes." Interpreting her statement as an outright challenge to the court, Hathorne demanded an explanation during her examination: "Now tell me the truth will you, why did you say that the Magistrates & Ministers eyes are blinded [and] you would open them?" Cory held her ground: "Yes, to accuse the innocent." But when Hathorne reiterated the same question, Cory's response was apparently laughter. Hathorne replied reprovingly, "Is it a laughing matter to see these afflicted persons?" To laugh at a magistrate's question was an insult to the court and a fatal mistake. Hathorne chose this moment to pounce on Cory: "Do not you beleive there are Witches in the Countrey?" Cory again stood her ground: "I do not know that there is any." This was another honest but fatal response. Cory's laughter (whether nervous or derisive) was undoubtedly provoked by the girls' incessant challenges and demonstrations, which she knew to be false.

The examination of Rebecca Nurse followed that of Martha Cory. Depositions from Ann Putnam Sr. and her nephew John Putnam Jr. reveal that they believed that Nurse's mother was a witch who had passed on her knowledge of witchcraft to her daughters, Rebecca Towne Nurse, Sarah Towne Cloyce, and Mary Towne Esty, and that the sisters had used witchcraft to retaliate against the Putnams by bewitching a number of the Putman children. The Putnams' suspicions stemmed from a boundary dispute between the Putnam and Towne families. This long-standing controversy over adjoining lands along the Topsfield border was still rankling in 1692.[24] Ann Sr. mentioned that she saw the specters of "six children in winding sheets which called me aunt," whose deaths she attributed to Rebecca Nurse. John Putnam recounted his own "strange fits" after he repeated "something which he had heard" about the mother of the Towne sisters, and he attributed the sudden death of his child to Towne's three daughters.[25] Thus, when

Ann Putnam Jr. saw a specter of a "pale-faced woman" sitting in her grand-mother's chair in her house, Ann's mother suggested it was the specter of Rebecca Nurse.[26]

Present during Rebecca Nurse's examination, Ann Putnam Jr., Ann Putnam, Abigail Williams, Mary Walcott, and Elizabeth Hubbard performed their afflictions on cue. Justice Hathorne badgered Nurse, asking repeatedly who it was that "hurt" the girls. Not wanting to give evidence against herself or anyone else, Nurse responded each time by saying that she "did not know."

Hathorne tried to trap her into admitting that the girls were genuinely afflicted. He asked: "Do you think these suffer voluntary or involuntary?" Nurse answered, "I cannot tell." Hathorne, clearly annoyed, responded, "They accuse you of hurting them, & if you think it is not unwillingly but by designe you must look upon them as murderers." This pronouncement was critical. Its meaning could not have been lost on Nurse or the young accusers. The girls were either bewitched (and therefore acting involuntarily), or their actions were fraudulent and malicious (and they were acting voluntarily). Nurse was under examination, but so were the girls, and their credibility, particularly when faced with the respected matriarch Rebecca Nurse, was at issue. Hathorne's question about whether they were acting "by designe" put them on notice. If they were faking their afflictions, that is, acting by deliberate effort, or voluntarily, the court would view their behavior as attempted murder. Hathorne asked Nurse one more time, "Do you think these suffer against their wills or not?" This time, the elderly and ailing Nurse waffled, perhaps tired from being badgered or failing to hear properly (she had difficulty hearing). Instead of saying again that she did not know what to say, she replied, "I do not think these suffer against their wills." Hathorne thus forced Nurse to commit to an interpretation of the girls' afflictions that appeared to endorse them. Using the ambiguous double negative (if the record is correct), Nurse had been cornered into admitting that the girls were not faking and were therefore bewitched.[27] After more intimidation she agreed, "I do think they are [afflicted]."

Hathorne followed up with a question that implied that Nurse was unsympathetic to the girls' plight. Why, he asked, did she never visit the afflicted girls? Nurse said she was afraid she "would have fitts too." Thus Hathorne forced Nurse again to admit that the girls' fits were genuine and that they could become contagious, as they clearly were among the group of girls, even to Nurse herself, who had voiced her uncertainty about their validity.

Nurse then apparently moved her body, and the girls immediately fell into fits, imitating her movements, to demonstrate that she was afflicting them and that their fits were involuntary. The court had taken a firm stand on the legitimacy of their afflictions, and the girls knew it. Thereafter, they would pounce upon anyone who questioned the veracity of their afflictions.

The recurrent theme of the girls' testimony in Cory's and Nurse's examinations was the claim that the defendants' specters tried to make them "sign the devil's book." The Reverend Lawson, who attended both examinations, explained what was going on: "They [the girls] are in their Fits tempted to be Witches . . . and are tortured, because they will not yield to Subscribe, or meddle with, or touch the Book, and are promised to have present Relief if they would do it."[28] To sign the devil's book was to make a compact with Satan, a charge the girls would level against nearly all subsequent defendants.

In the days following Nurse's examination, the records state, John Procter told Samuel Sibley that "if they [the young accusers] were let alone so we should all be Devils & Witches—quickly they should rather be had to the Whipping post." Procter's twenty-year-old maidservant, Mary Warren, had joined the young accusers about this time, and the court had summoned her to give evidence against Sarah Cloyce and Elizabeth Procter, who had been recently accused. John Procter, who lived in Salem Farms, near the southern border of the Village, apparently heard about Warren's summons to testify against his wife, and he went to fetch her home so that she would not be able attend court. He was overheard to say that he would thrash the devil out of Warren. He also let it be known that he would "drive the devil" out of John Indian, who by this time had joined in the accusations.[29]

Word had apparently got around about Procter's impugning the girls' testimony. He was charged with witchcraft and hauled into court. That Samuel Parris wrote down Sibley's deposition for the court indicates his interest in defending the girls' integrity. Sibley later swore to his deposition in court, and it was used against Procter at his trial.

After Mary Warren returned to Procter's home, her afflictions stopped, and she evidently began to doubt herself. She later confided to Edward and Sarah Bishop in jail that "when I was Aflicted I thought I saw the Apparission of A hundred prsons: for shee said hir Head was Distempered that shee Could Not tell what shee said, And . . . when shee was well Againe shee Could Not say that shee saw any of the Apparissions."[30] Rumors about Warren's misgivings apparently reached the afflicted girls, who viewed her change of mind as a betrayal.

One of the girls accused Warren of signing the devil's book, perhaps in retaliation for her perceived disloyalty in failing to appear in court against Elizabeth Procter. Arrested, Warren was taken to court on April 19. Hathorne asked her the obvious question: "You were a little while agoe an Afflicted person, now you are an Afflicter: How comes this to pass?" Elizabeth Hubbard spoke up and said that Mary had recovered from her afflictions and afterward had declared that "the afflicted persons did but dissemble." All five girls—Ann Putnam Jr., Mercy Lewis, Elizabeth Hubbard, Mary Walcott, and Abigail Williams—immediately fell into violent demonstrations, indicating that Warren was attacking them. Hathorne harried Warren: "Well here was one just now that was a Tormentor in her apparition, & she owns that she had made a league with the Devil." Warren immediately fell into a fit and claimed that she was being attacked by the specters of Martha Cory and John and Elizabeth Procter.

What follows next in Warren's examination record is a disconnected series of outbursts, as she struggled to gain control of her conflicted emotions and protect herself from her accusers. She fell silent, then tried to speak: "I will speak & cryed out, Oh! I am sorry for it, I am sorry for it, & wringed her hands, & fell a little while into a fit again." Was Warren struggling to say she was sorry for betraying the girls as frauds or for "tormenting" them, asking their forgiveness to gain their sympathy? After a few moments, she recovered and in desperation cried out, "Oh Lord help me, Oh good Lord save me!" She knew that she was being trapped by her accusers' outbursts and feared for her life. Then she cried, "I will tell, I will tell, they brought me to it; & then fell into a fit again." Who were "they"? Her former spectral tormentors, forcing her to become an accuser again? Having retreated into a fit and unable to speak, Warren was taken from the room. The magistrates later met with her privately in an effort to pry out incriminating evidence. She responded, "I shall not speak a word: but I will, speak I will speak satan— she saith she will kill me. Oh! she saith, she owes me a spite, & will claw me off." She imagined that unnamed specter was apparently trying to kill her, and she fell silent again. The court had turned against her, and she knew her life was in peril.[31]

Several days later, when they interrogated Warren in prison, the magistrates harassed Warren into turning against the Procters. She admitted that they had made her sign the devil's book. She was alone in her struggle with her conscience, and in her desperation called upon God to save her. The Village accusers were pushing her toward the gallows. Under the pressure of more interrogations, she confessed and accused others. Thereafter, in self-defense, she would join the ranks of the accusers, saving herself by acting for the prosecution.

Warren involved herself in nearly two dozen cases, including several in Andover. Having betrayed her conscience and risked her own life, she became one of the most demonstrative and self-wounding of the accusers, biting herself and sticking pins into her hands and bleeding in the courtroom. Hurting others, she hurt herself.

Recognizing the dramatic potential of Warren's doubts, the playwright Arthur Miller focused on Warren's predicament in the central scene of *The Crucible*'s pivotal third act. In the play, the embattled John Procter tells the magistrates that Warren had claimed that the girls were faking their afflictions. He presses her case in court before judge Thomas Danforth and makes Warren voice her doubts. For a moment it seems that Procter and Warren will prevail, but then Danforth and Abigail Williams browbeat Warren into submission. The records show, however, that in 1692 there was no such moment of uncertainty and debate in the courtroom. Warren's doubts never raised any suspicion in the minds of the magistrates about the honesty of the accusers. Warren's charge and her emotional state quickly collapsed under the demonstrations by the girls and the questioning of the court.

The girls were emboldened by the confession of fifteen-year-old Abigail Hobbs, which occurred on the same day as Warren's examination, and the accusation of the Reverend George Burroughs, and their accusations accelerated exponentially. They were soon testifying in court against people they did not know and had never seen. The young accusers would become the witch-finders not only for Salem Village but for neighboring Andover and more distant communities in Essex County. Historians rightly assume that as word of the witchcraft excitement in Salem Village spread across Essex County, the girls and their parents picked up malicious gossip and rumors about people in nearby communities who had long been suspected of witchcraft.

One of the most dramatically successful accusers was Mercy Lewis. The story, as it appears in the records, began in mid-April with the sudden death of John Putnam Jr.'s two-month-old child. His infant was normal and healthy, Putnam reported, until he mentioned "something he heard" about the mother of Rebecca Nurse, Sarah Cloyce, and Mary Esty. Immediately thereafter, he suffered "strange fits." Putnam soon recovered, but his child fell into fits, which seemed to be similar to those suffered by the "poor bewitched persons." John Putnam sent for his mother, who told him that his child had definitely been afflicted by the "evil hand." A doctor was called, but the baby continued to suffer, and after two days it died.

Nurse and Cloyce were already in jail. On April 21, Thomas Putnam and John Buxton, who had secured a warrant for the arrest of several people, also named Mary Esty. The next day Abigail Williams, John Indian, Ann Putnam, Mary Walcott, and Elizabeth Hubbard testified against Esty at her examination. Not all of the witnesses in court were certain of her identity, and several fell silent, appearing unable to speak, but Esty was sent to jail and held for trial. After three-and-a-half weeks (on May 18), however, she was set free, apparently because the charges against her did not appear substantial. Two days later, Mercy Lewis went to the home of John Putnam Jr. and became afflicted so severely that she was confined to bed in his house.

Attributing her torments to Esty, Lewis fell into what was reported to be a comatose state. As she lay in bed, Putnam summoned nine people—seven men and two girls—to observe her condition. They related that she was in a "very Dreadful and Solemn Condition," as if "death would have quickly followed." Upon receiving that information, George Herrick, the marshal of Essex County, issued a warrant for Mary Esty's arrest, dated May 20. Elizabeth Hubbard and Ann Putnam Jr. were summoned to identify the specter that continued to afflict the nearly lifeless Lewis, which they identified as the specter of Mary Esty. All told, the visitors to Lewis's bedside generated two indictments and ten depositions, signed by seventeen people. Esty was tried on September 9 and executed two weeks later with seven others.[32]

Was Mercy Lewis's behavior deliberately contrived, or was she gripped by a pathological fear of what she believed was Esty's demonic power? The records can be read either way, and both interpretations might be valid.

The records contain several complaints and warrants submitted by adults that list the names of as many as eleven people on a single complaint. Most are women identified only by their husbands' names, which suggests that they were not otherwise known to the Village complainants.

The suspects were arrested and examined; the girls dutifully performed their "torments"; the accused were sent to jail to await trial. Some individual or group of individuals was clearly responsible for collecting the names that appeared in the complaints. Most likely it was the parents of the most aggressive accusers—Putnam, Lewis, Walcott, Hubbard, and Williams—who kept the records of the girls' afflictions and the dates of their fits for use in the court. The girls' depositions refer to the exact dates when their torments took place, sometimes several months prior to the dates of the depositions. Three examples of such lists survive, and all were written by Samuel Parris.[33]

The most active of all the young Village accusers, twelve-year-old Ann Putnam Jr., was involved in cases against sixty-nine defendants, thirteen of whom were executed. Her father was the author of nearly all her depositions, which he prepared together with many others for the grand jury.

On April 20, as accusations were rapidly multiplying, Ann Putnam accused the Reverend George Burroughs of attacking her. Burroughs was the former minister of Salem Village whom the Putnams had forced to leave. Ann's dramatic account was drawn from her knowledge of Village gossip, as well as her own vivid imagination. "I was tortored by him," Putnam wrote on his daughter's behalf, "being Racked and all most choaked by him: and he tempted me to write in his book which I Refused with loud out cries and said I would not writ in his book tho he tore me al to peaces." The deposition concluded with references to more torments suffered at the hands of Burroughs's specter, whom Ann accused of "greviously tortoring me by beating pinching and almost choaking me severall times a day."[34] The deaths of Burroughs's two wives were not from natural causes, she said; they were "bewitched to death" by the abusive Burroughs. Out of malicious revenge, he had also murdered the wife and child of his successor, Deodat Lawson.

The impression given by the deposition is that of a brave child suffering heroically for the sake of her Christian faith. Wracked by Burroughs's torments, no one was more worthy to reveal the identity of the fiendish and brutal leader of Satan's plot than twelve-year-old Ann.

Ann was not the only young accuser who became accustomed to using florid language to describe spectral threats and injuries. Various depositions on behalf of the girls reveal that their throats were especially vulnerable to being choked or injured by invisible hands. Eighteen-year-old Susannah Sheldon reported that Mary Ireson's specter said she would "tear her throat out" if she did not sign the devil's book and that Martha Carrier would "cut my throat" if she did not sign. Mary Warren alleged that John Procter's specter threatened to "run ye hot tongs downe her throat."[35]

The court recorders also referred to the girls' necks as being severely bent and even "broken," an exaggeration surprisingly endorsed by the magistrates, who confirmed the accuracy of the examination records. Seeing that Mary Esty's head was bowed as she stood in the dock, Elizabeth Hubbard told the marshal standing next to her to "Put up her head, for while her head is bowed the necks of these [afflicted girls] are broken."[36]

One torment that the girls suffered "most grievously," sometimes "almost to death," was that of being painfully "pricked." This affliction was allegedly the result of sticking thorns or pins into small doll-like effigies of the victims, called poppets, made of rags or wood. Several confessors described seeing witches' specters in the courtroom. As the accusers grew bolder, they produced pins stuck into their hands. During the examination of George Jacobs Sr., "Ann Putman and Abigail Williams had each of them a pin stuck in their hands, and they said it was this old Jacobs." During Mary Parker's examination, Mary Warren went up to the defendant and showed "a pin run through her hand. And blood runeing out of her mouth."[37] Claiming to be bitten by specters, the girls also displayed bite marks on their wrists and arms to the magistrates and ministers.[38]

Soon after the first trial, in which Bridget Bishop was convicted and executed, the Boston ministers cautioned the magistrates on their use of spectral evidence. The ministers did not question the authenticity of the girls' claims to see invisible specters. They questioned the reliability of such evidence, that is, whether the devil was impersonating someone in spectral form without the person's permission, and therefore that person was innocent, or whether the person had given permission and was therefore guilty. Chief Magistrate William Stoughton chose to ignore the question of uncertainty and the ministers' explicit counsel. He not only continued to convict on the basis of spectral evidence but accorded it a primary role. Nor did he doubt the severity or validity of the girls' afflictions. Here Stoughton was following Hathorne's lead. In the courtroom, the young accusers were afflicted only momentarily. But Stoughton's crucial decision to endorse spectral evidence not only legitimated the girls' performances in court, but it also made them central to the trial process. From now on, the outcome of nearly every grand jury hearing and trial would turn on the girls' courtroom demonstrations.

The trial of Rebecca Nurse, which followed Bishop's on June 29, is a case in point. When the jury brought back a verdict of not guilty, Calef tells us that all the afflicted "made an hideous out-cry, to the amazement, not only of the Spectators, but the Court also seemed strangely surprised." The girls' furious performance of their "torments" caused the chief justice to send the jury back to reconsider, which they did, and changed their verdict to guilty. The girls' behavior was hardly hysterical. It was calculated and in keeping with their role to identify, isolate, and condemn the evil they believed they saw and the community feared. To doubt them in this instance was to doubt the central role that Stoughton had assigned to them and thus to doubt the trials themselves. Calef tells us that when the governor issued a reprieve for Nurse, after the guilty verdict, "the Accusers renewed their dismal out-cries against her, insomuch that the Governour was by some Salem Gentleman [i.e., the magistrates] prevailed with to recall the Reprieve."[39]

From March 1 through September 17 (the Court of Oyer and Terminer's last session), the core group of five Salem Village girls, initially assisted by Abigail Williams, before she dropped out at the end of June, was almost constantly in court for more than one hundred examinations, thirty-five grand jury hearings, and twenty-six trials.

In June, when Rebecca Nurse was indicted, the Nurse family mounted an all-out effort to influence the outcome of her trial, which was scheduled for the end of the month. They organized a petition, written by the influential Israel Porter, a stalwart friend of the Nurse family, on behalf of Rebecca's innocence. It was signed by thirty-eight Village residents, including several Putnam men and women. Part of the Nurse family campaign involved discrediting two of Nurse's principal accusers, Abigail Williams and Elizabeth Hubbard.

The respected Village resident Joseph Hutchinson reported in an undated deposition that Abigail Williams had told him that she was not afraid to see the devil, the black man, who kept bringing his book for her to sign. She said she could speak to the devil as easily as she could speak to him, which Hutchinson took to be suspicious familiarity with the devil. Doubt was therefore raised about young Abigail. The dating of Hutchinson's deposition is absent, but the influential Hutchinson's views might have begun to arouse suspicion against Abigail. In any case, Parris effectively silenced her by not writing any more depositions on her behalf after the end of the court's first session on June 30.[40]

Nurse family supporters also generated two depositions that cast doubt upon the credibility of Elizabeth Hubbard and five depositions against thirty-six-year-old Sarah Bibber of Salem.[41] None of these depositions bears the designation *jurat in curia,* and they were therefore not introduced in court on Nurse's behalf. Sarah Bibber was never taken seriously by the court, but Elizabeth Hubbard was, and her depositions, mostly written by Thomas Putnam, continued to be effective.

Thomas Brattle's assessment, which he circulated privately in his "Letter" of early October, was the strongest criticism leveled at the afflicted females. "The Devill imposes upon their brains," he resolved, "and deludes their fancye and imagination." He went on to draw attention to dissension among the magistrates about the girls' credibility, noting that some of the judges would rather give up their commission than continue to base their judgments "merely on the accusations of these afflicted, possessed children."[42]

By "possession" Brattle meant that the minds of the young accusers were taken over by the devil and used for his purposes. He was not saying that the afflicted were mentally impaired or physically ill but that their minds and imaginations were being manipulated not by witches but by the devil. While he pointed to the devil as the ultimate cause, he also implicated the magistrates, suggesting that they prompted the accusers to perform their afflictions and then claimed it was evidence of witchcraft: "The Justices ask the apprehended why they afflict those poor children; to which the apprehended answer, they do not afflict them. The Justices order the apprehended to look upon the said children, which accordingly they do; and at the time of that look, (I dare not say by that look, as the Salem Gentlemen do) the afflicted are cast into a fitt."[43]

The Village girls feared for their lives. Given Samuel Parris's ominous sermons, their distress is understandable. When ministers and magistrates expected them to produce evidence of spectral attack, they obliged. But the part they played admitted no exit. Early on, Hathorne had informed the girls that if they were not genuinely afflicted, they were murderers. Even if they began to entertain doubts, there was no turning back, a lesson Mary Warren had learned at her peril. Parris had also sent his nine-year-old daughter, Betty, to live with Stephen Sewall in Salem, thus taking her out of the line of fire and out of the reach of the authorities so that she could recover, which she did.[44] But Parris kept Abigail Williams at home and endorsed her denunciations against fifteen people, all of whom were executed.

If the girls' initial fear of the devil was genuine, as seems likely, the court, in requiring them to reenact their trauma in the presence of every new defendant, was retraumatizing them on an almost weekly basis in the courtroom. One can suppose that they saw each new suspect as an agent of Satan's malice, as their words indicate, who was causing them to relive their anxiety—first experienced outside of court—face-to-face in the courtroom. The girls were manipulated by the magistrates, and the courtroom became a theater for their post-traumatic behavior. They were playing a deadly role assigned to them, and they did everything they could to be convincing, even strategically performing their afflictions during the magistrates' interrogations, deliberately biting their lips until blood flowed, and sticking pins into their hands. The theatrical display was a stage-managed collaboration between the magistrates and the young, frightened, manipulated accusers, as well as the local ministers who were present. Thus the courtroom was transformed into a spectacle of invisible forces. As Cotton Mather wrote about the trial of Bridget Bishop, "There was little occasion to prove the *Witchcraft,* it being evident and notorious to all beholders."[45] The young accusers produced convincing symptoms of extreme physical torment—and they did so in insidious and pitiless ways, often taking cues from each other, as the court records reveal. Satan may not have been compelling the girls to contort themselves into the classic character of bewitched victims, but the magistrates and the community's fear of the devil in their midst certainly did.

THE MAGISTRATES

4

The Justices have given ear to the Devill.
— *Thomas Brattle*

Arguably, the most important question generated by the Salem tragedy is why the Salem magistrates believed the "afflicted" girls. If the magistrates had initially decided not to act on the girls' accusations, the legal process would never have started, and Salem would hold a very different place in America's historical self-consciousness.

The historical context of the trials makes the court's reliance on the girls' spectral evidence even more perplexing. As the seventeenth century progressed, magistrates and juries grew increasingly reluctant to convict people of witchcraft. The zeal of the Salem magistrates in 1692 went against thirty years of judicial restraint in New England witchcraft cases. Between 1665 and 1692, only one individual was executed. Puritan theology also reinforced the overall reluctance to convict alleged witches on the basis of spectral evidence. Historically speaking, the odds were very much against the judicial proceedings ever happening, or at least getting very far.

Why, then, did the Salem justices initially treat the girls' afflictions as genuine, and why, three months later, did the specially appointed Court of Oyer and Terminer continue to emphasize dubious spectral evidence, especially when the leading ministers of Boston warned against using it? With the arrival of the new charter of 1691, which diminished the political power of the Puritan church, were Boston's ministers initially hesitant to assert their views more strongly, delivering instead an ambiguous opinion? The trials broke with legal precedent in other significant ways as well.

The Salem magistrates went against customary procedure and conducted the preliminary hearings not in private but in public before large and prejudicial crowds. The magistrates also disregarded legal precedent in initially failing to require the complainants to post a monetary bond with their complaints, which was mandatory in all capital cases. Finally, the Salem justices violated all precedent in never executing anyone who confessed to witchcraft. Acting under pressure, perhaps, the court eventually did convict four confessors in late September but did not send them to the gallows. This particular aspect of the Salem trials is unique in the history of witch-hunts in Western civilization. The rampant confessions fueled more accusations as confessors named more and more suspects, which, in a vicious judicial circle, continued to legitimate the court's arrests and convictions.

As we shall see, the magistrates' attitudes and actions were shot through with a dire, overwhelming sense of urgency: the Puritan church, New England's central institution, was under attack in Salem Village. As the accusations spread, the threat widened and the Bay province as a whole became "miserably harassed," as the governor put it. From March through May 1692, the Salem magistrates had seen to it that the jails were "thronging" with suspects. When Governor Phips arrived in mid-May, empowered by a new royal charter, something urgent had to be done.[1]

In seventeenth-century New England, capital crimes were adjudicated in accordance with English common law practice, which involved three basic stages. The first encompassed complaints, arrest warrants, and preliminary hearings, called "examinations" in the Salem court records. If the examination yielded sufficient evidence, the defendant was jailed and held for the second phase of the process, which consisted of a formal indictment and a grand jury hearing (also called a "jury of inquest"), which could either acquit the defendant or uphold the indictment. If the indictment was upheld (a "true bill"), the proceedings moved to the final stage, a jury trial, which resulted in either conviction or acquittal. Because witchcraft was a felony and a capital offense, conviction meant execution by hanging.

Normally, the grand jury stage immediately followed the examination, but one of the peculiarities of the Salem episode is that this stage did not take place for three months. During this period, from March 1 to June 2, accusations and examinations continued unabated, and the jails were filled. In the view of some scholars, the long delay between the examinations and indictments encouraged more accusations and arrests in the absence of the possibly dampening influence of trials and executions.[2] But even after the trials and executions began, the impact of the legal process and its deadly consequences did not have a controlling effect; the accusations continued to pour in from throughout eastern Essex County.

The unusual delay in holding the grand juries and trials was due to the fact that until mid-May 1692, the Province of Massachusetts lacked both a royal charter and a royal governor. England had revoked the Massachusetts charter in 1684, and Boston leaders revolted and overthrew the royally appointed governor, Edmond Andros, in Boston in 1689. This bold action followed the "Glorious Revolution" in England, which unseated the Catholic monarch James II and installed the Protestant monarchs William and Mary. Until the new governor and new charter arrived in Boston, the elderly former governor Simon Bradstreet served as the acting governor. Increase Mather, Boston's most respected minister and president of Harvard College, had gone to London in 1688 to negotiate a new charter for Massachusetts. After the overthrow of the Andros regime in Boston, Mather stayed on in London to advise the Crown about the new charter and the selection of a new governor.

When the witchcraft proceedings began in Salem in March 1692, Mather was still in London. In late 1691, he had succeeded in securing both a new charter and a new governor, the thirty-one-year-old Sir William Phips. A ship captain and military leader who had been born in Maine, Phips had recently become a member of Cotton Mather's church. But neither Increase Mather nor Phips would sail for Boston until late March, and they did not arrive until mid-May.

In the meantime, on March 1, the Salem justices Hathorne and Corwin began making arrests and conducting examinations. But the interim governor, Simon Bradstreet, would not permit the examinations to proceed to indictments, which prevented the witchcraft cases from proceeding to a grand jury and, if deemed necessary, to trial. Bradstreet may have been exercising caution in acting on witchcraft allegations, as he had during his former gubernatorial tenure, which was the traditional approach in New England.[3] Whatever his reasons for doing so, Bradstreet deliberately blocked the magistrates from holding grand jury hearings and trials for the witchcraft defendants. He left the matter for the new governor and his Council to handle. Nevertheless, the Salem magistrates Hathorne and Corwin went ahead and continued with arrests and examinations through May without the possibility of indictments and grand juries. Since late January 1692, it had been known that a new governor and the new charter of October 1691 had been arranged in London and were presumably on the way, and in mid-February a copy of the new charter arrived.[4] So far as Hathorne and Corwin knew, the new governor would sail into Boston at almost any time. The Salem magistrates may not have wanted to appear soft on witchcraft during this crucial interim period. Word may also have reached them that they had been appointed by the Crown to the new Governor's Council and thus would hold positions of power once the governor appeared.[5] By initiating the legal process against the first three suspects, Hathorne and Corwin were undoubtedly trying to stop what must have seemed at the time to be a small but irritating threat in their own backyard and maintain local government control until Governor Phips and the new charter arrived.

The intercharter period was nevertheless an uncertain time. Since the overthrow of Governor Andros, all sorts of extralegal procedures and illegal activities had occurred. It must have appeared to Hathorne and Corwin that with multiple witchcraft accusations in the air, the situation had to be subjected to legal constraints.[6] Under the circumstances, the Salem magistrates could hardly have known that the initial allegations against three likely suspects would quickly swell into a flood that would fill the jails before the new governor appeared. As more accusations poured in, the magistrates continued to make arrests and hold hearings, perhaps hoping that their actions might suppress the witchcraft activity in their community.

It is also important to recognize that the afflicted girls belonged to the families of Salem Village's power structure and had received the full backing of the local ministers. Two of the girls were members of Parris's family, and their claims of bewitchment had occurred in the midst of Parris's repeated warnings about the devil's attempt to undermine his ministry. The other two, Ann Putnam and Elizabeth Hubbard, were members of households headed by prominent men, Thomas Putnam and Dr. William Griggs, both of whom were well known to the magistrates. Neighboring ministers also supported the girls' witchcraft accusations. John Hale, the minister of Beverly, and Nicholas Noyes, the assistant minister of Salem, who had ordained Parris in 1689, sided with Parris, and they held prayer sessions in their own churches to help remedy the girls' afflictions. The ministers' and doctor's views would have carried significant weight with the magistrates. With such backing and with the expected arrival of the new governor, the magistrates were under a certain amount of obligation to take legal action.

For a New England minister's family to be attacked by witchcraft was unprecedented. Justice Corwin had already come to Parris's aid in the fall of 1691, when the Village revolted and refused to provide him the firewood it was obliged to supply.[7] Now covert conflict was emanating from the invisible world, and Justices Corwin and Hathorne would have to intervene to rescue Parris and prosecute the accused.

As we have seen in chapter 2, Justice Corwin may also have had a strong personal interest in the unfolding crisis. During Tituba's examination, he seemed to have wanted to know whether his son's undiagnosed "hurt" was the result of witchcraft. When Hathorne asked Tituba, undoubtedly on Corwin's behalf, whether she had hurt his child, she confirmed that Sarah Good and Osborne had bewitched the boy. Perhaps Corwin suspected that his son was suffering in retaliation against his rescue of Parris by providing a fresh load of firewood, thus frustrating Satan's efforts to drive the clergyman out of the Village. Tituba's confirmation that Corwin's child was bewitched would have underscored the seriousness of the situation. Not even a magistrate's family was safe from Satan's plot against the community.[8]

Salem Village leaders and the local ministers must have been persuasive in their urgency, for after Governor Phips arrived he instituted the special Court of Oyer and Terminer. "The loud cries and clamours of the friends of the afflicted people . . . prevailed with me," he explained.[9] Thus, within a few days after Phips's arrival, New England's tradition of legal caution toward witchcraft accusations completely evaporated.

Despite the magistrates' readiness to proceed, they could not act on the basis of the charges advanced by three young girls, no matter how tortured they seemed. Nine-year-old Betty Parris, eleven-year-old Abigail Williams, and twelve-year-old Ann Putnam were too young to testify in court on their own. Seventeen-year-old Elizabeth Hubbard, Dr. Griggs's grandniece, who lived in his house as a maidservant, may have feared that she herself might become a target of the devil's torments in retaliation for her uncle's exposure of the devil's activities. After all, Satan had struck at Parris through his daughter and niece, and he had struck at Thomas Putnam, one of Parris's strongest supporters, though his wife, daughter, and maidservant. Hale indicates that Hubbard's affliction was indeed the turning point: "neighbours complained to the Magistrates at Salem, desiring they would come and examine the afflicted . . . after Hubbard became afflicted."[10]

As the records show, the "neighbors" making the initial complaints to the Salem court were the heads of the families of three of the girls and their friends. The first complaint was issued jointly by Thomas Putnam; his brother Edward Putnam, who was a church deacon; and Joseph Hutchinson Sr., who had given the land for the meetinghouse. Thomas Preston, who was not a church member, also subscribed to the complaint.

In preparation for the examinations, Hale tells us that the magistrates Hathorne and Corwin consulted English common law books as well as Puritan legal treatises.[11] In these books, the justices found remarkable parallels to their current situation and relevant legal precedents to follow. English common law tradition endorsed "specter evidence" for both examination and conviction. By contrast, English Puritan divines were more cautious and considered spectral evidence merely "presumptive," to be used for purposes of arrest and examination only, and not for conviction. Despite the discrepancy, both traditions supported spectral evidence for arrest and examination, and the two sources offered Hathorne and Corwin a legal foundation for moving forward. Tituba's legally potent "eyewitness" testimony, as a confessed witch, against the first two suspects provided solid grounds. From Tituba they also learned that there were more witches to be found. Examinations of new suspects would yield additional evidence, and there would be depositions from other witnesses.

Hale also tells us that the Salem magistrates had consulted Cotton Mather's recent account of a similar case involving spectral torment of the Goodwin children in Boston in 1688. Hale saw the parallels and noted that the Salem Village girls "in all things [were] afflicted as bad as John Goodwin's Children."[12] In the Goodwin case, legal proceedings began after a physician pronounced the children bewitched. The children had accused an Irish washerwoman, Ann Glover, who confessed to using witchcraft against them. The magistrates had also made her demonstrate in court how she manipulated the dolls representing them, called poppets, to which one of the frightened children responded by falling into "*sad* fits before the whole Assembly." While in prison, Glover confessed to tormenting the son of a woman who testified against her. She was tried, found guilty, and executed on the basis of spectral evidence, the dolls, and her own confession. Although the Goodwin children still exhibited torments and named additional suspects after Glover's death, Cotton Mather had taken the oldest and most agitated, a thirteen-year-old girl, to his home and calmed her fears through prayer, thus forestalling further legal action and a larger witch-hunt.

Initially, Parris appears to have tried to resolve the Village girls' tribulations in much the same manner, through prayer and counseling. But after Dr. Griggs's diagnosis and Mary Sibley's secret instigation of the witch-cake procedure, followed by Betty's and Abigail's naming of their tormentors, there was no turning back. "The devil had been raised," as Parris put it. He and the church members went on the attack, and the legal process commenced.

From the outset, the magistrates made two crucial departures from legal tradition that helped to generate more accusations. First, they waived monetary bond, called a "recognizance," that complainants in capital cases were normally required to pay. Without needing to post bond money, it was easier for complainants to initiate their accusations and to continue issuing new charges against suspects, sometimes naming multiple individuals in a single complaint. Recognizances in the Salem cases were not required until mid-July, well into the crisis. By that time, seventy-five people—half the total number of victims of the entire episode—had been arrested, incarcerated, and were awaiting trial. When bond was finally required, the amount varied from twenty to a hundred pounds, unlikely sums for Village farmers to have readily to hand for each complaint.[13]

This breach of legal procedure cannot have been an oversight. The bond requirement was stated in all the English law books, especially Michel Dalton's widely used *Countrey Justice* of 1618, which was available in many reprintings, including the updated 1690 edition.[14] If the Salem magistrates had insisted upon bond money before accepting the complaints, it might have forestalled the Village complainants from taking hasty action. If anything, however, the justices were removing barriers to facilitate the complainants and to assist their supporters in the Village congregation.

The second legal departure was the justices' decision to bring the accusers into the courtroom together instead of keeping them "apart, and not within hearing of one another," as Richard Bernard advised in his legal manual.[15] The magistrates further departed from normal procedure by opening the preliminary examinations to the public, which almost certainly spread fear and suspicion in the Village community. As Hale reports, the magistrates had given in to popular pressure: "Neighbours complained to the Magistrates at Salem, desiring they would come and examine the afflicted and accused together; which they did."[16] Thus the decision was made to place the girls together in the dramatic spotlight in front of the defendants and the whole Village.

The crowd that showed up for the first examinations was so large that it could not be accommodated at Ingersoll's tavern, where the hearings had been planned. The magistrates shifted the proceedings next door to the much-larger Village meetinghouse, where the examinations gained maximum exposure to the community. The meetinghouse was "Thronged with Spectators,"[17] and from our vantage point, the results were predictable. The girls not only identified the defendants as the cause of their torments, but followed the magistrates' cues to act out their torments in court, just as the Goodwin children had done. Over time, the magistrates permitted the young accusers to gang up and overwhelm the defendants' claims of innocence by the sheer force of their collective screaming and "falling into fits."

By allowing the girls to testify collectively in the public eye, the justices turned the courtroom into a theater where the performances of the afflicted provided what appeared to be visible evidence of unseen witchcraft powers employed by the defendants. This procedure would satisfy the "two eyewitnesses" requirement for the prosecution of witchcraft cases. The girls were the witnesses to the invisible, and their enacted "fits" and "torments" made the invisible visible to all. The girls also did their best to assist the magistrates in forcing the defendants to confess or incriminate themselves in the face of the girls' torments. The court-appointed recorders noted down the key points in the proceedings—the dialogue between magistrates, defendants, and accusers—as required in capital hearings. The accuracy of the examination records was confirmed by the magistrates, and they were used as evidence at the grand jury hearings and the trials.

The Reverend Deodat Lawson, who arrived in Salem Village on March 19, three weeks after the examinations began, described what he perceived to be the chief characteristic of the girls' afflictions: "That their Motions in their Fits are Preternatural, both as to the manner, which is so strange as a well person could not Screw their Body into; and as to the violence also it is preternatural, being much beyond the Ordinary force of the same person when they are in their right mind."[18]

The Salem magistrates had in fact invited Lawson to observe and validate the girls' afflictions. This appears to have been a deliberate move by the justices to gain additional clerical backing for the increasing number of accusations. There were five accusations already, and more were in the air. Lawson tells us that the magistrates then "Revised and Corrected" his account for publication.[19] Lawson's narrative was published in Boston on April 5, just over four weeks after the accusations began. Lawson, or more likely his publisher, the tabloid-style printer Benjamin Harris, gave Lawson's account a title that was meant to sell: *A Brief and True Narrative of Some Remarkable Passages Relating to Sundry Persons Afflicted by Witchcraft, at Salem Village.*[20] The magistrates may therefore have called in Lawson to publicize their efforts in the courtroom in order to gain wide support for the prosecution. Lawson and the magistrates were also joining company with Increase and Cotton Mather, who had attempted to revitalize Puritan faith in God's Providence and regenerate New England's flagging church membership by publishing popular accounts of Satan's forces attacking New England. The Mathers' similarly titled books described witchcraft cases and demonic attacks as instances of God's intervention in the world. Cotton's *Memorable Providences* described the spectral torments of the Goodwin children, and the magistrates were using it as a guide to their own proceedings.[21]

The many officials whose names appear in the court records also lent their authority to the girls' performances. In addition to the local magistrates and ministers, the accusations were backed by the various court recorders, the sheriff of Essex County, several town constables, neighboring ministers, and local physicians. From the beginning, the local legal and religious establishment, including several doctors besides Griggs, was fully behind the prosecutions.[22] The legal process was not simply the work of a few frightened adolescents and the Village minister.

From March through May, complaints, arrests, and examinations proceeded at an orderly but relentless pace. Defendants filled the four jails in Salem, Ipswich, Cambridge, and Boston without any trials taking place. When the newly appointed governor, Sir William Phips, stepped ashore in mid-May, he found a "Thronging of the Gaols at this hot season of the year."[23]

Phips, like the magistrates before him, decided that there was no time to lose. Rather than wait a few weeks until the newly constituted General Court in Boston could legislate the appropriate superior court into existence, as would later happen, the governor exercised his royal prerogative to establish the interim court.[24] He appointed a special Court of Oyer and Terminer ("To Hear and Determine") to deal with the growing crisis. The records show that by the time the special court began its work on June 2, 1692, there were sixty-eight prisoners in jail on witchcraft charges.

Seeking to justify his haste in setting up the Court of Oyer and Terminer, Phips graphically portrayed the scene he encountered in Boston: "When I first arrived, I found this Province miserably harrassed with a most Horrible witchcraft or Possession of Devills which had broke in upon severall Townes." "Some scores of poor people were taken with preternatural torments," he reported, "some scalded with brimstone, some had pins stuck in their flesh, others hurried into the fire and water, and some dragged out of their houses and carried over the tops of trees and hills."[25] The charge to the Court of Oyer and Terminer, Phips explained, was to hold grand jury hearings to discover "what witchcraft might be at the bottom or whether it were not a possession." As indicated in chapter 3, the distinction between witchcraft and demonic possession was a critical one. "Demonic obsession," sometimes called "Satanic possession," was voluntary insofar as it resulted from an individual's consorting with the devil or with some other evil spirit. The "possessed" person was the culprit, and anyone he or she accused was a victim, the innocent object of the possessed person's wrath. Only those learned in theology and the law, the ministers and magistrates, could properly make the distinction. Thus, Phips told officials in London that he had commissioned the Court of Oyer and Terminer to do just that: determine whether the accusers were suffering from demonic possession or from "reall witchcraft."[26]

In New England, the rare cases of demonic possession were left to ministers to treat with prayer, fasting, and counseling. A well-known case in Groton, Massachusetts, in 1671 had been described in detail by the Reverend Samuel Willard. Willard's careful supervision of the Elizabeth Knapp case had prevented it from resulting in witchcraft charges.[27]

Phips's second letter to London was more precise on this point. The court was focused on witchcraft, he explained, because "the generality of the People represented the matter to me as reall witchcraft." Here, in retrospect,

Phips may have been trying to shift the blame to his advisers for what turned out to be a legal disaster. Among the "people" who represented the situation to him were undoubtedly his lieutenant governor and the Salem justices Hathorne and Corwin, who were members of his Council.[28]

By the time Governor Phips and Increase Mather arrived with the new charter, Hathorne and Corwin had filled the jails, thus creating a legal and social crisis. Indeed, in mid-May, before Phips established the Court of Oyer and Terminer and before any grand jury hearings had been conducted, Hathorne and Corwin were already referring to future legal proceedings as "tryalls," which indicates that in their opinion the preliminary examinations had produced enough evidence to lead directly to trial.[29]

The court's procedure is not surprising. For the government to have interpreted the girls' afflictions as demonic possession instead of bewitchment would have been a defeat for the leaders of Salem Village, as well as the neighboring ministers. And it would have been a rejection of the preliminary findings of Hathorne and Corwin, both of whom were now sitting on the Governor's Council. The purpose of the Court of Oyer and Terminer was clearly to issue indictments and put the accused on trial.

Phips appointed nine members of the Governor's Council to serve as magistrates and designated his lieutenant governor, William Stoughton, to serve as the chief magistrate. Phips explained in his letter to London that he had chosen the "persons of the best prudence and figure that could then be pitched upon." Stoughton was one of the most respected men in the new provincial government. His fellow magistrates had also served in previous governments and as justices on various courts and were among the most experienced and politically influential men in the country.[30]

William Stoughton, stern and conservative, has been rightly characterized by Mary Beth Norton as "a man certain of his judgments and unwilling to entertain any opposition."[31] He held a master's degree in theology from Oxford and served in parishes in England and Massachusetts. But he eventually turned to a career in politics. His friend Cotton Mather had supported his appointment as the lieutenant governor.[32] In a letter endorsing Mather's justification of the Salem trials, published in Mather's *Wonders of the Invisible World,* Stoughton praised his friend's effort. Stoughton's letter to Mather emphasized the apocalyptic times that he believed New England was experiencing: "Such your Discerning of Divine Providences and Periods, now running on apace towards their Glorious Issues in the World; and finally, Such your [Mather's] Good News of The Shortness of the Devils Time, That all Good Men must needs Desire the making of this your Discourse Public to the World."[33] It seems clear that Stoughton, like Mather, saw the witchcraft trials as part of an ultimate showdown between God and Satan in New England. No doubt deeply influenced by witnessing the young accusers' dramatic torments, Stoughton is reported to have said that "when he sat in judgment he had the fear of God before his eyes,"[34] and that he hoped to have "cleared the land of these [witches]."[35]

Stoughton's job as chief magistrate was to preside over the proceedings of the Court of Oyer and Terminer and to set the rules of evidence for the trials. Disregarding Puritan authorities, Stoughton chose to follow the procedure of the preliminary examinations by relying heavily on spectral evidence, as was common in English law. The spectral evidence would be supplemented by as many testimonies as possible about the acts of *maleficium*—instances of permanent physical harm caused by witchcraft—that were alleged in hundreds of depositions. In defense, Cotton Mather would later claim that the acts of *maleficium* described by witnesses played as strong a role as spectral evidence in the court's verdicts. But on this point Mather was betraying his own repeated cautions to the court about privileging spectral testimony.

It was Stoughton, however, who gave the attorney general and the jury instructions about the interpretation of the witnesses' evidence. Thomas Brattle expressed astonishment at Stoughton's bias in favor of the spectral. According to Brattle, Stoughton told the jury "that they were not to mind whether the bodies of the said afflicted were really pined and consumed as expressed in the indictment but whether the said afflicted did not suffer from the accused such afflictions as naturally *tended* to their being pined and consumed, wasted, etc. This, (said he,) is a pining and consuming in the sense of the law." Brattle's point was that Stoughton wanted the jury to find the defendants guilty solely on the basis of the accusers' behavior in the courtroom when, as Brattle observed, "they were at intervals hale and hearty, robust and lusty, as tho' nothing had afflicted them." The jury, said Stoughton, was not to concern itself with whether the young accusers were permanently harmed in any way, which they were not, but only whether they "tended" to appear that way on the basis of observation. In any case, the results of Stoughton's instructions to the jury were predictable: the innocent were condemned. The jurors admitted as much in their apology five years later. "We do therefore hereby signifie . . . sorrow for our Errors, in acting on such Evidence to the condemning of any person."[36]

The first trial was that of middle-aged Bridget Bishop. She was tried and convicted on June 2, and executed by hanging on the morning of June 10. The execution took place on common land, a large hillside grazing pasture to the west of Salem Town in an area that later became known as Gallows Hill. The warrant for Bishop's execution, signed by Stoughton, said that she had been found guilty on the charge of witchcraft whereby she "hurt, afflicted pined, consumed, Wasted, and tormented" the bodies of Williams, Putnam, Lewis, Walcott, and Hubbard.[37] The qualifying word "tended," which gave the jurors the latitude to convict her, was absent from the execution warrant and from all four of Bishop's surviving indictments.[38] Bishop died simply for having "tended" to—that is, for having appeared to—harm the Village girls.

Given Stoughton's departure from the standard theological rationale of his day, his reliance on the spectral torment section of the Witchcraft Act of 1604 set up an inevitable clash between the government and the Boston clergy. The key clause of the act specified that "any evill and spirit, or shall consult[,] covenant with[,] entertaine[,] employ, feede, or rewarde any evill and wicked Spirit to or for any intent or pupose . . . wherebie any pson shall be killed, destroyed, wasted, consumed, pined or lamed in his or her body . . . shall suffer pains of deathe."[39]

Immediately after Bridget Bishop was tried and executed, Governor Phips asked Boston's leading clergy to advise him on the issues involved in the trial. Phips, who was himself fully committed to the court's procedure, was likely seeking the clergy's endorsement of Bishop's trial as a test case to see if Boston's ministers would support the government's reliance on spectral evidence for conviction. It was the first trial of several that were scheduled in June, and Phips, perhaps on the Mathers' advice, sought the ministers' backing for the court's methods. The result was an unfortunate equivocation.

The ministers replied on June 15 in a document entitled "Return of Several Ministers." Their statement began by emphasizing "the need of a very critical and exquisite caution" in the court's reliance on spectral evidence, asserting that the evidence used to condemn someone for witchcraft "ought certainly to be more considerable, than barely the accused persons being represented by a Spectre unto the Afflicted." The ministers pointed out that it was well known that a devil, with God's permission, "may take the shape of an innocent." Just because the devil made a particular individual's specter appear in a vision to the accusers and hurt them did not mean that that person was a witch, but only that the devil was a master of delusion. The ministers further added that by ignoring spectral evidence, the Salem court might well "put a period unto the progress of the dreadful calamity."[40] Here was the opportunity for the court to reconsider.

It is clear that the Boston ministers were not in favor of the English common law practice of giving significant weight to spectral evidence.[41] They followed the enlightened views of the Puritan divines Richard Bernard and William Perkins, who rejected spectral evidence as grounds for conviction, believing that the devil could take the shape of an innocent person. Bernard asserted that to convict a person it was necessary "to prove a league made with the Devil. In this only act standeth the very reality of a Witch." But "if this be not proved, all the strange fits, apparitions, naming of the suspected in trances, sudden falling downe at the sight of the suspected, the ease which some receive when the suspected are executed, bee no good grounds for to judge them guiltie of Witchcraft."[42] Bernard had made himself clear: an accuser's visions and fits could not be used as evidence to convict the accused.

The ministers also spoke against the court's use of the so-called "touch test": "nor can we esteem alterations made in the sufferers, by a look or touch of the accused, to be an infallible evidence of guilt, but frequently liable to be abused by the Devil's legerdemains."[43] In other words, the same logic applied to both visual and tactile evidence of spectral activity.

Nevertheless, the Boston ministers failed to entirely condemn the court's privileging of spectral evidence and the touch test. Instead, the "Return," which was written by the avid witch-hunter Cotton Mather, reached the opposite conclusion: "we cannot but humbly recommend unto the Government the speedy and vigorous prosecution."[44]

Why this obvious ambiguity in the ministers' counsel? Historians have supposed that they were reluctant to oppose the magistrates because several of the magistrates were members of their own churches. The document also shows that the ministers themselves were in a quandary about how to proceed and so offered conflicting views. "Speedy and vigorous prosecution," however, was all the court wanted to hear. Historians agree that the ministers' reply had sent an ambiguous message. But the court, under Stoughton's leadership, chose to ignore their cautionary statement, and, relying primarily on spectral evidence and the precedents of English common law, it proceeded to bring witchcraft cases to trial.

Although all of the magistrates were experienced justices of the peace and had served on various courts for years, none of them was a professional lawyer or had received formal legal training. The court proceeded under the supervision of two English lawyers, Thomas Newton and Anthony Checkley, who served as the Crown's attorneys general for the Bay Province. Newton served until late July and was succeeded by Checkley. Both clearly approved of Stoughton's emphasis on spectral evidence and ensured that the justices followed the procedures of English law.[45] Newton's and Checkley's signatures and handwriting on court records show that they selected the evidence, depositions, and witnesses to be used at the grand jury hearings and prepared the indictments and arranged the grand jury's schedule. It is also likely that they argued the cases before the grand jury.[46]

When the grand jury hearings and trials began, Stoughton decided to base the trials on the evidence documented from the preliminary examinations and used depositions taken from dozens of accusers in Salem Village and other communities. The grand jury hearings and trials unfolded largely as a replay of the testimonies about spectral evidence used in the preliminary examinations conducted by Salem justices John Hathorne, Jonathan Corwin, Bartholomew Gedney, and (later) John Higginson. This evidence was supplemented by numerous depositions alleging *maleficium,* such as unexplained deaths and injuries, especially of women and children. The records show that the afflicted accusers were present at the grand jury hearings and performed their specter-caused torments.

As Phips and the Governor's Council went about restoring governmental institutions, their immediate concerns were the Indian attacks along the Maine frontier and the burgeoning witch-hunt crisis, which continued to spread across eastern Essex County. The court records and sermons indicate from early on that the local ministers and magistrates believed they were dealing with a general plot against the church. Under these circumstances, the Court of Oyer and Terminer, guided by Stoughton's zealous leadership, overextended itself and employed ever more unusual methods to discover and prosecute witchcraft suspects. As far as the government was concerned, Boston's spiritual leaders were free to theologize, but desperate times called for the newly empowered civil authorities to act decisively to quell the apparent chaos.

In mid-April, the magistrates Hathorne and Corwin presided over several confessions that described satanic masses attended by witches' specters that occurred in the pasture next to Parris's house. The most shocking news, revealed at this time, was that these masses were led by George Burroughs, a former controversial minister of Salem Village. The identification of George Burroughs attached a name and a face to the demonic attack on Salem Village, and it was the face of a Puritan minister gone over to Satan. It confirmed the Puritans' worst fears, voiced by Lawson in late March: Satan wanted to make Salem Village the seat of his kingdom. As Stoughton's letter to Cotton Mather indicated, Satan was inflicting an organized assault on New England, "Coming like a Flood upon us." God would ultimately defeat him, but meanwhile Salem Village was ground zero in an all-out war between the forces of good and evil.[47]

Despite the urgency of the situation and the need for the court to take decisive action, the June 10 execution of Bridget Bishop elicited criticism. The Reverend William Milborne, a Baptist clergyman in Boston, sent a petition to the legislature warning of the danger of the court's proceeding on the basis of spectral evidence. Formerly a minister in Saco, Maine, Milborne probably knew George Burroughs, who was living at that time in the neighboring settlement of Black Point. "Several persons of good fame and of unspotted reputation stand committed to several gaols . . . upon bare specter testimonies," Milborne noted, and cautioned that continuing to proceed as the court had done in Bishop's case would trigger "a woeful chain of consequences." Phips and the Governor's Council would hear none of it. They ordered Milborne to pay two hundred pounds in bond money, a large and punitive fee, and to promise good behavior or be put in jail.[48]

However determined the government was to stifle public criticism, sermons and private letters began to be directed at the court. The highly regarded Samuel Willard, the minister of Boston's liberal Third Church and formerly the Groton minister who had saved Elizabeth Knapp from prosecution for witchcraft, was the first to address the situation in a sermon. He had initially endorsed the trials, cognizant that three of the judges on the court were seated in his congregation.[49] In a sermon preached on May 29, just before the trials would begin, Willard warned his congregation, "Be sober and vigilant because your adversary the devil, a roaring lion walketh about seeking whom he may devour; [and] whom resist steadfast in the faith." Samuel Sewall, one of the judges appointed to the court, was a member of Willard's congregation and noted in his diary Willard's warning about the devil stalking the land. But not long afterward, following the arrest, on spectral evidence, of the distinguished Captain John Alden, who was a member of Willard's church, Willard began to raise doubts about the proceedings. On June 19, a little more than two weeks after Alden's arrest, Willard spoke again from the pulpit and bluntly posed the critical question: "whether the devil can represent the person of a good man doing a bad action." His answer directly challenged Justice Stoughton's position: "I do assert that the devil may represent an innocent, nay a godly person, doing a bad act." Willard also insisted that the devil can "perswade the person afflicted that it is done by the person thus represented"; indeed, "the devil can represent the Image of any man in the world."[50] Willard was as clear as he could be: the devil had deluded the afflicted accusers, and the judges were making a grave mistake.

Shortly after his outspoken sermon, which likely became the subject of criticism in Salem, Robert Calef noted that "one of the Accusers cried out publickly of Mr. Willard, Minister in Boston, as afflicting of her." Willard's high status as one of Boston's leading ministers and his personal relationship to the magistrates protected him, and "she [the accuser] was sent out of the Court, and she was told that she was mistaken in the person."[51] Although the charges never stuck, Willard's boldness showed that openly challenging the trials could be dangerous.

Less risky than the public sermon was the private letter. Two days before the court convened for its first session, Cotton Mather wrote to Justice John Richards, a member of Mather's congregation who had recently been appointed to the court. Mather came directly to the point: "I must most humbly beg you that in the Management of the affair in your most worthy hands, you do not lay more stresse upon pure Spectre testimony than it will bear." He emphasized that "it is very certain that the devils have sometimes represented the shapes of persons not only innocent, but also very virtuous." He warned Richards that "if mankind have thus far once consented unto the Creditt of Diabolical representations the Door is opened!"[52]

But Mather all too frequently undercut his own advice, a sign of his ambivalence and reluctance to dispute with the civil authorities. "There is cause Enough," he wrote, "to think that it is a horrible Witchcraft which hath given rise to the troubles wherewith Salem Village is at this day harassed." Thus he endorsed aggressive judicial proceedings, and his warning against spectral evidence was entirely ignored.

By August, however, Mather was anxious about the court's reckless behavior. He reiterated his caution about relying on spectral evidence in a letter to Justice John Foster, who had asked Mather for his appraisal. He suggested that Foster question the effects of a defendant's looking at or touching the afflicted and not take for granted an accuser's testimony about animal familiar spirits—all typical features of the court's proceedings. He also counseled that if the court was uncomfortable with any of its convictions, it might well reconsider them, as "it would certainly be for the glory of the whole transaction to give that person a reprieve." Yet again, Mather undermined his moderating advice as he urged the court to move forward to "cleanse the land of witchcrafts, and yet also prevent the shedding of innocent blood, whereof some are so apprehensive of hazard."[53] Taken together, Willard's public pronouncements and Mather's letters served as a warning to the court that serious doubts were now being raised.

More detailed than Mather's August letter was Robert Pike's carefully argued objection, addressed to Justice Jonathan Corwin and dated August 8. Both Pike and Corwin were members of the Governor's Council and thus were political equals. Pike, an experienced magistrate from Salisbury, had supported the accusations that five of his neighbors had lodged against Salisbury resident Susannah Martin in May. Three months later, after Martin's execution, Pike was having second thoughts. In a long and tactfully written letter to Justice Corwin, someone he considered a personal friend, Pike set forth the clearest case yet against the court's use of spectral evidence. The main points of his argument are summarized in his own words:

[In] the enclosed, I further humbly present to consideration the doubtfulness and unsafety of admitting spectre testimony against the life of any that are of blameless conversation, and plead innocent, from the uncertainty of them and the incredulity of them; for as for diabolical visions, apparitions, or representations, they are more commonly false and delusive than real, and cannot be known when they are real and when feigned, but by the Devil's report; and then not to be believed, because he is the father of lies.[54]

It is not difficult to appreciate Pike's criticism. Although the court presented other kinds of testimony at the grand jury hearings, such as suspicious bodily injuries and the sudden and unexplainable deaths of various people (mostly children), all the bills of indictment issued by the grand juries had specified the charge of spectral "pining, tormenting and wasting" as the grounds on which the defendants would be tried. Everyone executed on Gallows Hill was condemned on this charge.

Pike also wondered, as did Brattle, why witches would so easily incriminate themselves. It seemed illogical that defendants would "plead innocent, when accused of witchcraft, and yet, at the same time, [be seen] to be acting witchcraft in the sight of all men, when they know their lives lie at stake by doing it. Self-interest teaches every one better." Pike went on to question whether "the eye [of the accuser] is abused and the senses deluded, so as to think they do see or hear some thing or person, when indeed they do not." Translated into modern terms, Pike was proposing that the magistrates should determine whether the accusers were hallucinating.

Pike concluded his letter by saying that given all the uncertainties involved in trying to prove that someone was a witch, "it may be more safe, for the present, to let a guilty person live till further discovery, than to put an innocent person to death. First, Because a guilty person may afterward be discovered, and so put to death; but an innocent person to be put to death cannot be brought again to life when once dead."[55]

The July and August criticisms of Samuel Willard, Cotton Mather, and Robert Pike were but a prelude to the detailed and authoritative case against the trials written by Cotton's father, Increase Mather, Boston's most respected theological voice. Unfortunately, the elder Mather took his time. He spent two full months, from early August to early October, writing his treatise, which he titled *Cases of Conscience Concerning Evil Spirits Personating Men*. Strategically, he may have worked with deliberate slowness in order to allow public criticism to arise. Within that eight-week time frame, however, fell the court's deadliest period, the last weeks of August and the first weeks of September. During this period, six men and eight women had been put to death. Chief Magistrate Stoughton, knowing of Mather's work and that the court might soon be closed, rushed through more defendants to trial and execution.

REPORTS OF WITCHES' MEETINGS 5

They did eat Red Bread like Mans Flesh.
— Mercy Lewis, April 1692

They mett there [next to Samuel Parris's house] to destroy that
place. . . . Satans design was to set up his own worship.
— William Barker Sr., August 1692

Among the several factors that drove the magistrates
recklessly forward were the many dramatic and often bi-
zarre testimonies about witches' meetings taking place
in Salem Village and, later on, in neighboring Andover.
Around four dozen records out of approximately 950
contain accounts of witches' meetings and references
to performances of the devil's sacrament in Salem Village and Andover. The reports of these demonic rituals
make clear the threat that Satan was believed to pose to
the Salem Village community, to the Village church, and,
as one Andover confessor indicated, to all the churches
in the Massachusetts Bay Province. Although historians
have not given these particular testimonies much attention, contemporary observers noted that they played a
significant role in confirming the validity of the accusations, thus helping to legitimate the legal process and pro-
pel it onward.[1]

The witches' meetings were entirely spectral in nature.
That is, they were visible only to the afflicted accusers and to those who confessed. Accusers and confessors sometimes gave elaborate descriptions of the satanic
masses and acts of witchcraft they witnessed. From the
beginning, these testimonies alarmed the authorities be-

cause they described not only individual bewitchments within the community but also Satan's larger plot to undermine the church in Salem Village. Witches were not just targeting the minister's family and church members, a fact that was obvious to Reverend Lawson soon after he arrived in Salem Village, but were also establishing their own covenant community. These allies of the devil were holding satanic masses next to the Village parsonage in a brazen attempt to destroy the Christian faith and supplant it with a church of Satan on Parris's own property. This was the same property that Parris's opponents claimed he had no right to possess in the first place. Satan was now laying claim to it.

Nothing of this sort had ever been mentioned before by witchcraft suspects or accusers in New England. To be sure, New England Puritans had long believed that their errand in pagan Indian North America to establish a Puritan utopia inevitably involved a direct assault on Satan's empire, and they knew that the devil was responsible for some of the unexplainable misfortunes that they suffered. The Prince of Demons' usual method was to empower a few degenerate and willing souls to use his evil magic in order to take revenge on some of their neighbors. Satan was also believed to be directly responsible for inciting the devastating Indian attacks on English settlements, as happened in King Philip's War of 1675–78, and later in what became known as King William's War of 1688–97.

In 1692, it was revealed in Salem Village that Satan was striking a direct blow at the spiritual core of New England—the church—at a time when, under the new charter, the Puritan church would no longer be central to the government of the country.[2] It soon became apparent that the devil was recruiting agents from all over Essex County. As time went on, accounts of witches' meetings revealed that destroying the Salem Village church was only the beginning. Satan's ultimate goal was to destroy all the churches in the land.

We have seen that Tituba was the first to tell about witches gathering in the Village. She described encountering the specters of four of them, led by a man dressed in black. They had gathered in the lean-to chamber at the back of Parris's house, and they had come from Boston. The meeting, Tituba said, was unseen by Parris or anyone else. The court record of Tituba's second examination continues in question-and-answer form, with Hathorne prompting her to tell what the man dressed in black said she must do:

> A: [H]e tell me they must meet together.
> Q. When did he Say you must meet together?
> A. He tell me Wednesday next att my master's house, & then they all meet together thatt night I saw them all stand in the Corner, all four of them, & the man stand behind mee & take hold of mee to make mee stand still in the hall.[3]

Tituba's eyewitness testimony about the witches' specters meeting inside Parris's house hit the courtroom like a bombshell. It meant that Satan's attack against the family of the minister was an organized assault led by outsiders, and it captivated the imagination of the Village and the Salem magistrates. Finally, Tituba revealed that there were nine witches' marks in the man's book, thereby doubling the number she had initially seen meeting in Parris's house.

The young accusers immediately picked up on Tituba's report about witches gathering in the minister's house. Three weeks after Tituba's testimony, the accusers boldly confronted Martha Cory during her examination in the meetinghouse, asking "why she did not go to the company of Witches which were before the Meeting house mustering? Did she not hear the Drum beat?" This challenge was the first independent confirmation of Tituba's report that witches were meeting in the Village. They were now gathering in a threatening manner outside the meetinghouse, where magistrates were interrogating a new suspect. This news came from the court's star witnesses, and it increased the number of witches to the size of a "company," which Lawson reported to be about twenty-three or twenty-four.[4]

A week later, Abigail Williams and Mercy Lewis told the Reverend Lawson that they had just witnessed a performance of the devil's mass in the Village. This was on the same day (March 31) that a public fast was being held in Salem Town for the benefit of the afflicted Village girls. Thus Williams and Lewis were privy to a counterritual in the Village, a demonic feast opposing the Christian fast. According to Lewis, "they [the witches] did eat Red Bread like Mans Flesh, and would have her eat some: but she would not; but turned away her head, and Spit at them, and said 'I will not Eat, I will not Drink, it is Blood,' etc."[5]

On Sunday, April 3, a Sacrament Day at the Village church, one of the afflicted girls told Lawson that she had seen the specter of Sarah Cloyce shortly after she had stormed out of the meetinghouse during a Sunday worship service without having taken communion. " 'O Goodw[ife]. C[loyce],' " said Lawson's informant, " 'I did not think to see you here!' (and being at their Red bread and drink) said to her, 'Is this a time to receive the Sacrament, you ran-away on the Lords-Day, and scorned to receive it in the Meeting-House, and Is this the time to receive it? I wonder at you!' "[6] The implication was that Cloyce, who was a sister of the accused Rebecca Nurse and who left the church (slamming the door) on Sunday without taking communion, did so in order to attend a satanic mass elsewhere in the Village. The location was not mentioned. The next day Sarah Cloyce was accused and joined her sister in jail.

On the basis of these reports, Lawson declared from the pulpit that the devil was trying to make Salem Village "the Rendezvous of Devils" and attempting to "set up his Kingdom in opposition to Christ's Kingdom."[7] Enthralled by what he heard and saw, Lawson did not think to question the large number of witches reported by the girls, thus confirming the growing scale of Satan's attack.

A week later, the former deputy governor Thomas Danforth presided over the examinations of Sarah Cloyce and Elizabeth Procter. He was apparently well-informed about the subject of witches meetings on Samuel Parris's property. During the examination, he asked Abigail Williams for an eyewitness account: "[D]id you see a company at Mr. Parris's house eat and drink?" Williams replied that she saw "their sacrament" and added, "they said it was our blood, and they had it twice that day."[8] Williams's statement that the devil's sacrament was "our blood"—that is, the blood of the afflicted girls—in addition to her confirmation that Parris's property was the site of the meetings must have been deeply alarming to the Village. On this occasion, Williams estimated that there were about forty witches in attendance at the meal, which doubled the number recorded by Lawson a week earlier. The magistrates, apparently convinced, did not question Williams's claim. From this point onward, the field next to Parris's house would be the location of all reported witchcraft meetings in Salem Village. It was the site of Satan's counterfaith, which was rapidly growing while Parris's congregation stagnated and some full members had begun to stay away.

On April 19, fifteen-year-old Abigail Hobbs of Topsfield confessed that she "was at the great Meeting in Mr Parris's Pasture when they administered the Sacramt'tt, and did Eat of the Red Bread and drink of the Red wine att the same Time." Hobbs was the first to explain how witches afflicted their victims by sticking thorns into effigies: "the Devil in the Shape of a Man came to her and would have her afflict Ann Putnam, Mercy Lewis, and Abigail Williams, and brought their images with him in wood like them, and gave her thorns and bid her prick them into those images, which she did accordingly." By stabbing doll-like effigies, called poppets, witches afflicted their victims with painful torments, making them cry out that they were being "pricked" by specters. For their part, the magistrates were fully convinced of the efficacy of sticking thorns and pins into effigy dolls. They made several defendants demonstrate the procedure in the courtroom, using dolls and pins. They asked Hobbs about the death of a certain Mary Lawrence, who had died at the time when Hobbs lived in Casco (Portland), Maine. "Where did you stick the thorns? . . . Was it about the middle of her body?"[9]

Two days later, Abigail's stepmother, Deliverance Hobbs, who had also been accused, knowing that the magistrates were seeking evidence against the Reverend Burroughs, confirmed Ann Putnam's and Abigail Williams's reports that the high priest of the satanic masses was the former Village minister the Reverend George Burroughs, who was now minister at Wells, Maine. According to Deliverance's account, "Mr Burroughs was the Preacher, and prest them to bewitch all in the Village, telling them they should do it gradually and not all att once, assureing them they should prevail." Hobbs added that she had seen Burroughs conduct a satanic mass next to Parris's house: "He administered the sacrament unto them att the same time Red Bread, and Red Wine Like Blood. . . . The meeting was in the Pasture by Mr Parris's house."[10] Hobbs herself admitted to being a "Covenant Witch" and proceeded to name nine suspects at the devil's sacrament, referencing Tituba's initial count of nine witches in the Village, all of whom had been previously named.

It was at this climatic juncture, with the new confessions by Abigail Hobbs, Deliverance Hobbs, and Mary Warren, and with the accusations of George Burroughs by Ann Putnam and Abigail Williams, that the floodgates of accusations opened. Before April 12, only ten people had been accused. Then the accusations escalated. By April 22, Burroughs and thirteen more had been accused, and there were three new confessions. The identification of Burroughs as the leader of a large-scale conspiracy helped to crystallize the surge of fear in Salem Village. He was the perfect choice to escalate the unfolding drama: a renegade minister turned to devil worship was using the field next to Parris's house to attack the very ministry he once led. The frightened Salem community now had a scapegoat who represented their fear of the devil active in the community, and the news reverberated throughout Essex County.

By May, reports of satanic masses being held in Parris's pasture had become a common theme. Mary Warren, having decided to cooperate with the court, told the magistrates that "she saw this Woman [Sarah Buckley] & a great company & that this Woman would have her the said Warren go to their Sacrament up to Mr Parris." Warren also testified that Burroughs had tried to bewitch Justice Hathorne.[11]

On June 1, the day before the grand jury heard the first cases, Attorney General Thomas Newton sought additional testimony from Abigail Hobbs and Mary Warren. Newton interviewed them in the Salem jail, and they named fourteen more suspects whom they claimed to have seen at witches' Sabbaths in Parris's field. Hobbs named five, including Burroughs, and Warren named nine more and identified them as the people who had tortured her in an attempt to make her attend a devil's sacrament in mid-May. Warren also identified Rebecca Nurse and Elizabeth Procter, both jailed suspects, as Satan's deacons who assisted Burroughs (in spectral form) at the meeting. Nurse and Procter "would have had her [Warren] eat some of their sweet bread & wine & she asking them what wine that was one of them said it was blood & better then our wine but this depon't refused to eat and drink with them."[12]

The purpose of Newton's interview was to obtain Hobbs's and Warren's sworn testimony about Sarah Good and John Procter for the grand jury hearings that he had scheduled for June and July. He needed eyewitness evidence in order to satisfy the two-witness rule required in witchcraft cases. Testimonies about who attended witches' meetings, mainly from confessed witches, would therefore play an instrumental role in moving the trials forward from June through September. Confessed witches thus made sure they named a few suspects whom they saw at satanic meetings to satisfy the court's demand. In preparation for Sarah Good's grand jury hearing, Newton noted down that Deliverance Hobbs had seen Good at a "meeting of witches in Mr Parris' field when Mr Burroughs preached [and] administered the sacrament to them."[13]

In mid-July, the elderly Ann Foster of Andover told the magistrates that she had flown on a stick in the air "above the tops of the trees" in the company of several other witches on her way to meetings in Salem Village. The court records contain three of Foster's accounts, and all were selected for use at the September grand jury hearings. Foster attested that she saw Martha Carrier, a witchcraft suspect from Andover, sticking pins into poppets to bewitch children in Andover, making one of them ill and killing the other. "[S]he further Saith that she hard Some of the witches say that their was three hundred & five in the whole Country. & that they would ruin that place ye village." The Salem magistrate John Higginson added the comment that Foster "further conffesed that the discourse amongst the witches at the meeting at Salem village was that they would afflict there to set up the Divills Kingdome."[14]

Mary Toothaker followed up at the end of the month by saying a man "Whose Name Is Burroughs yt preached at ye Village Metting of witches, & She Heard yt they Used bread & wine at thes Metting & yt they did talk of 305 Witches in ye Country . . . [and] Saith their Discourse was about pulling Dwone ye Kingdome of Christ. & Setting Vp the Kingdome of Satan."[15]

From July onward, magistrates repeatedly asked confessors to identify whom they had seen attending witches' meetings and, apparently, to estimate the size of the gatherings. Mary Lacey was asked, "[D]id you see your daughter at the meeting?," "What sort of worship did you do the Devil?," and "What meeting have you been at, at the village?"[16] The magistrates assumed that meetings were being held frequently and seem to have hoped that continuing arrests and examinations would stem the tide. They did not. Instead, during July, August, and September, the court records refer to witches' meetings more than fifty times and the estimated number of witches increased alarmingly, as the confessors attempted to give weight to their testimonies.

In neighboring Andover, accused suspects, pressured by their families and the authorities, confessed in large numbers and offered elaborate descriptions of witches' meetings. Twenty-two-year-old Elizabeth Johnson Jr. told the court that there were "about six score," that is, 120, at the witches' meeting in the Village. "[S]he s'd they had bread & wine at the witch Sacrament att the Village & they filled the wine out into Cups to drink she s'd there was a minister att theat meeting & he was a short man & she thought his name was Borroughs: she s'd they agreed that time to afflict folk: & to pull done the kingdom of Christ & to set up the devils kingdom."[17] A few days later, twenty-seven-year-old Susannah Post of Andover said at her examination that she saw 200 at a meeting in Andover, and "she heard there were 500 witches in ye country."[18]

On August 29, forty-six-year-old William Barker Sr. of Andover offered the most detailed description to date of the devil's meetings. He explained that Satan had initially recruited followers in Salem Village because of discord over the minister. Furthermore, Satan's congregation in the Village had grown to hundreds of followers, led by Burroughs and another minister, the Reverend John Busse, a former preacher in Wells, Maine. Most important, the devil's attack on the Village church was but a prelude to his attack on all the churches in the Massachusetts Bay Province:

> He said they mett there [next to Samuel Parris's house] to destroy that place by reason of the peoples being divided & theire differing with yr ministers Satans design was to set up his own worship, abolish all the churches in the land, to fall next upon Salem and soe goe through the countrey. . . . He sayth there was a Sacrament at yt meeting, theire was also bread & wyne. . . . [H]e has been informed by some of the grandees yt yr is about 307 witches in the country. . . . He sayth the witches are much disturbed with the afflicted persones because they are discovered by ym, They curse the judges because their Society is brought under.[19]

After the closure of the court in late October 1692, critics and supporters alike took up their pens to dissect the trials. In the process, they drew attention to the significance of the testimonies about witches' meetings. Thomas Brattle, in a privately circulated letter, wrote that the testimonies of witches' meetings were the result of psychological delusion and judicial coercion and should never have been admitted in court. He also noted that many of his neighbors disagreed, saying: "Will you not believe men and women who confesse that they have signed to the Devill's book? that they were baptized by the Devill; and that they were at the mock-sacrament once and again? What! will you not believe that this is witchcraft?" To this charge, Brattle responded that "the witches' meeting, the Devill's Baptism, and mock sacraments, which they oft speak of, are nothing else but the effect of their fancye, depraved and deluded by the Devill, and not a Reality to be regarded or minded by any wise man."[20]

The Boston merchant Robert Calef's trenchant criticism of the Salem trials, published in 1700 in *More Wonders of the Invisible World,* pointed out that the magistrates prompted the confessions by asking loaded questions that coached the defendants into giving the desired response: "were you at such a Witch-meeting, or have you signed the Devil's Book, etc. upon their replying, yes, the whole was drawn into form as their Confession."[21] Calef's observation is important because it establishes a connection between the confessors' reports of witches' meetings and the evidence sought by the magistrates.

The Reverend John Hale, who described some of the early proceedings, also concluded that the testimonies about witches' meetings played a crucial role in driving the Salem trials forward:

> [T]hat which chiefly carried on this matter to such an height, was the increasing of confessors till they amounted to near about Fifty: . . . their relating the times when they covenanted with Satan, and the reasons that moved them thereunto; their Witch meetings, and that they had their mock Sacraments of Baptism and the Supper, . . . and some shewed the Scars of the wounds which they said were made to fetch blood with.[22]

By contrast, Cotton Mather was convinced that the testimonies about witches' meetings were valid evidence. In *Wonders of the Invisible World,* his justification of the trials, he wrote that "at prodigious Witch-Meetings the Wretches have proceeded so far as to Concert and Consult the Methods of Rooting out the Christian Religion from this Country."[23] Mather quoted at length from several accounts of satanic masses to prove his case and thereby justify the actions of the court.

The testimonies about a witchcraft conspiracy against Parris and the church, which included dozens of "eyewitness" reports of satanic masses in Parris's pasture, endowed otherwise ordinary accusations among neighbors with the heightened significance of a Satanic plot against the Village ministry. The reports, prompted by the magistrates, confirmed Parris's preaching that Satan was trying to "pull down his church." With such "evidence," the accusations were driven forward.

6

THOMAS PUTNAM

Beholding Continually the Tremendous Works of Providence . . .
we remain yours to serve in what we are able.
— *Thomas Putnam to Salem magistrates, 1692*

I saw the Apperishtion of Sarah osborn . . . who did Immediatly
tortor me most greviously.
— *Thomas Putnam on behalf of Ann Putnam Jr.*

When Ann Putnam Jr., along with Betty Parris, Abigail
Williams, and Elizabeth Hubbard began to suffer torments from specters sometime in mid-February 1692,
Ann's father, Thomas Putnam, joined by Samuel Parris
and other Putnam men and elders of the church, were
the first to write out the official complaints that launched
the witch-hunt. Before the witch trials ended in October, Thomas Putnam would write more than 120 depositions and testimonials, mostly on behalf of himself and
the afflicted girls. This number accounts for one-third
of the surviving 346 depositions and testimonies of the
Salem trials.[1] It is striking evidence of Putnam's aggressive support for the prosecution, and all the more significant because most of his efforts took place during the
crucial early phase of the legal process when the accusations began to accelerate. Altogether, twelve members of
the extended Putnam family, drawn from all three of its
branches, would become involved in the prosecution of
no fewer than fifty-eight people, more than one-third of
the total number of people accused and arrested. Thomas
Putnam and the women in his household—his wife,
daughter, and maidservant—were responsible for more

than 160 accusations. His brother Edward and his nephew Jonathan Walcott participated in twenty-five cases. As the local historian Charles Upham rightly observed, the Putnam family "seemed to have been carried away by the witchcraft delusion in its early stages, and were more or less active in pushing the prosecutions."[2] If anything, Upham's observation is too moderate: Thomas Putnam and his family were central players in pushing forward the unfolding drama of Satan's apparent attack on Salem Village.

Forty-year-old Thomas Putnam Jr. was the eldest son of Thomas Putnam Sr., one of the wealthiest men in Salem Village. His younger brother Edward and his two uncles, Nathaniel and John, were the Village's largest landholders and among its most influential men. In 1678, Thomas married seventeen-year-old Ann Carr, the daughter of the wealthy John Carr of Salisbury. Ann's sister Mary was married to the Reverend James Bailey of Salem Village, who had been the Village's first minister. By 1692, Thomas and Ann Putnam had had seven children in the space of twelve years. The seventh child, Sarah, died in infancy in December 1689. Their oldest child was twelve-year-old Ann Jr.

From 1684 to 1687, Putnam served as the Village clerk and recorded the proceedings of meetings in the Salem Village record book. He was also a member of the Village tax-rate committee, a group that the Putnams usually dominated. His father and two uncles were often elected to the influential office of selectman in Salem Town. The Putnam family was used to having its hands on the reins of power in the Village as well as a voice in the affairs of the prosperous Salem Town.

Thomas was one of seven Putnam men who, together with four of their wives, became founding members of the Village church under Samuel Parris. The Putnam family, along with the other members of Parris's new congregation, supported Parris's rejection of the Halfway Covenant and his retention of the older and more exclusive rules of church membership. By 1692, the Putnam surname comprised one-fourth of the total church membership and close to 30 percent of the male membership. Thomas's brother Edward was one of the church deacons, and his brother-in-law Jonathan Walcott was a former deacon. From 1691 onward, Samuel Parris selected several senior Putnam men to represent the congregation against his Village opponents. In 1695, after the witch trials were over, a total of twenty-one Putnams signed a petition to retain Parris as the Village minister over the objections of his opponents. Thomas and Edward's young stepbrother Joseph and his wife,

Elizabeth Porter Putnam, were the only family members to stand apart from the rest of the Putnam clan in opposition to Samuel Parris.

Given Thomas Putnam's central role in the early phase of the accusations in the Village, it might be supposed that he was the leader of a conspiracy that started the witch-hunt. But there is no evidence of a plot of this kind. On the other hand, once the accusations began and Thomas's daughter, wife, and housemaid became deeply involved, there is ample evidence that he collaborated with family members, church leaders, and Samuel Parris in turning the Village inhabitants' fears and suspicions into a legal onslaught against what he perceived to be Satan's alliance with several of his neighbors. Most important in this respect were his efforts during the first three months, when the arrests grew to sixty-eight individuals. In addition to his collaboration with Samuel Parris, Putnam teamed up with three of his relations (Edward Putnam, John Putnam Jr., and brother-in-law Jonathan Walcott) and two prominent church members (Nathaniel Ingersoll and Ezekiel Cheever) to initiate forty-two accusations. Their complaints not only launched the legal process but sent it out of control in mid-April. There is no evidence that Thomas or anyone else realized that their initial four or five complaints would explode into a large-scale witch-hunt that would reach across Essex County. But it was the continued efforts by these men, spurred on by what they perceived to be Satan's continuing assaults on the terrified Village girls and two or three adult women, especially Thomas's wife, that enlarged the crisis.

It is apparent from the court records that Thomas Putnam's zeal was motivated by a desire to protect his family. The wording of his depositions shows his unquestioned belief in the reality of the spectral torments suffered by his wife, Ann; his daughter Ann Jr.; his maidservant Mercy Lewis; and his niece Mary Walcott. His many depositions on their behalf describe in graphic detail the afflictions that he observed on an almost daily basis. He used the most dramatic phrases he could muster, and used them repeatedly, to describe their condition: "greviously afflicted," "dreadfully tormented," "pinching and almost choking." Hence his frequent concluding formula: "I verily believe in my heart that [so-and-so] is a witch." His unique spelling of the words "apparition" (apperishtion) and "deposition" (deposistion) make his depositions easy to identify. He was undoubtedly present in the meetinghouse during the first examination, when his daughter Ann testified that Sarah Good's specter threatened to "Cut of hir own head" with a knife.[3]

One can only surmise Thomas's paternal reaction to his young daughter's dramatic claim.

Thomas recorded his distraught wife's account of being threatened by the specter of Martha Cory, which "almost pressed and choked her to death," causing "dreadful tortures," and was "allmost redy to kill" her.[4] In a separate deposition written by Stephen Sewall, clerk of the court in Salem, Thomas's troubled wife described a spectacular vision in which several ghosts of the deceased children of her neighbors and relatives appeared at her bedside in their burial shrouds. The ghosts cried out to her that John Willard had murdered them, and they threatened that if she did not tell the magistrate John Hathorne, "they would tare me to pieces." John Willard's specter also said that Willard had killed the Putnams' six-week-old child, Sarah, as well as several other recently deceased children in the Village. In this deposition, Ann Sr. confirmed her daughter's gruesome charge that Willard, who had once tended to Ann Jr. as a child, "had whiped my little sister Sarah to death."[5]

What was a God-fearing man like Thomas Putnam supposed to make of it all? During March and April, his house was the scene of a constant series of apparent supernatural wonders. Desperate visions of apparitions, spectral shapes of living witches, ghosts of victims crying for vengeance, and specters of demons were daily occurrences. Putnam's depositions describe scenes of his wife, daughter, servant, and niece repeatedly falling into trances, contortions, and choking spasms, screaming and crying out against their tormentors. To Thomas, it must have appeared that his family was the target of the most vicious demonic assault.

Three weeks after the accusations began, the Reverend Lawson described his visit to the Putnam house, where he found Putnam's wife, Ann, in the bedroom, suffering a hysterical fit:

[She was] lying on the Bed, having had a sore fit a little before. She spake to me, and said, she was glad to see me; her Husband and she both desired me to pray with her, while she was sensible . . . when Prayer was done, her Husband going to her, found her in a Fit; he took her off the Bed, to set her on his Knees; but at first she was so stiff, she could not be bended; but she afterwards set down; but quickly began to strive violently with her Arms and Leggs; she then began to Complain of, and as it were to Converse personally with, Goodw. N[urse]., saying, "Goodw. N[urse]. Be gone! Be gone! Be gone!"[6]

In another deposition, Thomas wrote down his wife's account of a spectral torment: "I being wearied out in helping to tend my poor afflicted child and Maid: about the middle of the afternoon I laid me down on the bed to take a little Rest: and Immediately I was almost pressed and choked to death: that had it not been for the mercy of a gracious God and the help of those that ware with me: I could not have lived many moments."[7]

Faced with this kind of perceived malice, Thomas countered the danger as best he could. God was sending a message to the Village through satanic attacks that he knew to be "tremendous work of divine providence,"[8] and he wanted the culprits to be dealt with. He had been the Village clerk and could write legibly and effectively. He was also well acquainted with the workings of the court in Salem. He therefore put his position and skills to use by submitting detailed accounts of his family's sufferings in the form of complaints and depositions against the accused. He would do this week after week, obviously well supplied with paper and ink. During the first seven weeks, he and his allies wrote eight complaints against twenty-one people in an attempt to halt the demonic scourge against their families and friends. It would become an obsession. The fact that the Salem court under the supervision of the magistrates Hathorne and Corwin did not require posting monetary bond for the prosecution of capital complaints during the first four and a half months gave Thomas, his relatives, and friends free rein to "paper" the court with complaints against dozens of people.

In late March, when the visiting Deodat Lawson stood in the Village pulpit to preach, Ann Putnam Jr. shouted out that she saw the specter of a yellow bird. Here in the church was a demonic spirit, first identified by Tituba, sitting on Lawson's hat, which hung on a peg next to the pulpit. It was during this sermon that the congregation heard Lawson declare that the devil had singled out "this poor village for the first seat of Satans Tyranny, and to make it . . . the Rendezvous of Devils." The next day, after Cory and Nurse were examined, the congregation heard Parris preach on the theme that "the Lord Jesus Christ knows how many Devils there are in his Church, & who they are."[9] Seven Putnam family members, including the servant girl Mercy Lewis, were involved in the accusations against Cory and Nurse, both of whom were convicted and executed.

In early April, when there was talk of witches' specters attending a devil's sacrament in the Village, Abigail Williams reported that a devil's sacrament was held at the house of an unnamed resident. Mercy Lewis said that she had been forced to attend this sacrament, where "they did eat Red Bread like Mans Flesh." In mid-April, Abigail Williams let it be known that about forty witches' specters participated in the devil's sacrament held in the field next to Parris's house. When Danforth asked Williams what witches "[did] eat and drink," Williams replied, "it was our blood," a revelation that must have been deeply troubling to Parris and Putnam.[10]

Neither Williams nor Lewis, however, said anything about the identity of the witch who performed the sacrament. Who was the leader of the devil's worship in Salem Village? Was he the same person whom Tituba had referred to as "the man" dressed in "black clothes"? The afflicted girls had appropriated this figure in their testimonies as "the black man," but so far he was unnamed.

On April 20 and 21, Ann Putnam and Abigail Williams had visions that the Reverend George Burroughs was the leader of the witches in Salem Village.[11] An excited Thomas Putnam wanted to convey the significance of this news immediately by letter to the magistrates in Salem. He wrote a cryptic note addressed to the "much Honored" Hathorne and Corwin. He began his missive by assuring the magistrates that they were working for the "cause and interest" of God and would be rewarded with "a crown of Glory in the day of the Lord Jesus Christ." To give himself credibility, he reminded the justices that he was standing in the midst of God's intervention in Salem Village, witnessing "continually the tremendous works of Divine Providence, not only everyday but every hour," by which he undoubtedly meant the afflictions to his family and the Village girls. Then, using phrases from the Old Testament prophets Ezekiel and Jeremiah, he wrote "to inform your Honours of what we conceive you have not heard which are high and dreadful—of a wheel within a wheel, at which our ears do tingle." He did not reveal the Reverend George Burroughs's name, but he knew that word of Ann's and Abigail's sensational accusations of Burroughs would spread quickly through the community. Putnam himself would write out two depositions on behalf of his daughter against Burroughs after his arrest.[12] For the present, Putnam wanted to convey the notion that his daughter's and Williams's shocking revelations were prophetic, as divinely portentous as Ezekiel's mysterious vision of "a wheel in the middle of a wheel" (Ez 1:16) and as fearsome as Jeremiah's prophecy about God bringing "evil upon this place, the which whosoever heareth, his ears shall tingle" (Jer 19:3). Putnam concluded his letter by encouraging the magistrates to act boldly against the evil in their midst: "so praying almighty God continually to prepare you that you may be a terror to evil-doers."[13] That he believed his letter would have effect suggests his confidence in his ability to manipulate the magistrates' judgment.

Now that Burroughs was identified as Satan's chief agent, the chaos in Salem Village had a name and a face behind it. It was a darkly plausible explanation. A Puritan minister who had been thrown out of the ministry in Salem Village had turned to Satan out of jealousy. He had killed the wife and daughter of his successor, Deodat Lawson, and was now taking vengeance upon Parris by attacking the girls in his house and by attacking the daughters and wives of his closest allies. Burroughs was immediately perceived as the high-profile threat. The magistrates quickly sought out confirmation from the three new confessors, Abigail and Deliverance Hobbs and Mary Warren, who obligingly named him as the leader of Satan's onslaught; Burroughs was bent on establishing his own church of Satan next to the Village parsonage.

_____

Reading through Thomas Putnam's many depositions turns up the stock phrases mentioned above. These phrases are unique to Putnam's descriptions of spectral afflictions. His repeated use of them suggests they were probably not the words of his deponents but his own attempts to rhetorically heighten the depositions' impact. The phrase "most greviously" appears 172 times in descriptions of various sufferings (pinchings, prickings, tortures, torments, choking), and it stands out as the signature phrase in dozens of depositions. The phrases "greviously tortured" and "greviously tormented" appear forty-five times. The expression "pinching and almost choking me" appears in seventeen different depositions. Whether it was due to the impact of these phrases or Putnam's own social standing in the Village or the fact that he served as a paid assistant to the court, his depositions achieved a high success rate in getting grand juries to indict the accused.

_____

In his capacity as an assistant to the court in preparing depositions for the grand jury, Putnam also tried to strengthen some of the depositions by adding incriminating information. After the establishment of the Court of Oyer and Terminer in May, he worked together with Stephen Sewall, the clerk of the court, and with the attorneys general, who selected the cases for the grand juries. Putnam's abundance of depositions on behalf of the afflicted girls clearly influenced the judgment of the attorneys general and played a key role in the majority of cases that they selected. And he strove to strengthen some when they were used in court.

For example, on May 9 Elizabeth Hubbard testified that the specter of George Burroughs appeared to her, told her he was a wizard, and tried to make her sign his book by pinching and threatening to kill her. On August 3, in preparation for Burroughs's grand jury hearing, Putnam added further testimony to Hubbard's statement:

> Also on the 9th May Being the time of his Examination George Burroughs or [his] Appearance did most greviously afflict and torment the bodies of Mary Walcott, Mercy Lewis, Ann Putnam, and Abigail Williams. For if he did but look upon them he would strick them down or almost choke them to death. Also several times since he has most dreadfully afflicted and tormented me with a variety of torments and I believe in my heart that Mr. George Burroughs is a dreadful wizard.[14]

Hubbard swore to this enhanced statement, and it was used as evidence at Burroughs's trial. Thomas Putnam made similar additions to Mercy Lewis's testimony at the time of Burroughs's hearing, which Thomas and Edward Putnam signed as witnesses. It, too, was used at Burroughs's trial.[15]

More significant than his occasional strengthening of the evidence was his knowledge of the court's docket schedule. He knew when to seek out and write up the relevant depositions to fit the schedule of grand jury hearings and trials. For example, the first session of the Court of Oyer and Terminer met on June 2 and 3, when it was scheduled to hear the cases of Bridget Bishop, Rebecca Nurse, and John Willard. Putnam signed as a witness to all five indictments brought against Bridget Bishop. He wrote up seven of the eleven depositions against Rebecca Nurse, and three of them were under his own name. In the case of John Willard, who appeared before the grand jury on June 3, Putnam wrote three depositions against him; Samuel Parris wrote two; and one was written by Stephen Sewall on behalf of Ann Putnam Sr.

Putnam and Parris were the two Village men who were most intimately involved with the legal process of the witch trials. As such, they were best positioned to feed the court's insatiable appetite for "evidences," as the depositions and written testimonies were called. Thomas Putnam persisted in supplying depositions until the very end. The special court's last trial was on September 17, when it heard the case of forty-year-old Abigail Dane Faulkner Sr. of Andover. Putnam wrote all six depositions against her. She was indicted for bewitching sixteen-year-old Martha Sprague of Boxford and ten-year-old Sarah Phelps of Andover. Putnam wrote the depositions on behalf of Sprague and Phelps, as well as those of his daughter, Mary Walcott, and Mary Warren. Their depositions were sworn before the grand jury and used at Faulkner's trial, and she was convicted. After the trials were over, the court paid Putnam five pounds for his work.[16]

On September 18, Thomas Putnam wrote his second urgent letter to the Court of Oyer and Terminer, this time to Judge Samuel Sewall. His purpose was to assuage Sewall's conscience about the torturous death of seventy-one-year-old Giles Cory. He may also have wanted to bolster the sensitive Sewall for more trials to come. The court itself was coming under public criticism, and Sewall was known to be sympathetic to the plight of the condemned.

Giles Cory had been accused by Ann Putnam Jr., Mercy Lewis, Abigail Williams, Mary Walcott, Elizabeth Hubbard, and Abigail Hobbs. He was examined in late April and arraigned before the grand jury on September 9, the day after his wife, Martha, had been convicted and sentenced to die. Giles knew that he would face the same accusers and that he had no chance of proving himself innocent. Therefore, after making sure that his valuable farm had been legally deeded to his sons-in-law so that the land could not be confiscated from him or tied up under legal attainder, he decided to deny the court the opportunity to impose either of these fates upon him. Cory stood mute and refused to enter a plea or stand trial.[17]

Under British law, the refusal to stand trial was punishable by *peine forte et dure* (hard and forceful punishment). In Cory's case, large heavy rocks were placed on him as he lay on the ground in a field near the Salem prison house. Even the pleading of his friend Captain Thomas Gardner of Nantucket failed to change Cory's mind. According to tradition, when Sheriff George Corwin asked Cory as he was suffering under the weight, "how do you plead?" Cory answered, "More weight! More weight!" He died on September 19, a date that Judge Sewall noted in his diary.[18]

Putnam's letter to Sewall was a masterpiece of deception based on a grain of truth. In 1675, Cory had severely beaten a servant on his farm, named Jacob

Goodale, with a hundred blows of a stick, and Goodale had subsequently died of his wounds. But the court records show that Cory was not accused of his death. Cory was charged instead with physical abuse and fined.[19] In his letter to Sewall, however, Putnam said that Cory had once killed a man by crushing him with his feet. He related that the apparition of a man whom Cory had killed appeared to his daughter Ann, saying that Cory had murdered him. According to Putnam, Cory had killed him by "pressing him to Death with his feet; but that the Devil there appeared unto him, and Covenanted with him, and promised him, He should not be Hanged." Putnam's letter continued, repeating his daughter's words: "God Hardened his Heart, that he should not hearken to the Advice of the Court, and so Die an easy Death; because as it said, 'It must be done to him as he has done to me.' "[20] Crushing Cory to death was therefore a fitting punishment from God.

Sewall naively accepted Putnam's tale and noted in his diary: "Now, I hear from Salem about 18 years ago, he [Cory] was suspected to have stamped and press'd a man to death, but was cleared. Twas not remembered till Ann Putnam was told of it by said Corey's Spectre the Sabbath-day night before the execution."[21] It would be unreasonable to assume that a small community like Salem Village could forget Cory's trial, even though it had occurred almost two decades earlier. Nor would it be forgotten that Cory had not been tried for murder but for giving a man a harsh beating, contrary to Putnam's claim. "Now Sir," Putnam wrote, "this is a little strange to us; that no body should remember these things. For all people now Remember [it] very well, (and the Records of the Court also mention it)."[22]

Sewall was apparently so emotionally relieved by Putnam's letter that he misunderstood that the specter Ann had supposedly seen was not Cory's but the man Cory had allegedly killed. How fitting it was that Cory should have died in the same way by being crushed to death.

Putnam's two letters reveal his willingness to try to manipulate the judges even to the point of deception. His comparing his daughter's and Abigail's revelations about Burroughs to Old Testament prophecy suggests the scope of his ambition: God had selected his daughter for a providential role. His second letter was equally ambitious and succeeded in deceiving the liberal-minded Sewall that Cory's cruel death was justified by his own murderous behavior.

Putnam's letter to Sewall was his last communication with the court. His last depositions were written on behalf of his daughter, Mary Walcott,

Mary Warren, and sixteen-year-old Martha Sprague, all against Abigail Dane Faulkner Sr. They succeeded, and Faulkner was tried and found guilty on September 17. Putnam most likely attended the eight executions on Gallows Hill that took place on September 17, those of Martha Cory, Mary Esty, Alice Parker, Mary Parker, Ann Pudeator, Wilmot Redd, Margaret Scott, and Samuel Wardwell. His depositions on behalf of his daughter had played a major role in six of these cases. The court would now go into recess. It was scheduled to resume on November 1. Putnam undoubtedly hoped it would continue to try the backlog of cases.

In the immediate aftermath of the trials, Thomas Putnam remained a loyal supporter of Samuel Parris and aligned himself with those who strove to keep him in his post. But by 1697, even the indefatigable Putnam had had enough of the stubborn and domineering minister. He joined the effort to dismiss Parris from the Village and helped collect the payment for Parris's back salary and received Parris's deed for the return of the parsonage to the Village.[23]

Thomas Putnam died at age forty-seven in May 1699. His wife, Ann, died two weeks later. He lived long enough to see the arrival of the Reverend Joseph Green, Samuel Parris's successor, and to witness the institution of the popular Halfway Covenant, which he had once opposed. He also lived to experience the great Fast Day of 1697, which asked God to forgive the "mistakes" that caused the tragedy of the witch trials. At his death, Thomas Putnam's diminished landholdings were heavily indebted, and he was able to leave only small bequests to his children.

He would never know that seven years later his daughter Ann, then age twenty-six, would begin her apology for the role she played in the witch trials by referring to "that sad and humbling providence that befell my father's family in the year about 92." This amounted to an implicit admission of her father's responsibility as the head of her family, which God had chosen as the instrument by which to impose his vengeance upon the Massachusetts Bay Province.

ANDOVER

7

[T]hree hundred & five [witches] in the whole Country.
— Ann Foster, Andover

Satan's design . . . was to abolish all the churches in the land.
— William Baker, Andover

The arrest of Martha Carrier at the end of May signaled an eventual shift of focus in the 1692 witch-hunt away from Salem Village and Town to Andover and the surrounding communities. But the accusations did not accelerate in Andover until mid-July, with the arrest of elderly Ann Foster. During August and September, the total number of accused people in Andover swelled to forty-six, more than in any other town in Essex County and more than in Salem Village and Salem Town combined. Unlike Salem, most of the Andover defendants confessed, giving the Salem court new evidence of a widespread satanic conspiracy and justifying its proceedings.

———————

In 1690, thirty-eight-year-old Martha Allen Carrier and her family moved from nearby Billerica to Andover and stayed in the house of Andrew Allen, Martha's brother. At the time, a smallpox epidemic was ravaging New England, and some of the Carrier children began to fall ill with the disease. Andover's town fathers warned the Carriers to leave, lest they infect the rest of the community by their "wicked carelessness."[1] But the Carriers refused. The town then quarantined them in the house and provided food at the town's expense. More than a dozen Andover residents died of smallpox, including six members of the Allen family.

Martha was a feisty character who soon became the subject of town gossip. She made ominous threats against a neighbor who tried to encroach on the Allen land, and the town's hostility toward the Carrier family made her a likely target for witchcraft suspicions.[2]

On May 28, 1692, four Salem Village girls accused Martha of afflicting them. Abigail Williams, Mary Walcott, Elizabeth Hubbard, and Ann Putnam Jr. made the allegations. They also accused Martha's sister, Mary Carrier Toothaker, who lived in nearby Billerica, and Mary's nine-year-old daughter, Margaret Toothaker.

The court record of Martha Carrier's examination reveals that she was one of the most outspoken victims of the Salem episode. She challenged the magistrates and her accusers at every point. The examination came to a climax when Carrier, frustrated by the girls' repeated charges and staged afflictions, denounced both the magistrates and her accusers: "It is a shamefull thing that you should mind these folks that are out of their wits." A magistrate responded by pointing to the girls' afflictions and declaring, "Do not you see them?" Carrier shot back, "If I do speak you will not believe me?" "You do see them," said some of the accusers. Carrier responded sharply, "You lye, I am wronged." The girls hit back with a collective display of torments, and the courtroom fell into chaos. The magistrates had Carrier bound and taken away before an excited crowd. The examination record notes: "The Tortures of the afflicted were so great that there was no enduring of it, so that she [Carrier] was ordered away & to be bound hand & foot with all expedition the afflicted in the mean while almost killed to the great trouble of all spectators Magistrates & others."[3]

Nothing more was heard from Andover until mid-July, when constable Joseph Ballard of Andover, who had been troubled by the lingering illness of his forty-six-year-old wife, Elizabeth, began to suspect that witchcraft was the cause of his wife's illness. He called in two of Salem Village's most active witch-finders to diagnose the cause of his wife's condition. The records do not say which two girls he brought to his house, but they were most likely Mary Walcott and Elizabeth Hubbard, both of whom were later named in indictments as being afflicted by Ann Foster.[4] The two girls went to Ballard's home, where they saw the specter of a seventy-two-year-old widow named

Ann Foster afflicting the bedridden Elizabeth Ballard. Both girls then became afflicted by Foster.

The sources do not indicate why Foster was selected as the culprit. Whatever the reason, it is clear that Joseph Ballard, assisted by two of Salem Village's young witch-finders, initiated Andover's massive witch-hunt.

Ann Foster readily confessed. Guided by the magistrates' questions, she filled her confession with borrowed themes from the confessions of Tituba, Abigail Hobbs, and Deliverance Hobbs. Although the court records were accessible only to the court officials, gossip had apparently spread the details of previous confessions. Foster said that Martha Carrier had made her a witch. She said that Carrier stuck pins into poppets, or effigies, to bewitch two of her brother's children who had become ill, one of whom died. Foster also described flying through the air on a pole to witches' meetings in Salem Village, where she saw George Burroughs and two other ministers conduct a satanic mass.

For the magistrates, Ann Foster's several examinations were as pivotal as Tituba's for Salem Village because Foster revealed the scope of Satan's activity at the beginning of the extensive Andover phase of accusations, hence the magistrates' multiple interrogations. Each time Foster added more detail, saying Martha Carrier had bewitched another child to death and that the devil would set up his kingdom in Salem Village. Her third examination conveyed the alarming revelation that there were "three hundred & five [witches] in the whole Country, & that they would ruin that place ye [Salem] Vilige." She concluded by saying that the witches in Salem Village told her "they would afflict there to set up the Divills Kingdome."[5]

The day after Foster's second examination on July 18, Joseph Ballard, whose wife was now near death, submitted a new complaint, this time—in keeping with the belief that witchcraft was passed from mother to daughter— against Foster's forty-year-old daughter, Mary (Foster) Lacey Sr., and her eighteen-year-old daughter, Mary Jr. Mercy Lewis and Elizabeth Hubbard immediately confirmed Ballard's suspicions and testified that they saw Mary Lacey and her daughter bewitching (and killing) his wife. The record shows that the desperate Ballard posted one hundred pounds to prosecute his case, a significant amount of money. This was the first time the Salem court had required a monetary guarantee, usually a requirement in capital cases, but the large amount of money did nothing to stop the determined Ballard.

At Foster's third examination, the magistrates tried to make her confirm that her daughter was a witch, and Mary Lacey Sr. was then called in. Suspecting that the judges were trying to manipulate her mother into saying she had made her a witch, Mary greeted her mother and confessed that she had already given herself over to the devil. "Oh, mother! How do you do? We have left Christ, and the Devil hath gat hold of us. How shall I get rid of this evil one?" The magistrates bore down upon Mary, trying to make her say that her mother led her to the devil. But she deflected their charge by saying that the devil had already baptized her three years previously in the Fall River.[6]

The court then called in the granddaughter, Mary Lacey Jr. One of her accusers, Mary Warren, immediately fell into a "violent fit." Warren's fit stopped when the magistrates made Lacey touch Warren, thus proving that Lacey was a witch. As an experiment to make her confess, the magistrates told Lacey to look upon Warren in a "friendly way," but "she trying so to do, struck her [Warren] down with her eyes." In this way, young Lacey, who had previously run away from her father, was forced to confess she was a witch. She confessed to afflicting Timothy Swan of Andover and said that she joined Richard Carrier in causing afflictions. The magistrates wanted Lacey to tell them how many witches there were in Andover, but she said she knew only of the Carriers and her mother and grandmother. Asked to tell about going to witches' meetings in Salem Village, Lacey said she saw a minister there who was in prison. The magistrates asked pointedly whether there were not two ministers there, fishing perhaps for evidence against the Reverend John Busse, who had been a preacher in Wells, Maine, prior to Burroughs's arrival, and was mentioned by Mary Warren a month earlier. Lacy said she saw only Burroughs.[7]

Two days later, the magistrates again hauled the two Laceys into court, this time accompanied by fifteen-year-old Andrew Carrier and eighteen-year-old Richard Carrier. The two Carrier boys were accused of afflicting Mary Warren. At first, the brothers refused to confess or to accuse their mother of witchcraft. Then Mary Warren fell into "a bad ffitt & blood Runing out of her Mouth," and Mary Lacey said that Andrew Carrier did it. The account then says that "Richard and Andrew were Carried out to another Chamber—And there feet & hands bound a little while after Richard was brought in again." According to John Procter, the Carrier brothers were tied "Neck and Heels till the Blood was ready to come out of their noses." After being tortured, Richard confessed volubly to everything he could think of. He saw the devil, who looked like a black man; he signed the devil's book and gave the devil permission to use his shape to afflict Timothy Swan and Elizabeth Ballard. He also confessed to sticking pins in images of Swan and Ballard to afflict them. He said he rode on a pole to Salem Village, where he saw seventy witches meeting in Samuel Parris's pasture. Mary Lacey Jr. then joined in and said that "She heard ym talk of throwing Dwone ye King-dome of Christ & Setting up ye Diuel on his throwne they ware to Doe Soe throughout all ye Whole Country—& were Enjoyned by ye Diuel to Make as Many witches as we Could." Mary Lacey Sr. also admitted to afflicting Abigail Williams, Betty Parris, Parris's wife, and Mary Walcott. Then Lacey herself became afflicted.[8]

Next was Andrew Carrier's turn. Having been tortured, he admitted to everything, including signing the devil's book and hurting a child in the Frye family of Andover. Mary Warren said she saw Andrew baptized by the devil in Andover's Shawsheen River. Richard interrupted, saying that he had at-tended the devil's sacrament, where he drank the wine but did not eat the bread, which had been handed out by Rebecca Nurse. Two weeks later, eight-year-old Sarah Carrier and ten-year-old Thomas Carrier Jr. were to be accused by ten-year-old Sarah Phelps of Andover and Ann Putnam Jr.[9]

Meanwhile, from July 15 onward, several Andover residents, following Ballard's lead, brought Mary Walcott, Elizabeth Hubbard, and Mercy Lewis from Salem Village to their homes to diagnose sick family members who were suspected of being bewitched. According to Robert Calef's account, "Horse and Man were sent from several places [in Andover] to fetch those Accusers [from Salem Village] who had the Spectral sight, that they might thereby tell who afflicted those that were any ways ill. When these came into any place where such were, usually they fell into a Fit; after which being asked who it was that afflicted the person, they would, for the most part, name one whom they said sat on the head, and another that sat on the lower parts of the afflicted."[10]

By the end of July, there were seven new cases in Andover. August brought twelve more, and by mid-September the number had grown to forty-five.

As in Salem Village, the context of the witch-hunt in An-dover was one of festering community conflict.[11] Andover's first group of twenty-four settlers came into the area in 1644. They were known as proprietors and were given large tracts of land of more than two hundred acres each. These initial allotments comprised the whole area of the town. The proprietors established themselves primarily in the northern end of the town, where they erected a church and created the village center. The plan was that the proprietors would take parts of their initial holdings as personal property and gradually divide the rest into parcels to be distributed among newcomers to the town. The proprietors, however, ensured that the power to govern the town remained in their hands. Over the years, they continued to appoint the selectmen and the ministers.

By the 1680s, Andover had grown into two divergent settlements: the North End, consisting of the lands of the original settlers, and the South End, made up of smaller portions allotted to the newcomers. Many of the original families had also grown in size and dispersed to new houses in the South End. Because of the distance between the residents of the South End and the church in the North End, the South Enders desired to relocate the church building to a more central area for their convenience. When this idea failed, the South End proposed the establishment of a separate parish in the South End with its own minister. In 1681, the talk of a new parish merged into the question of the lapsed activity of Andover's aging minister, the Reverend Francis Dane, who was failing to hold regular worship services. Francis Dane was then sixty-six years old and had been Andover's minister for twenty years. "Church and town" eventually sent a complaint to the General Court in Boston to obtain a solution.

Meanwhile, the local magistrates arranged for the appointment of a new minister, the Reverend Thomas Barnard, who would take over from Francis Dane. With Barnard's appointment, the town decided to stop paying Dane's salary, expecting that he would "subsist and not be burdensome to them." A year later, the General Court in Boston sent along a committee to advise on the matter. The committee proposed that Dane should assist Barnard to the extent that he was able and that the town should pay Dane thirty pounds annual salary. The town was also told to pay Barnard a salary of fifty pounds and that he should live in a part of Dane's house. It was also decided that the whole town, not just the church members, would be responsible for the ministers' pay. The committee advised that henceforth Dane should "carry it [his ministry] to his people with that tender love and respect (forgetting all former disgusts) as becomes a minister of the gospel."[12]

Not everyone was satisfied when Barnard was hired. He began to associate himself with the residents of the North End, and there was disagreement about the requirement to pay Dane's salary. The South Enders continued to want a separate church of their own with their own minister (which they eventually achieved after Dane's death), and they chafed under the control of the powerful proprietor families.

The witch-hunt targeted the old proprietor families, especially the women related to the elderly Francis Dane. At least eight of the accused were Dane's near family, including two of his daughters, a daughter-in-law, and five grandchildren. By one count, as many as twenty-six of Andover's accused were related to Dane by blood or marriage.[13] These relations included the Carrier, Allen, and Howe families. If Dane could be discredited by accusations against members of his family, perhaps he would be deemed unworthy of the town's support and the new meetinghouse would be built closer to the South End.

The Reverend Dane himself was too respected in the Puritan clerical establishment to be accused directly. The records suggest, however, that he was a target of suspicion. When Ann Foster confessed in July, she said that she had seen a man with gray hair standing together with Burroughs, conducting a satanic mass in Salem Village. Dane's daughter, forty-year-old Abigail Faulkner Sr., was accused in mid-August and convicted in mid-September. Two of Dane's young granddaughters confessed and became afflicted accusers themselves.

The July accusations in Andover were but a prelude to the surge that occurred between the end of August and mid-September. The accusations were occasioned by a unique and ominous act on the part of Andover's junior minister, Thomas Barnard. Sometime in early September, Barnard arranged for a number of people, against whom complaints had been made, to gather at Andover's meetinghouse. Then, according to several women who were present on this occasion,

> after Mr. Barnard had been at prayer, we were blindfolded, and our hands were laid upon the afflicted persons, they being in their fits and falling into their fits at our coming into their presence, as they said; and some led us and laid our hands upon them, and then they said they were well, and that we were guilty of afflicting them: Whereupon, we were all seized, as prisoners, by a warrant from the Justice of the peace and forthwith carried to Salem.[14]

The touch test had been used in the Salem court for some time to identify witches and hold them for indictment. Barnard's innovation was to make it a group test. As the above description indicates, suspects were required to touch an afflicted person. If the afflicted immediately recovered, this was taken as evidence that the suspect was a witch.[15] Cotton Mather, consistent with Puritan doctrine, regarded the touch test as presumptive evidence and as grounds for arrest and examination. But he had cautioned the court that it was "frequently liable to be abused by the Devil's legerdemains."[16]

After Barnard's group touch test, Andover's magistrate, Dudley Bradstreet, wrote out the arrest warrants, and "forthwith [the accused were] carried to Salem" to jail. Francis Dane was conspicuously absent from the scene.

Twenty-eight years old and a recent graduate of Harvard College, Thomas Barnard belonged to the second generation of ministers in New England. The older Dane had shown himself to be a cautious man in witchcraft cases, refusing to give evidence against the notorious figure named John Godfrey, who had been tried three times for witchcraft.[17] Dane's behavior was in keeping with his generation's reluctance to become involved in witchcraft cases, a reluctance that helped to limit their number. With the exception of Goody Glover in Boston in 1688, there had not been a successful witchcraft prosecution in New England for thirty years.

Harvard's second-generation clergy, however, were brought up according to what the historian Harry Stout has called "a habit of mind constantly attuned to the invisible realities and metaphysical principles around which the visible universe revolved." Moreover, the younger generation was trained to be community leaders, men set apart as the "watchmen and prophets of their generation."[18] With witchcraft accusations gathering momentum in Andover, Barnard seems to have given in to local pressure from the South Enders and helped to organize the mass touch test as a way of asserting his leadership. The result was an explosion of arrests, with cartloads of Andover suspects taken off to Salem's jail.

As in Salem Village, the impact of such strong legal action only inspired more accusations. The mass touch test was Andover's tipping point. The court records show that in the first week of September, fourteen Andover residents were examined and jailed in Salem Town. Two weeks later, the total was forty-five.

The Andover witch-hunt included a total of twelve children, ages eight to fifteen, all of whom confessed. The obvious question arises, did the magistrates actually intend to execute the children or would they be exempted because of their age? The records indicate that the children were treated no differently from the adults. They were arrested on the basis of warrants, taken to jail in Salem, sometimes put in shackles, and examined before the magistrates. Some initially declared their innocence, such as thirteen-year-old Mary Barker, who under pressure of the interrogation "at last acknowledged" that Rebecca Johnson, who had been previously accused, had made her a witch and that she had signed the devil's book. In some cases, the children, under pressure, accused their mothers of making them witches (e.g., ten-year-old Thomas Carrier and seven-year-old Abigail Faulkner Jr.). All confessed to afflicting their accusers, often by sticking pins in effigies, and many testified that they attended witches' meetings in Salem Village, traveling there by flying on a pole. Some said that they promised to worship the devil in return for his pardoning of their sins or for fine clothes that he offered. This was the standard confession, sometimes embellished with details such as baptism by the devil in a local river. The court was ended before any of the children were put on trial.

Andover's forty-five confessions, which occurred mostly in August, became a major problem, indeed, an embarrassment. Was witchcraft really that rampant in Andover, or was there something wrong with the court's eagerness to extract confessions, especially from children? The next chapter looks at what may have motivated the court to spare the lives of confessors and how the court extracted confessions, as well as the fate of the confessors.

8

CONFESSIONS

If I would confess I should have my life.
— *Margaret Jacobs*

They tyed him Neck and Heels till the Blood gushed out at his Nose.
— *John Procter*

[The] most violent, distracting, and dragooning methods [were] used . . . to make them confesse.
— *Thomas Brattle*

Confessing was the only way to obtain favour.
— *Andover ministers*

From the beginning of the Salem witchcraft proceedings, the many confessions spurred on the legal process, legitimating it at critical points along the way. Confession had long been deemed the best possible evidence of witchcraft because, as David Hall puts it, "it made visible the hidden (no one ever saw the occult lines of force that witches were supposed to use), and it confirmed that the root of witchcraft was a compact with the Devil."[1]

The confessions began with Tituba's dramatic testimony about the devil appearing to her in the shape of a man dressed in black and his trying to make her sign his book. She also told about the devil recruiting witches in Salem Village and about witches' specters meeting together, first in Samuel Parris's house and then elsewhere, and tormenting the children in the Village. These themes became the distinctive features of the Salem narrative and the substance of subsequent confessions. Were it not for Tituba's initial confession of a satanic plot unfolding in Salem Village, with witches congregating there and with more to be found, the Salem story might have been very different.

Equally important was the afflicted girls' reaction to Tituba's testimony: their torments suddenly stopped. Tituba was sent to jail, and the girls never accused her of hurting them again. Henceforth, this would become the standard reaction to confessions made in the presence of the afflicted. It was taken as evidence that the confession was genuine and that the confessed witch was thereby rendered harmless, as Parris and Thomas Putnam testified after Tituba's confession.[2] The same phenomenon happened after Abigail and Deliverance Hobbs confessed. Samuel Parris, who recorded both examinations, noted that afterward "All the sufferers [were] free from affliction."[3]

It is possible that this understanding—that confession took away a witch's powers—helped to influence the Court of Oyer and Terminer's decision not to execute confessors, which had the effect of encouraging more confessions by those accused. Confessed witches were never restrained by shackles while in jail because of their harmlessness, unlike those who maintained their innocence.[4]

The next to confess after Tituba was Sarah Good's five-year-old daughter, Dorothy. When Dorothy entered the courtroom, the record says that she cast her eye upon her accusers, Mary Walcott and Ann Putnam, and they became tormented. Dorothy also showed the magistrates marks of a "small set of teeth" on her arm. A day or two later, the magistrates interrogated Dorothy in prison for the purpose of obtaining a confession. Dorothy showed them a red spot on her finger where she said that a little snake had sucked. The magistrates asked whether the snake was given to her by the "great Black man." She told them it was her mother.[5] Dorothy's was hardly a significant confession. But her examination reveals the magistrates' fanaticism in their intimidation of a young child to obtain a confession.

A month later, the second major confession was made, this time by fifteen-year-old Abigail Hobbs. Abigail was a rebellious teenager who lived in neighboring Topsfield. She was reportedly rude to her neighbors and bragged about having "Sold her selfe boddy and Soull to the old boy." One neighbor, who was provoked by Abigail's rude behavior when she came to her house, mentioned that Abigail had called upon the "old nick," that is, the devil, whom she said was present in the house and, as Abigail's ally, would put a stop to the neighbor's criticism. Hobbs and her family were refugees from Maine who had settled in Topsfield. Abigail's mother had died in Casco, Maine, though not as a result of an Indian attack. Her father, William Hobbs, had remarried, and her stepmother was named Deliverance Hobbs. Abigail apparently disliked Deliverance. She taunted her in front of a neighbor for not having been baptized, and then proceeded to sprinkle water on her, saying, "I will baptize hir in the name of the father Son and Holy Ghost." Abigail's disrespectful behavior insulted both her stepmother and the Puritan sacrament of baptism. Abigail's stepmother remarked derisively that "shee little thought to have bin the mother of such a dauter."[6]

Not surprisingly, Abigail's blasphemous behavior attracted the attention of the Village girls, and they accused her of witchcraft. Abigail took to the spotlight in the courtroom and eagerly confessed. Her confession proceeded along the lines of Tituba's, with Hathorne asking the same questions he put to Tituba and Abigail giving the same answers. The devil, she said, looked like a black man, and she made a covenant with him by putting her mark in the devil's book. She described several animal spirits and named other witchcraft suspects to support her confession. Like Tituba, Abigail also concluded her testimony by falling silent, alleging that the specter of Sarah Good prevented her from speaking. Samuel Parris, who recorded her examination, noted down that during the course of Abigail's confession, the afflicted girls were "none of them tormented." Parris thereby implied that Hobbs's testimony freed her from the devil's powers and that she was no longer able to hurt them.[7]

Abigail's confession, occurring as it did on April 19, six weeks after Tituba's revelations, was a significant validation of the magistrates' proceedings. Equally important was the confession of her stepmother, Deliverance Hobbs, which occurred three days later on April 22. Deliverance was accused by Ann Putnam, Mercy Lewis, and Mary Walcott. Perhaps they believed that if Abigail was a witch, her stepmother was one, too, since it was commonly assumed that witchcraft was passed down from mother to daughter. That Deliverance Hobbs was not baptized, a significant lapse, may also have added to their suspicion.

Deliverance Hobbs's confession followed Ann Putnam's and Abigail William's revelations on April 20 and 21 about George Burroughs being the leader of the witchcraft plot in the Village. Deliverance not only confirmed the girls' accusations of Burroughs but, upon further questioning, said that she saw his specter conducting a satanic mass on Parris's property, thus legitimating her confession by utilizing the latest revelations about Satan's plot.

On the day of Deliverance Hobbs's examination, huge crowds appeared at the Village meetinghouse, with "many in the windows" looking on. Her examination was one of eleven that occurred between April 19 and 22. Momentum grew as a result of the Hobbses' two confessions and the identification of Burroughs as Satan's ringleader. Complaints poured in, and warrants were issued for the arrest of fifteen more people by the end of the month.

One of those examined on April 21 was the troubled twenty-year-old Mary Warren. She had been examined twice before, after accusing the other Village girls of "dissembling," and confessed as the result of the magistrates' badgering. The magistrates interrogated her on three separate occasions, and she finally confessed in order to save herself. She admitted to signing the devil's book and to afflicting her young Village accusers. For good measure, she named George Burroughs as the leader of the plot against the Village. She also said that Burroughs had tried to bewitch Justice Hathorne and that his specter had told her that he "Killed his Wife off of Cape Ann."[8] Warren was thus the third confessor in two days to confirm that Burroughs was Satan's spectral high priest in Salem Village.

Warren's confession on April 21 was the fourth substantial confession and the third in three days. Like the others, hers was shaped by Hathorne's questions. Hathorne used Warren's vulnerability to obtain incriminating evidence against John and Elizabeth Procter, in whose household she was a maidservant. Warren complied by saying that when Procter took her home, away from the other accusers, he had told her that she was trying to expose "innocent persons," that is, alleged witches, thus revealing Procter's true purpose of trying to protect the people Warren had accused. When Hathorne asked if she saw any poppets in the Procters' house, she said Elizabeth Procter had one that represented either Ann Putnam or Abigail Williams. She related that she stuck a pin in the doll's neck while Procter held it, and she did the same with poppets held by other suspects whom she named.[9] Thereafter, Warren was allowed to rejoin the group of Village accusers. She became one of the most aggressive, testifying in twenty-three examinations and appearing in fifteen indictments. Warren's confession was a turning point not only for her but for the afflicted girls' efforts to prevent any further defections from their group.

The confession of the seventy-two-year-old widow Ann Foster of Andover on July 15 was the first of forty confessions in Andover that continued through August to mid-September. According to the Reverend Francis Dane, the people of Andover understood that confession was the way to gain freedom from trial. The Andover confessions followed a standard formula: stories of spectral threats by witches to sign the devil's book, tales about witches' meetings in Salem Village (in the field opposite Parris's house), the naming of several people seen at witches' meetings, and estimates of the total number of witches seen at these meetings. Magistrates elicited these responses by posing the standard checklist of questions. The process became relentless and fed upon itself: confessions generated more accusations, which generated more confessions and accusations.

Puritan theological principles required that confessing witches be kept in jail for a period of time and not be brought immediately to trial. The justification was that they needed time to reconcile themselves with God before they were tried and executed. As the Reverend John Hale explained in the case of Dorcas Hoar, who had confessed, she wished for "a little longer time of life to realize & perfect her repentance for the salvation of her soul."[10] Thus, according to Hale, confession was a way for defendants "to seek Mercy for their Souls in the way of Confession and sorrow for such a Sin."[11]

Previously in New England, any defendant who confessed to being a witch was brought to trial and executed, except in the rare cases in which the individual was found to be mentally unbalanced. The most recent execution of a confessed witch in New England prior to the Salem episode was that of Ann Glover, who confessed at her trial in Boston in 1688. But in Salem, none of those who confessed were executed. Moreover, the number of confessed witches amounted to fully one-third of those accused. As the historian Perry Miller observed, there was such a flood of confessions as the Salem trials progressed that their value "depreciated spectacularly."[12] John Hale came to the realization that because confessions appeared to ensure that one would not be put on trial, there was no certainty that the confessors "would stand to their Self-condemning confessions, when they came to dye."[13] Hale was correct. By the end of the trials, the number of recanted confessions raised doubts about the court's procedures and helped to bring it down.

Most historians have assumed that the reason for Salem's large number of confessions was that the accused realized that confessors were not being brought to trial. Confession appeared to save them not only from immediate trial but also from being put on trial at all. It was well known, of course, that all who maintained their innocence were convicted and executed. If the court was following a policy of not putting confessors on trial, it was unique and unprecedented in Western history. The court records do not contain reference to such a procedure, but there are statements from defendants saying they were told—in some instances by other confessors—that confession would prevent their execution. Some of the records also suggest that Justice Hathorne promised leniency if defendants confessed.

On May 31, before the Court of Oyer and Terminer began its first session, Cotton Mather wrote a letter to Judge John Richards, who was also a member of Mather's church. Mather began by imploring the court not to rely on spectral evidence because "the devils have sometimes represented shapes of persons not only innocent, but also virtuous." He suggested that in such cases God would provide a "speeding vindication" of the accused. He therefore reminded Richards that spectral evidence was only a "presumption" of guilt and could not be used for conviction.

Mather then went on at length to advise Richards to distinguish between "what confession may be credible, and what may be the result of only a delirious brain, or a discontented heart"; and he proposed that the court consider leniency for those who confessed. Mather knew that the jails were filled with suspects, and he voiced his doubts about the seriousness of their guilt. "I begin to fear," he wrote, "that the devils do more easily proselyte poor mortals into witchcraft than is commonly conceived." Some confessing witches, he proposed, might therefore be considered "lesser criminals" and should not be executed. He emphasized that not "every wretched creature that shall be hooked into some degrees of witchcraft" should be hanged or burned, provided they be "scourged with lesser punishments" and made "some solemn, open, Public & Explicit renunciation of the Devil." Just before the trials began in June, Parris, Putnam, and Ezekiel Cheever submitted a statement in preparation for Sarah Good's trial confirming that the devil had stopped tormenting the girls once Tituba confessed. Thus, the judge's notion that confessors were harmless, as evident from the Salem girls' behavior, taken together with Cotton Mather's letter requesting that the court show leniency to confessors, may have been the grounds for the court's unusual policy of sparing confessors.

New England had never seen such a staggering number of witchcraft suspects, and Mather was suggesting that if they voluntarily confessed, they might not be as dangerous as supposed. He proposed that when defendants arrived in the courtroom they might become so "thunderstruck" by God "as to make them show their deeds" by free confession. By their thus disavowing the devil, the devil might then "cease afflicting the neighborhood." Some of the accused, he believed, had become "entrapped" by the devil. When they found themselves "treacherously" abandoned, they might be thrown into such "toiling vexations that they discover all." Thus Mather reasoned, "what if the death of some of the offenders were either diverted or inflicted, according to the success of such their renunciation?"[14]

Even before Mather's letter to Richards, the examination records contain hints that Hathorne was offering clemency to obtain confessions. During the examination of John Willard, Justice Hathorne seemed to propose a plea bargain. Hathorne told him that "if you can therefore find in your heart to repent it is possible you may obtain mercy." Hathorne might also have been suggesting that Willard seek Christ's mercy through confession. Willard, however, did not take Hathorne's apparent offer of the court's mercy and courageously refused to confess "that which I do not know."[15]

When Abigail Hobbs confessed in court, she added, "I hope God will forgive me." The magistrate, whom we can assume was Hathorne, immediately responded with the reassuring affirmation, "The Lord Give you Repentance." Hathorne was no minister, but by asking God to forgive Abigail, he may have been suggesting that God would look upon her with favor, thus giving her an incentive to confess, which she did.

Over time, Hathorne appears to have become more explicit, especially after the acceleration of the accusations in Andover. In mid-July, during the examination of eighteen-year-old Mary Lacey Jr., Hathorne suggested that confession would lead her to salvation:

[Hathorne:] You are now in the way to obtain mercy if you will confess and repent. She said: The Lord help me. [Hathorne:] Do not you desire to be saved by Christ? Lacey: Yes. [Hathorne:] Then you must confess freely what you know in this matter.[16]

Hearing Hathorne's proposal that confession would lead to mercy and salvation, Lacey chose to confess. From the beginning, Hathorne was intent on obtaining confessions, and in this exchange he appears to be offering her freedom from the court's judgment. At the start of the hearing, Mary had said to her mother, "We have left Christ, and the Devil hath gat hold of us. How shall I get rid of this evil one?," thus providing Hathorne with an opening to remind her of Christ's mercy and implying the court's mercy as well. Confessors, it turned out, would not be executed.

Thomas Brattle, too, realized that the court was favoring confessors and not holding them responsible. He believed that some who confessed were "known to be distracted, crazed women" or had been "deluded by the devil." Brattle was therefore surprised to hear that "the Judges vindicate these confessours, and salve their contradictions, by proclaiming, that the Devil takes away their memory, and imposes upon their brain." Brattle scoffed at the justices' apparent irrationality in accepting the testimony of such addle-brained witnesses rather than simply "discarding them." He fumed: "the Justices have given ear to the Devil."[17] It is speculation, of course, but the court's behavior would make sense if the judges were following Mather's advice to show leniency to confessors as "lesser criminals," while keeping them locked away as punishment. The problem was that the mounting number of confessions, which named more and more people as witches, convinced the court to keep pursing its relentless witch-hunt.

Brattle also recognized that some of the confessions were the result of deliberate coercion. Reports of severe interrogation and underhanded methods began to appear soon after the trials started.

In early June, after Bridget Bishop's execution, twenty-five-year-old Sarah Churchill told her friends Sarah Ingersoll and Anna Andrews that the confession she had made a few days earlier was a lie. Churchill was a maidservant in the house of eighty-year-old George Jacobs Sr. She was a witness at Jacobs's examination on May 10, and she claimed to have seen his name in the devil's book. Jacobs's specter, she said, had tormented her and made her sign it. Prior to this, Churchill had apparently joined the company of the afflicted Village girls, one of whom, Mercy Lewis, had complained that the specter of Jacobs had beaten her with his canes. Churchill, who was apparently sympathetic to Lewis's accusation, told Jacobs that afterward she refused to "doe her service" for him. She reported that he had called her a "bitch witch" and was apparently beaten by him. Much like Mary Warren, who had been beaten by her master, John Procter, when she claimed to be afflicted, the records imply that Sarah Churchill was beaten by George Jacobs in an effort to stop her tormented behavior. When Sarah stopped saying that she was afflicted, Mercy Lewis turned on her and accused her of being a witch. Sarah was then taken to court and examined as a suspect on May 9.

The record of Sarah's examination is no longer extant, but she apparently accused Jacobs in court because the next day she appeared as one of the witnesses at Jacobs's examination. The magistrates forced her to admit that she had seen Jacobs's specter and to admit that she had signed the devil's book and seen his name in it: "Sarah Churchwell, when you wrote in the book, you was showed your Masters name, you said." Sarah agreed and urged Jacobs to confess.

Afterward, she tearfully told Ingersoll and Andrews that her confession was false. Anna Andrews was George Jacobs Sr.'s daughter and clearly had reason to tell the justices that Churchill's confession was a lie. According to Ingersoll, "After her [Churchill's] examination, . . . she came to me Crieng and wringing her hands seeming to be much troubled in Spirit," saying that "she had undone herself." She admitted that she had confessed falsely. "I have belied myself, Churchill cried, saying she had set her hand to the devil's book whereas she said she never did. I told her I believed she had set her hand to the book. She answered Crieng and said no no no: I never, I never did." She explained that "they threatened her: and told her they would put her in to the dungeon." Churchill did not indicate who "they" were. But one of them was Mercy Lewis, who later said that she had "perswaded her to confess." The other was the Reverend Nicholas Noyes, the assistant minister of First Church in Salem. According to Churchill, "if she told Mr. Noyes but once she had set her hand to the book, he would believe her, but if she told the truth and said she had not set her hand to the book a hundred times he would not believe her."[18]

From the beginning, forty-five-year-old Nicholas Noyes, who had ordained Samuel Parris, was a strong advocate of the trials. The records show that he was present at several preliminary hearings and supported the accusers' testimonies. Attorney General Thomas Newton wrote down Churchill's confession on June 1, which Churchill signed as evidence in preparation for the trials of Bishop, Procter, and Ann Pudeator. Bishop was tried and convicted the next day, June 2, and executed on June 10.

Churchill undoubtedly realized the consequences of her confession when she was called upon to swear to it the next day at Bishop's trial, and she would have known that it had helped to send Bishop to the gallows. Afterward, Churchill sobbed out her feelings to Ingersoll and Andrews. The two women submitted their account of Churchill's retraction to the Court of Oyer and Terminer,[19] perhaps hoping that it would overturn Churchill's testimony against Jacobs. But their statement was never used in court, and Churchill never formally retracted her confession. She almost certainly realized that to have done so would have forced the judges to put her on trial. Despite her initial agony of conscience, she stuck by her confession and put her name to indictments against Jacobs and Pudeator, aware that it would help to convict them as well.[20]

In July, John Procter of Salem Village, who was awaiting execution in the Salem jail, sent a petition to Increase Mather and several other Boston ministers known to be sympathetic to the plight of the accused. Procter reported that his seventeen-year-old son, William, had been tortured by being tied up "Neck and Heels till the Blood gushed out at his Nose" and thereby forced to confess. Procter also said that the same technique had been used on two of Martha Carrier's sons, eighteen-year-old Richard Carrier and fifteen-year-old Andrew, in order to extract confessions and accusations against their mother. Procter closed his petition by observing that "these actions are very like the Popish Cruelties," by which he meant the notorious Catholic Inquisition.

The court transcript of the Carrier brothers' preliminary examination says that the two boys initially denied the charges against them. The transcript continues: "Richa'd and Andrew were Carried out [of the courtroom] to another Chamber—And there feet & hands bound." When they were brought back before the magistrates, Richard was asked: "Rich'd, though you have been Verry Obstinate, yet tell us how long ago it is since you ware taken in this [the devil's] Snare." The record continues, "many questions [having been] propounded, he answered affirmatively." That is, Richard admitted his guilt.[21] The torture of the Carrier brothers is the only example of judicially approved physical torture mentioned in the surviving court records.[22]

In mid-July, after the execution of six people, all of whom were women, a spate of accusations was immediately followed by confessions. Two of the confessors were the middle-aged Elizabeth Johnson Sr. and her twenty-two-year-old daughter, Elizabeth Johnson Jr. The elder Johnson was the daughter of the Reverend Francis Dane of Andover, and her daughter was Dane's granddaughter. Both described spectral masses held in Salem Village and Andover. According to Dane, his daughter was "weak, and incapacious, fearful and . . . falsely accused herself." She denied she was a witch when arrested but gave in to pressure when brought to court. Dane referred to his granddaughter as "simplish at best" and said that she confessed because of the rumor in Andover that confession was the only way for the accused to obtain freedom.[23]

Statements by seventeen-year-old Margaret Jacobs indicate that the magistrates forced her to choose between confession and execution. Arrested and examined in early May, she succumbed to courtroom pressure and accused George Burroughs and her grandfather George Jacobs Sr., both of whom had already been accused. In a letter written to her father, George Jacobs Jr., in August, following the trial and conviction of her grandfather and George Burroughs, Margaret explained that she had made a false confession, which she blamed upon the "magistrate's threatenings." She also said that when she tried to retract her confession, the magistrates refused to believe her. Later, in a separate statement to the Superior Court of Judicature, she wrote that "they told me, if I would not confess, I should be put down into the dungeon and would be hanged, but if I would confess I should have my life." In this statement, Jacobs does not say who "they" were who made her choose between death and confession, but her previous letter appears to indicate that it was the magistrates.[24]

Jacobs's dramatic story illustrates the moral dilemma faced by those who felt forced to confess to save themselves, and Margaret struggled with her conscience. If she confessed, she would have to live with her conscience and give evidence against others, in her case against her grandfather and Burroughs. If she did not confess or retracted her confession, she would be executed. "Oh!" she exclaimed, "the terrors of a wounded Conscience who can bear!" Conscience stricken, she chose the latter alternative: "What I said, was altogether false against my grandfather, and Mr. [George] Burroughs, which I did to save my life and to have my liberty."[25] Both her grandfather and Burroughs had been accused before, so mentioning them was nothing new. Because Margaret was a family member, her testimony against her grandfather would have weighed significantly at his trial.

Two months later, unable to bear the pangs of conscience, she recanted, knowing the penalty was death and realizing that she had helped to convict her grandfather and George Burroughs. She hoped that by righting her wrong and sacrificing herself for the truth she might gain salvation. She concluded her letter to her father by saying: "God knows how soon I shall be put to Death. Dear Father, let me beg your Prayers to the Lord on my behalf, and send us a Joyful and Happy meeting in Heaven."[26]

Although indicted for witchcraft in mid-September, Margaret was not put on trial at this time because of a cyst or abscess on her head. The swelling likely saved her life.[27] English policy prohibited executing anyone who was ill at the time. A month later the court was closed. In January 1693, Margaret was tried and acquitted by the new Superior Court of Judicature, in which spectral evidence was disallowed. Her behavior stands in marked contrast to that of the older Sarah Churchill, mentioned above. Unlike the courageous Margaret, Churchill was apparently too frightened to formally recant her confession and risk the gallows. She let her confession stand, and its evidence was used to condemn others.

Fifty-one-year-old Rebecca Eames of Boxford confessed due to intimidation by her young accusers, Abigail Hobbs and Mary Lacey. Hobbs and Lacey had confessed earlier and were in jail together with her. They persuaded Eames to confess, perhaps in an attempt to get her to confirm their confessions that had named her. She was one of the four confessors who were tried and condemned in mid-September. But the court did not send her or the others to the gallows with the rest of the condemned on September 22. Eames later petitioned the government for a pardon, saying that her August confession "was altogether false and untrue." She explained that Hobbs and Lacey persuaded her to confess by telling her that otherwise she would be immediately hanged:

> I, being hurried out of my Senses by ye Afflicted persons Abigail Hobbs and Mary Lacye, who both of them cryed out against me charging me with witchcraft ye space of four dayes mocking of me and spitting in my face saying they knew me to be an old witch and if I would not confesse it I should very Speedily be hanged. . . . which was ye Occasion with my owne wicked heart of my saying what I did say.[28]

Hobbs and Lacey clearly believed themselves to be free from trial because of their confessions, and this turned out to be correct. In mid-September, fifty-eight-year-old Mary Towne Esty of Topsfield, who had been convicted and was in the Salem jail awaiting execution, petitioned the governor and the court to put the confessors on trial: "I Petition to your honours not for my own life for I know I must die and my appointed time is sett but the Lord he knowes it is that if it be possible no more Innocent blood may be shed which undoubtidly cannot be Avoyded." She was certain that some of them had lied. She did not say that coercion was used; she knew only that she had been falsely named, and she believed that the confessors would be exposed if the court would question them separately and put them on trial. She asked Governor Phips and the court to try some of these confessing witches, "I being confident there is severall of them has belyed themselves and others as will appeare . . . I question not [but] youle see an alteration of thes things they say my selfe and others having made a League with the Divel."[29] Whether or not Esty suspected that coercion had been used to obtain false confessions or that promises of freedom had been made, she believed that confessors would be exposed and recant their testimony when put on trial.

Esty's noble effort to set the court straight for the sake of others is recognized as one of the high points of conscience exhibited during the Salem tragedy. She would eventually be proven correct in early October, when some confessors recanted, but she did not live to see it. Nevertheless, her timing was critical. She raised her voice in mid-September, when confessions and executions were reaching their peak, and when the public opinion was turning against the court. Her petition was an intelligent and well-calculated stroke. Historians agree that Esty's letter, which was addressed to the governor, the judges, and the Boston ministers, helped to bring the embarrassingly high number of confessions to the fore. Soon four confessors would be put on trial and convicted, and support for the trials would begin to unravel as others began to recant their confessions.

Also in mid-September, elderly Ann Pudeator, who was condemned and awaiting execution, insisted that she had been falsely accused and petitioned the Salem court. She named Sarah Churchill as one of her accusers and asked "that my life may not be taken away by such false Evidences and wittnesses as these."[30] Her petition was to no avail. She was executed on September 22, the third person named by Churchill to be hanged.

In a statement to the Superior Court of Judicature written in January 1693, the Reverend Francis Dane confirmed that Andover residents believed that promises of freedom had been made to defendants in exchange for confession: "the common speech that was frequently spread among us, [was] of their liberty, if they would confesse."[31] Dane does not indicate the source of this opinion, but it appears to explain why so many of the Andover suspects, who were otherwise model Christians, confessed falsely and "belied themselves."

Soon after Esty's and Pudeator's petitions, the court decided to put some of the confessors on trial. The public had begun to question the court's practice of ignoring them, although Thomas Brattle reported that there was still strong faith in the genuineness of the confessions: "The great cry of many of our neighbours now is, What, will you not believe the confessours?"[32] At about this time, Samuel Wardwell of Andover recanted his confession. He did not indicate that he had been forced to confess but said that he believed he would die whether he recanted or not. So he recanted, apparently for reasons of conscience. He was immediately tried, convicted, and executed. The court also found four other confessors guilty and sentenced them to death but did not send them to the gallows.[33] September 22 concluded the fifth session of the Court of Oyer and Terminer, and it went into recess for the month of October. It was scheduled to resume on November 1 with a new round of trials, but not before the Governor's Council and General Court met in October and was scheduled to take up the matter. According to one account, four graves had been dug at the execution site in preparation for the hanging of the four who had been convicted. Fortunately, they were never used.[34]

Meanwhile, during the month of August, Increase Mather had been occupied with the writing of *Cases of Conscience,* which was aimed at nullifying the court's use of spectral evidence and the touch test. At the same time, Increase's witch-hunter son Cotton wrote a letter to his grandfather John Cotton and expressed his satisfaction at the execution of five more witches, whose hangings he had gone to Salem to witness. Cotton Mather also noted that "immediately upon this [the executions], our God miraculously sent in five Andover witches, who made a most ample, surprising, amazing confession of all their villainies."[35] Ironically, while the younger Mather was celebrating the deadly work of the court, his father was preparing a detailed argument that would shut it down.[36]

On October 3, Increase Mather finally finished *Cases of Conscience.* He immediately sent the manuscript to the governor and presented a summary of his findings to Boston's assembly of ministers for their approval. Before the work's publication, however, he added a postscript that strongly upheld the integrity of confessions: "More than one or two of those now in Prison, have freely and credibly acknowledged their Communion and Familiarity with the Spirits of Darkness."[37]

The recantations by confessors probably began in late September, perhaps after Mather wrote his postscript. Thomas Brattle took it upon himself to expose the existence of these recantations. His "Letter" of October 8 is dated four days before the start of the session of the General Court, the legislative body of Massachusetts, which might take up the question of continuing the witchcraft court. He was a cautious critic, and it is likely that he wrote to communicate his views to a small circle of friends, some of whom were undoubtedly members of the General Court and perhaps the Governor's Council. Brattle was careful not to question the motives of the judges while at the same time questioning their methods. The informal style of a private letter allowed him to indulge his rhetorical skills without fear of official retribution.

Brattle went on to express his "wonder" at the court's acceptance of confessions by individuals who had been coerced. He reported that some of the confessors "had denied their guilt, and maintained their innocency for above eighteen hours after [the] most violent, distracting, and dragooning methods had been used with them to make them confess." He continued: "Such methods they were, that more than one of them said confessors did since tell many, with teares in their eyes, that they thought their very lives would have gone out of their bodyes."[38]

Encouraged perhaps by Brattle's letter, and seeing the opportunity to influence the delegates meeting in Boston, Andover's two ministers, Francis Dane and Thomas Barnard, sent a petition to Boston a few days later stating that many confessions had indeed been obtained by coercion. The petition was signed by former governor Simon Bradstreet and twenty-four relatives of the Andover confessors. The Reverend Barnard's endorsement was significant because he had been a strong advocate of the trials but had obviously changed his mind. "[W]e have reason to think," the petition said, "that the extreme urgency that was used with some of them by their friends and others who privately examined them, and the fear they were then under, hath been an inducement to them to own such things, as we cannott since find they are conscious of; and the truth of what we now declare, we judge will in time more plainly appear. And some of them have expressed to their neighbours, that it hath been their great trouble, that they have wronged themselves and the truth in their confessions."[39]

About this time, Increase Mather also appears to have realized that some of the confessions were false, and he went to the Salem jail to hear for himself. He may have wanted to uphold the Andover ministers and expose the fact that forceful methods had been used. If the court were to resume as scheduled in early November or if another court were to continue with the trials, as later happened, the confessors would have to be put on trial. The confessions had been recorded, often in great detail, and they were deemed to be the best grounds for conviction, as Mather had indicated in his postscript. Moreover, four confessors had been condemned by the court in mid-September and were awaiting execution when the court resumed in early November. Several children, ages five through fourteen, had also confessed and were in jail awaiting trial.[40] Would they be executed on the basis of their confessions? Mather, it seems, felt an urgent need to address the problem of coerced confessions, a subject he had omitted from *Cases of Conscience* and had not considered in his laudatory postscript. Because he was Boston's most respected religious leader, his response would carry significant weight.[41]

Mather had likely been aware of previous reports of coerced confessions addressed to him and others by John Procter and Margaret Jacobs. But Procter and Jacobs had been indicted at the time, and their petitions would have been suspect. Mather's investigation of coerced confessions occurred only after stories of intimidation began to surface in October from Brattle and the ministers in Andover. Mather apparently felt compelled to visit the Salem jail to see for himself whether "extreme urgency" had been used, as Brattle had said and the Andover ministers had claimed.

Mather's account of his interviews with women in the Salem prison is dated October 19, 1692. He heard of the same coercive methods that Brattle had described a week earlier. Both men are said to have been there, and they may have been there at the same time.[42] Mather chose to write down the accounts of eight women in their own words, and he found their stories of intimidation emotionally moving. The elderly Mary Osgood explained that her confession was "wholly false" and the result of "the violent urging and unreasonable pressings that were used towards her." Deliverance Dane and Abigail Barker said "they were press'd, and urg'd, and frightened; that at last they did say anything that was desired of them; they said that they were sensible of their great evil in giving way at last to own what was false, and spake all with such weeping, relenting, and bleeding, as was enough to affect the hardest heart." Mary Barker "bewail'd and lamented her accusing of others . . . and said that she was told by her examiners that she *did* know of their being witches and *must* confess it . . . [and] by the renewed urgings and charging of whom at last she gave way."[43]

Mather chose to dwell at length on the story of forty-year-old Mary Tyler. She reported that her brother-in-law, John Bridges, and the Reverend John Emerson of Charlestown stood on either side of her in the Salem jail and

did tell her that she was certainly a witch, and that she saw the devil before her eyes at that time . . . and so they urged her to confess, that she wished herself in any dungeon, rather than be so treated. Mr. Emerson told her once again, Well, I see you will not confess! Well! I will now leave you, and then you are undone, body and soul forever. Her brother urged her to confess, and told her that in so doing she could not lie; . . . [He] said that God would not suffer so many good men to be in such an errour about it, and that she would be hang'd, if she did not confess, and continued so long and so violently to urge and presse her to confess, that she thought verily her life would have gone from her, and became so terrifyed in her mind, that she own'd at length almost any thing that they propounded to her; but she had wronged her conscience in so doing, she was guilty of a great sin in belying of herself, and desired to mourn for it as long as she lived. This she said and a great deal more of the like nature, and all of it with such affection, sorrow, relenting, grief, and mourning as that it exceeds any pen for to describe and express the same.[44]

Mather's moving account would serve as his final argument against the procedures used by the Court of Oyer and Terminer, and it would cast doubt upon the heretofore unquestioned validity of the confessions. His intended audience was not the judges on the court, which was in recess, but the governor and the legislators who were meeting in Boston and might be taking up the question of whether to continue the witch trials. While pointing out that many admissions of guilt were coerced, Mather chose not to address the question of determining whether all confessions were forced. Instead, he relied on the emotional power of the women's stories. The report's purpose was to show that the confessors' claims to intimidation were genuine and by implication that the court's methods were flawed.

Four confessors were awaiting execution when Phips closed the court in late October, and they escaped the gallows.[45] The zealous chief magistrate, William Stoughton, knowing that opposition to the trials was gaining influence, had hurried more defendants to trial and to the gallows in August and September in an attempt, as he said, "to have cleared the Land of these [witches]."[46] By September, the Court of Oyer and Terminer had become a victim of its own success, crushed by the weight of nineteen executions and by the fifty-four confessions.[47]

The Boston merchant Robert Calef's trenchant criticism of the Salem trials, published a few years later in his *More Wonders of the Invisible World*, reinforced Brattle's and Mather's point about the use of intimidating methods. These tactics included promises of freedom, especially by family members, which were calculated to generate confessions:

Concerning those that did Confess, that besides that powerful Argument, of Life . . . There are numerous Instances, too many to be here inserted, of the tedious Examinations before private persons, many hours together; they all that time urging them to Confess (and taking turns to persuade them) till the accused were wearied out by being forced to stand so long, or for want of Sleep, etc., and so brought to give an Assent to what they said; they then asking them, Were you at such a Witch-meeting, or have you signed the Devil's Book, etc. Upon their replying, yes, the whole was drawn into form as their Confession.[48]

The Reverend John Hale, writing six years after the event, emphasized the fact that the confessions played a crucial role in driving the witch trials forward:

That which chiefly carried on this matter to such an height, was the increasing of confessors till they amounted to near about Fifty. . . . And many of the confessors confirmed their confessions with very strong circumstances . . . their relating the times when they covenanted with Satan, and the reasons that moved them thereunto; their Witch meetings, and that they had their mock Sacraments of Baptism and the Supper, . . . and some showed the Scars of the wounds which they said were made to fetch blood with.[49]

Cotton Mather, by contrast, took the confessions to be valid evidence that justified the court's actions. In *Wonders of the Invisible World,* Mather quoted at length from selected confessions in order to justify the court's convictions.

The testimonies of confessed witches had contributed what was assumed to be the most convincing evidence for the prosecution, legitimating the court's actions from the very beginning and propelling it forward. Most of the confessions also reinforced the notion that the ministry in Salem Village was Satan's target. If the accusers ignited the witchcraft crisis in Salem, then the court poured fuel on the flame in the form of confessions wrought by intimidation and apparent extortion.

THE APPARITION AND TRIAL
OF GEORGE BURROUGHS

[O]h dreadfull dreadfull here is a minister com:
what are Ministers wicthes to[?]
— *Ann Putnam Jr.*

In 1680, Salem Village invited the Harvard-educated, thirty-year-old Reverend George Burroughs to replace the Reverend James Bailey as its minister following a dispute about Bailey's qualifications. Burroughs was unable to smooth over other conflicts that had developed within the community and instead concentrated on his preaching. Two years later, as we have seen, the Village resident Jeremiah Watts wrote to Burroughs lamenting the disputes in the community that pitted "brother . . . against brother and neighbor against neighbor." The conflict was about whether Salem Village should become a town, independent of Salem Town.[1] Given the fractiousness of Village politics, Burroughs was powerless to stop the quarreling. His opponents were the Putnams, and his presence must have upset them, as they had been Bailey's supporters. The following year, the Putnams prevailed upon the rest of the Village to have Burroughs dismissed, and the Village refused to pay his salary. After two more years, subsisting on loans from John Putnam Sr., in whose house he and his family lived while the parsonage was being built, Burroughs suspended worship services in protest of his unpaid wages. He had used some of the borrowed funds to purchase wine for the funeral of his wife, who had died in 1681. Two years later, the coastal frontier town of Casco (later Falmouth, now Portland), Maine, which was resettled after King Philip's War, invited Burroughs to return as its minister. He had served as Casco's minister from 1673 to 1676, when he and his family, together with the rest of Casco's residents, were driven out by an Indian attack. In 1683, unwanted in Salem Village and having just remarried, Burroughs was invited to return to the Casco community, and he and his family left Salem Village to start a new life.

John Putnam Sr. subsequently sued Burroughs for failure to pay back his loans, and Burroughs was forced to return to face the charges. He won the suit, saying that he could not repay Putnam without first receiving the salary the Village owed him, thus forcing the Putnams to pay him first. He then left the Village for good. But he was a marked man.

In Casco he continued to serve as the minister for six more years until 1689, when a devastating Indian attack forced him to flee with his family again. The Indian attack lasted five days and burned down three or four hundred homes. Some two hundred people were killed, many scalped and brutalized, and about eighty were captured.[2]

Burroughs moved to the coastal town of Wells, Maine, and became its new minister. As a pastor in the small frontier communities of Casco and Wells, which did not have established congregations, Burroughs had never become an ordained minister, a fact that Cotton Mather threw in his face at his execution. On January 25, 1692, Candlemas Day, Indians raided the nearby town of York, Maine. Dozens of homes were burned, about fifty people killed, and a hundred captives taken away. York's minister, the Reverend Shubael Dummer, was shot on the doorstep of his house, and his body was mutilated. Burroughs wrote a report of the raid, painting a grim scene: "pillars of smoke, ye raging of ye merciless flames, ye insultations of ye heathen enemy, shouting, shooting, hacking . . . & dragging away captives [to Canada]." Afterward a militia officer in nearby Portsmouth reported, "Nothing remains Eastward of Wells." Portsmouth, to the south, began frantically to refortify itself. Indians attacked York again in June 1692, but were repelled with heavy losses.[3]

Burroughs, like Cotton Mather, saw the punishing hand of God in the shocking raids. He sent a report to Boston saying that "God is still manifesting his displeasure against this land."[4] God was again using the Indians to smite his wayward people. By contrast, militia leaders in Maine generally spoke of incompetence among the local militias and decried the delays in obtaining help from Boston, which left the frontier open to Indian predations. What had started in late April with accusations against the "dreadful minister" by young Ann Putnam and Abigail Williams developed rapidly through the interrogations and testimonies of subsequent confessors, which confirmed that Burroughs's specter was leading satanic masses in Salem Village next to Samuel Parris's house. In late July, as Burroughs's August 5 trial drew near, his apparition appeared frequently to Andover's confessors. Dozens of witches were said to attend spectral gatherings led by Burroughs, and each confessor reported increasing numbers at the meetings, eventually reaching five hundred in the whole country.[5] Burroughs was said to be tormenting people in Andover in an attempt to make them join Satan's cult in Salem Village. By August, the case against Burroughs had developed into a sensational story of revenge, spousal abuse, murder, bewitchment of English soldiers, and religious apostasy.

Burroughs, it appears, had become the scapegoat for Salem Village's repeated conflicts over its ministers. At long last, the satanic source of the Village's problems had been identified. After Burroughs had been forced to leave the Village, his specter had attacked the Reverend Deodat Lawson's family and was now leading the attack on the family of Samuel Parris as well as members of the Village congregation and the inhabitants of nearby Andover.

Increase and Cotton Mather also became interested in the Burroughs case. Though they had expressed doubts about the reliability of spectral evidence, they were remarkably confident about the spectral evidence presented against Burroughs. They seem to have projected onto him their own uncertainties about the future of the Puritan religion under the new charter. The charter of 1691 had dethroned Puritanism from its dominant position in New England, and here was Burroughs, a Puritan minister who seemed to have lost his faith or perhaps had become a dissident Puritan and joined the Baptists' camp.[6] It was known that Burroughs had baptized only the first of his eight children and that he had twice refused to take communion when he had the opportunity. For the Mathers, Burroughs may have represented all that was wrong in a colony that was moving away from its original Puritan religious origins and purpose. Now the devil was seen in Andover baptizing many of Satan's recruits, and Burroughs, known to have rejected infant baptism in his own family, was seen to be present. The devil made people renounce prior baptisms and become rebaptized, as the Baptists did.[7]

The powerful Putnam family also came forward with evidence of Burroughs's spousal abuse when he lived in the Village. Ann Putnam Jr. and Abigail Williams magnified the Village suspicions and accused him of killing his two wives who had died—one in Salem Village and the other later, after he left—and also of killing the Reverend Lawson's wife and daughter, who died in Salem Village after Burroughs was dismissed. For good measure, Ann Putnam threw in the Village gossip that he had bewitched "a great many" English soldiers "at the eastward" out of jealousy over Lawson getting the post of pastor to the soldiers in Maine, thus helping the Indians in their raids. All of these issues were raised at Burroughs's examination in early May and again at his trial on August 5.

John and Rebecca Putnam Sr. testified at the trial that when "Burroughs did live at our house he was a very sharp man to his wife." The Putnams told of a special covenant that Burroughs had wanted his wife to sign that "she would never reveal his secrets."[8] The Putnams recoiled with suspicion and refused to join in Burroughs's scheme to censure his wife, and the deposition implied that Burroughs was a wife abuser. Ann Putnam Jr.'s accusation revealed that the death of Burroughs's first two wives, the second of whom was the magistrate John Hathorne's sister-in-law, was no coincidence. Nor was it a coincidence that Burroughs's successor's wife and child had suddenly died. In Maine, Burroughs had gained a reputation among militia troops, whom he assisted, for phenomenal physical strength. It was reported that he could hold a musket at arm's length with his finger inserted in the muzzle of the barrel. Now he was identified as the recruiter of witches in Salem Village and the leader of satanic masses next to the Village parsonage.

The historian Bernard Rosenthal was the first to see the importance of the accusation of Burroughs, which brought the question of Puritan theological orthodoxy into the affair. Increase Mather and his son Cotton, who had otherwise been cautious about supporting the trials, took an interest because of Burroughs's religious unorthodoxy.[9] More recently, Mary Beth Norton has taken the subject of Burroughs's prominence a step further by seeing his connection to the Indian attacks on the Maine frontier as the key relationship that caused the escalation of the witchcraft accusations in late April.

But the targeting of Burroughs on April 20 took place in the midst of an escalation of accusations that was already under way, backed mainly by the Putnams and their friends. By April 11 the number of accusations had reached ten.[10] This was a relatively high number, but the affair was still contained within Salem Village and its immediate neighbors, Salem Town and Topsfield. But between April 18 and April 22, there were fourteen new accusations and three new confessions. In the middle of this frenzy, Burroughs was accused and named as the leader. The shocking scandal of a Puritan minister who had turned to Satan in order to destroy his former congregation was just too "dreadfull," to use Ann Putnam's phrase. When combined with the new accusations and supported by new confessions, an unstoppable course was set into motion. A week later, there were six more arrests, making a total of twenty-nine arrests by the end of April. There was no turning back.

What set off the rash of new accusations in April was the steady momentum of fear generated in late March by the claim that Salem Village was becoming the "first seat of Satans Tyranny . . . in opposition of Christ's kingdom," in the words of the Reverend Deodat Lawson. Parris followed up this shocking pronouncement three days later with the claim that there might be as many as twenty devils in the congregation itself.[11] Previously, during Martha Cory's examination, the Village girls had spied a whole company of spectral witches outside the meetinghouse. These alarming numbers, which no one questioned, inevitably turned into the flood of formal complaints and accusations from middle to late April. The accusation of Burroughs served as a catalyst for the escalation that had already begun.

The magistrates knew, of course, that Ann Putnam and Abigail Williams were too young for their stories about Burroughs to hold up in court. So they followed up their initial examinations of Deliverance and Abigail Hobbs by interrogating them again in prison in order to extract the information that Burroughs was the recruiter of witches in Salem Village. The Hobbses told them more: Burroughs was the leader of the witches' meetings and satanic masses in Salem Village in the field next to Parris's house. A few days later, the magistrates would obtain evidence from Mary Warren, who was now eager to cooperate. Burroughs, she said, tried to bewitch Justice Hathorne, and she confirmed that he had killed his second wife. Mercy Lewis also chimed in. She said that two days before Burroughs's examination on May 9, his specter carried her up to a high mountain and "shewed me all the kingdoms of the earth and tould me that he would give them all to me if I would writ in his book and if I would not he would thro me down and brake my neck." Thus within the space of two weeks, Putnam's and Williams's revelations about Burroughs were strongly corroborated. He was initially identified by the court's two star witnesses, Putnam and Williams, later followed by Mary Walcott and Elizabeth Hubbard, and immediately thereafter by three new confessors as the leader of a witchcraft conspiracy. With Burroughs as the catalyst, the number of accusations and arrests would continue to soar.

The sensation Burroughs generated did not concern the allegation that he had aided the Indians in Maine but rather that he was a turncoat clergyman who was taking revenge on Salem Village, which had expelled him, by setting up Satan's worship there. Thomas Putnam had already warned the magistrates that he had news, based on his daughter's terrifying vision of Burroughs, that would cause the ears of everyone to "tingle." Ears did tingle with Burroughs's name and not just in Salem Village but also in Salem Town and other communities in Essex County (Topsfield and Andover) among people who knew him or his reputation.

The next step in the developing plot was to tie Burroughs to Satan's evil blackness. Abigail Williams referred to him as "a lettell black menester," and Elizabeth Hubbard followed up by emphasizing some of the black aspects of Burroughs's appearance: "There apeared a little black-haired man to me in blackish aparill [and] I asked him his name. & he told me his name was borrous [Burroughs]."[12] The girls were saying that Burroughs's black hair, which he wore unusually long, and black clothing made him a human counterpart to the devil, thus identifying him with the spectral black man himself. Burroughs's short stature also received attention, and he had a swarthy complexion. Although Tituba had described the black man as tall in stature, Hubbard referred to Burroughs derisively as a "little" man, and Cotton Mather denigrated him as a "very puny" man. All the more suspicious, then, was Burroughs's showing off his extraordinary physical strength, which Cotton Mather would declare to be evidence of the "preternatural."[13]

Given Burroughs's importance as a Puritan minister, permission for his arrest had to be obtained from the governor and his Council. After Thomas Putnam and Jonathan Walcott issued their complaint against Burroughs on April 30, Major Elisha Hutchinson of Boston received the authorization from the governor to dispatch an order to John Partridge, marshal of Portsmouth, New Hampshire, to arrest Burroughs in Wells and bring him to Salem, which he did on May 4.[14]

Because of Burroughs's high status, the examination on May 9 was conducted by two members of the Governor's Council, Deputy Governor William Stoughton and Samuel Sewall, in addition to Hathorne and Corwin. The record indicates that the magistrates began their interrogation before calling the "bewitched" into the courtroom. The justices first wanted to know about Burroughs's Puritan orthodoxy. They learned that he had not taken the sacrament of the Lord's Supper when he had the opportunity on two different occasions, and that he had baptized only the first of his eight children. These were important matters. Burroughs's failure to baptize his children was a startling omission for a Puritan clergyman. It suggested that he did not believe in the Puritan custom of infant baptism and that he possibly harbored Baptist ideas. The Baptists, as Calvinist Protestants, agreed with the Puritans on almost every point of doctrine except the sacrament of baptism. Baptists held that baptism could only be given to persons of age who were able to profess their faith in full knowledge of baptism's meaning and significance. By contrast, Puritans believed that baptism incorporated children, even as infants, into God's covenant of faith.

As for Burroughs's failure to partake of communion, this could only mean that he harbored doubts about the central sacrament of the Puritan church. Whether Burroughs's behavior was the result of negligence or religious belief, it was tantamount to a rejection of the fundamentals of Puritan faith. Both Increase and Cotton Mather would condemn him for such religious deviance and justify his execution despite their doubts about spectral evidence.

The magistrates also asked Burroughs whether his house in Maine was haunted, perhaps having heard rumors about it from Abigail Hobbs. Burroughs denied it was haunted, but he commented, perhaps sarcastically, that his house had been inhabited by toads. Such a reply was not a joking matter for the magistrates. Burroughs also denied that he had prohibited his wife to write to her father without his permission, an allegation that had been made by the Putnams.

When the afflicted girls were let into the court for the examination, there was no question that many were "grievously tortured." Eighteen-year-old Susannah Sheldon of Salem Village was the first to speak up. She was the boldest of the young Village accusers and did not collapse in fits when asked to testify. Sheldon was a refugee from Black Point (in Scarborough), Maine, who had settled with her family in Salem Village. She had lost her uncle in an Indian attack at Saco, Maine, in 1675 and had recently lost a brother in an Indian attack in 1690. As Norton indicates, she and her family would have known Burroughs as the local minister in Falmouth.[15]

Sheldon repeated Ann Putnam's and Abigail Williams's accusations about Burroughs killing his wives, saying she saw a vision of their ghostly forms in winding sheets. She may have been asked something about the charge that Burroughs bewitched the soldiers in Maine, but the record of her response is illegible at this point, except for the word "souldiers." Whatever was said, the magistrates did not return to the subject for the rest of the examination. As members of the Governor's Council, they may have known that the famous Indian fighter Benjamin Church had in fact commended Burroughs in a report to the authorities in Boston for his part in the defense of Casco during the devastating Indian raid of September 1689.[16] Other documents indicate that Burroughs fought courageously alongside the militia soldiers in both Indian wars.

The magistrates did, however, raise the subject of bewitching soldiers during the second examination of Abigail Hobbs. Abigail was a refugee from Falmouth after the attack of 1688, and she undoubtedly knew George Burroughs as the minister of the Falmouth community. Pursuing, perhaps, Ann Putnam's claim about Burroughs bewitching soldiers in Maine, the magistrates asked Hobbs whether he had ever used poppets against his wives, children, or the "Eastward soldiers." Abigail denied it, and the subject was dropped.[17]

Burroughs's trial and conviction on August 5 began the court's most active—and deadliest—phase. From August 5 until September 22, when the court was terminated, fourteen trials and thirteen executions took place. Cotton Mather noted that Burroughs's trial on August 5 was a sensational affair, "whither a Vast Concourse of people is gone," Burroughs being said to be the witches' "ringleader."[18] Cotton Mather began his review of Burroughs's case by emphasizing the strength of the spectral evidence against him. At his examination, Mather pointed out, "the Bewitched People were grievously harassed with Preternatural Mischiefs, which could not possibly be Dissembled; and they still ascribed it unto the Endeavours of G[eorge]. B[urroughs]. to kill them." At his trial, Mather related, "one of the Bewitched

Persons testify'd, That in her Agonies, a little Black hair'd man came to her, saying his Name was B[urroughs]. and bidding her set her hand unto a Book which he show'd unto her; and bragging that he was a Conjurer, above the ordinary Rank of Witches." As Mather recounted Burroughs's trial, his usual skepticism about the reliability of spectral evidence disappeared, and he endorsed all such evidence as genuine and convincing. But Mather assured his readers that spectral afflictions were not "any part of his Conviction," even though Burroughs's four indictments referred only to spectral affliction and were all signed by the afflicted accusers.[19]

Mather then drew attention to the judges' interest in questions about Burroughs's deviations from Puritan orthodoxy, the deaths of his two wives, the sudden deaths of Lawson's wife and daughter, and his feats of unusual strength. The subject of bewitching soldiers in Maine was apparently not raised.[20]

The judges, according to Mather, were especially provoked by Burroughs's denial that spectral witchcraft existed. Burroughs had brought along a copy of a passage taken from a book written by the seventeenth-century witchcraft skeptic Thomas Ady. Ady was an English physician and humanist who wrote three books that raised doubts about witchcraft and witch-hunting. In *Candle in the Dark*, Ady had written that the Devil's use of specters had no foundation in the Bible, and Burroughs handed a copy of the passage to the jury. The quotation, according to Mather, claimed "that there neither are, nor ever were Witches, that having made a compact with the Devil, Can send a Devil to torment other people at a distance."[21] The court recognized the passage and accused Burroughs of copying it and passing it off as his own. Burroughs explained that he had not taken it from Ady's work but from a manuscript that a friend had given him. The court regarded this explanation as an evasion and took it as further evidence of his guilt.[22] Burroughs's open rejection of the Puritan view of witchcraft was an outright defiance of the court. As for his feats of unusual strength, Mather pronounced them to be "preternatural," performed with the help of the devil.[23]

Given Burroughs's prominence as a Puritan minister, Increase Mather made a point of attending Burroughs's trial on August 5. He said that had he been one of the judges, he would not have acquitted him, thus siding with the judges whose methods he would later reject.

Cotton Mather also decided to confront the evil up close, and he went to witness Burroughs's execution in Salem. In mid-August, Mather, who was recovering from poor health caused by his repeated bouts of fasting, traveled to Salem. He would lend his clerical authority to the momentous occasion. Robert Calef describes the scene:

When he [Burroughs] was upon the Ladder, he made a Speech for the clearing of his Innocency, with such Solemn and Serious Expressions, as were to the Admiration of all present; his Prayer (which he concluded by repeating the Lord's Prayer,) was so well worded, and uttered with such composedness, and such (at least seeming) fervency of Spirit, as was very affecting, and drew Tears from many (so that it seemed to some, that the Spectators would hinder the Execution). The accusers said the black Man stood and dictated to him.

Mather then spoke up.

As soon as he was turned off, Mr. Cotton Mather, being mounted upon a Horse, addressed himself to the People, partly to declare, that he [Burroughs] was no ordained Minister, and partly to possess the People of his guilt; saying, That the Devil has often been transformed into an Angel of Light; and this did somewhat appease the People.[24]

Cotton Mather wanted to show that the trials and executions were justified, especially in the case of George Burroughs. Mather chose the Burroughs case as his prize exhibit, describing it fully and concluding that Burroughs was undoubtedly "the King of Satan's Kingdom."

Writing after the trials had ended, John Hale set himself the task of evaluating what had happened, having changed his mind about their legitimacy. Even before George Burroughs was executed, Hale had questioned the truthfulness of some who had confessed and named Burroughs, suspecting that they had lied. He noted that "when G[eorge] B[urroughs] was Tryed, seven or eight of these Confessors severally called, said, they knew the said B[urroughs] and saw him at a Witch-Meeting at the Village, and heard him exhort the Company to pull down the Kingdom of God, and set up the Kingdom of the Devil." When Hale later questioned one of the confessors, "He denied all, yet said he justified the Judges and Jury in Condemning of him; because there were so many positive witnesses against him: But said he dyed by false Witnesses." Hale said of another confessor, "I seriously spake to one that witnessed (of his [Burroughs's] Exhorting at the Witch Meeting at the Village) saying to her; You are one that bring this man to Death, if you have charged any thing upon him that is not true, recal it before it be too late, while he is alive. She answered me, she had nothing to charge her self with, upon that account."[25]

In 1712, after twenty years of attempts by the Burroughs family to clear George Burroughs's name from the record and receive compensation for the cost of his imprisonment, his widow and surviving children received the amount of fifty pounds. His name was also cleared from the record, "as if no such Convictions, Judgments or Attainders had ever been had or given."[26] There was no compensation for his wrongful execution.

SAMUEL PARRIS,
"THE BEGINNER AND PROCURER"

God . . . has suffered ye evil Angels to delude us.
— Samuel Parris, 1694

Such implacable offenses . . . do render Mr Parris's
removal necessary.
— Increase Mather and Council of Elders, 1695

Historians have described Samuel Parris as an ambitious
and authoritarian personality who was given to confrontation. The nineteenth-century Salem clergyman Charles
Upham, whose classic study *Salem Witchcraft* was the
first to investigate the role that Parris played in the witch-
hunt, regarded him as a man devoid of "many of the
natural human sensibilities" and someone who "delighted
in the exercise of power and rejoiced in conflicts or com-
motions." Although Upham suggested that Parris's personality was "fraught with danger, and prolific of evil," he
did not regard him as a deliberate instigator of the witchcraft accusations.[1] More recent studies portray Parris as
an insecure man who was driven by his obsessions and
played a crucial role in the witchcraft crisis.[2] Parris's bi-
ographer, writing in 1990, concluded that his involvement
was a vital one, "not just important but decisive."[3]

Recent research into the chronology and authorship of
the court records in the *Records of the Salem Witch-Hunt*
makes it possible to shed more light on Parris's critical
role at the start of the legal process. He authored a num-

ber of preliminary examinations on behalf of the court during the first three months. He also wrote many depositions on behalf of more than a dozen different complainants and accusers, most of them being the young Village accusers, during the same period. The examinations and the depositions concerned the same people, mostly inhabitants of Salem Village; and it was their arrests and hearings that drove the rapid start-up.

These documents show Parris to have been a dedicated agent for the prosecution. His opponents in Salem Village believed his role was even more significant. After the trials were over, they would call him the "beginner and procurer," meaning that he was not only an advocate for the prosecution but also an "instigator" and "promoter," in the seventeenth-century sense of these terms.[4] Although Parris cannot be said to have caused or instigated the witch-hunts, since he was only one of several authorities initially involved, it seems clear that, before the accusations began, his aggressive preaching about the devil at work against his ministry created a dark and foreboding atmosphere that legitimated the accusations and shaped his congregation's reaction. His advocacy for the accusations at the very outset was also influential, as can be seen from his collaborations with others in issuing complaints and depositions. His zealous engagement in the legal process played a central role in setting the direction and scope of the proceedings. When it was all over, his opponents, who had been subdued by the zealousness of the Village accusers, had even more reason to wish him gone.

———————

In mid-August 1692, as the accusations and trials were continuing to accelerate, Parris had tried to take action against members of the Nurse family who were church members, for abstaining from communion. Just three weeks after Rebecca Nurse's execution, Parris led a delegation of church elders to seek out four members of the Nurse family in order "to know the reason for their absence" from the Lord's Supper. This was a deliberate act of confrontation.[5]

Parris had played a prominent role in writing depositions against Rebecca Nurse and her two sisters, Sarah Cloyce and Mary Esty. The Nurse family had made great efforts to save Rebecca from the gallows and organized petitions on her behalf signed by thirty-eight Village residents. To no avail. Twenty-eight-year-old Sarah Nurse had directly challenged one of the older accusers, Sarah Bibber, charging that she had seen Bibber take pins hidden in her clothes and stick them into herself in court while claiming that Rebecca Nurse's specter had "prict" her.[6] Parris must have been fully aware of the animosity of the Nurse family, but he would not leave the Nurses alone. Perhaps he wanted to provoke their anger in order to bring censure upon them and possibly arouse suspicion against them as the "Devil's instruments," which Nurse family spokesmen said they feared at the time.[7] But the attempt to create a confrontation failed. The two brothers-in-law John Tarbell and Peter Cloyce avoided contact with Parris,[8] and Nurse's son Samuel and his wife, Sarah, resumed attendance at communion. The Nurses later revealed that they kept their heads down until the crisis was over.

In the spring of 1693, the Nurse family wrote down their grievances against Parris and presented them to him as part of their plan to force him out. A Puritan minister could be dismissed only by the members of his congregation. With the exception of the four Nurses who were church members, Parris retained the backing of the rest of the congregation.

Parris knew, however, that if the Nurse family's complaints remained unresolved, and if they gained support among some in the congregation, his opponents could request a Council of Elders to render a ruling. This he wanted to avoid. A review by a Council of Elders or ministers from Boston and neighboring communities would expose his assistance to the accusers and his public condemnation of the accused from the pulpit well before they were tried in court.

Parris responded in two ways. He sought action from the county court to restore his salary, which had not been paid for a year and a half, and he tried to obstruct his opponents' attempts to settle their grievances by trying to trap them into giving him grounds for a libel suit. He insisted that the Nurses put their signatures to a document listing their charges: "I desired them to subscribe this paper with the hands to it." By obtaining a signed document, he likely intended to turn their ecclesiastical charges into a libel case, which he might assume that the Salem magistrates would decide in his favor. Parris's opponents anticipated this maneuver and listed their grievances in an unsigned document. None would "yield," as Parris expressed it, and put their names to the allegations. His opponents were also careful to say that their case was directed only against Parris, not against the congregation, and they focused their complaints on his conduct during the witch trials.[9]

The first step in the removal of a minister required a representative of the dissenters to meet with the minister and present their complaints. This procedure, vague as it was, followed the Gospel of Matthew 18:15–17, which states that disputes among Christians should be resolved in one-on-one meetings between the two parties. If the meetings proved unsatisfactory, then three dissenters should present their complaints together, in order for there to be witnesses. Parris tried to avoid such a meeting by seeing his opponents individually and without witnesses. On one occasion, Parris noted that John Tarbell, Rebecca Nurse's son-in-law, told him that "I was guilty of Idolotry, in asking the afflicted persons, who they saw upon other afflicted persons. He thought I was going to the God Ekron," that is, the devil. Tarbell also told Parris that "had it not been for me his Mother Nurse might have still been living, and so freed from execution; that I had been a great Prosecutor." Parris noted that Samuel Nurse "has the same objections."[10]

After a number of acrimonious meetings over a period of several months, Parris's opponents told him and his supporters that "by our maintaining and upholding differences amongst us, we do but gratify the Devil." They called for a Council of Elders to find out who was to blame in the dispute. Parris's refusal to meet together with the "dissenting brethren" created widespread dissatisfaction. In December 1693, the dissenters were able to gain the support of fifty Village residents, several of whom were church members. The group then sent a petition to Governor Phips and the General Court requesting that a Council of Elders decide the question of retaining Parris in his post. The petitioners said they had tried "all other methods of bringing matters to a good composure." The government agreed and a council was called.[11]

While the negotiations were going on, Parris expressed his frustration from the pulpit. He castigated the dissenting brethren for their "neglect" in staying away from communion. When the church did not turn against the dissenters, Parris shifted his target to the failings of the rest of the congregation, accusing them of abusing the Lord's Supper by "partaking unworthily." Such people, Parris said, failed to give their full attention during church services, whispering, nodding off to sleep, and gazing about during communion. By abusing the Lord's Supper in this way, such people "eat & drink damnation and judgment to themselves." These were harsh words directed at people whom he had personally admitted to the church. His congregation became spiritually disengaged and resisted his authority. In his later sermons, Parris lashed out and said that the suffering caused by the witchcraft crisis was God's will, and a punishment upon the Village.[12]

The dissenters charged that when the accusations began, Parris had allowed worship services to be interrupted by "distracting & disturbing tumults & noises made by the persons under Diabolical power & delusions preventing sometimes our hearing & understanding & profiting of the word preached."[13] Permitting the young accusers to perform their afflictions during church services must have heightened the atmosphere of demonic threat to the congregation. The Nurses said that these open displays by the young accusers in the meetinghouse made them feel "apprehensions of danger of ourselves."[14]

The Nurse family's statement suggests that the outbursts in church occurred more than once. As we have seen, Deodat Lawson was the target of one such attack during a service held on Sunday, March 20. The girls interrupted his prayers and challenged his selection of biblical readings in a bold display of Satan's power. Parris's opponents regarded this display as a calculated effort to instill fear into the community. The congregation could see that godly women and children were being transformed into agents of Satan. In light of these disruptions, it is no wonder that Lawson declared, just three weeks after the accusations began, that the devil was establishing his kingdom in the Village.

New England ministers at this time showed keen interest in direct encounters with manifestations of the devil as a way to stimulate religious revival: God was using Satan to punish his people for their sins. Increase and Cotton Mather had published popular accounts of demonic possessions and witchcraft in which they saw God's providential hand acting among them, for the devil could act only with God's direct permission.[15] But if Parris fancied himself to be another Cotton Mather, the strategy did not work. So divided was the community that no one came forward to join the congregation during the witch trials period. Nevertheless, the girls' possessed behavior in church undoubtedly increased Parris's standing among church members, and many joined him in supporting the accusers by issuing complaints and depositions.

After the execution of five people in mid-August, Parris preached a sermon aimed at his opponents. Two days after Martha Cory was condemned in early September, he painted a forbidding scene in which "Multitudes of

Witches & Wizards" were attempting "the overthrow of Religion." As the trials and executions were reaching their climax in September, Parris told his congregation that there were but two groups in the Village, that of Christ and that of the Antichrist: "Here are no Newters. Everyone is on one side or the other." Parris's meaning was harsh and clear. His opponents, including some abstaining church members, were on the side of the Antichrist. But by this time Salem Village's phase of the crisis had long passed and could not be revived.[16]

In early October, Boston ministers supported Increase Mather's *Cases of Conscience*, which rejected the reliance on spectral evidence in the trials, and then Governor Phips ordered the closure of the Court of Oyer and Ter-miner.[17] Parris knew he was on the wrong side. He had endorsed spectral evidence in his own complaints and depositions, and he realized that his advocacy for the accusers would be held against him.

In late October 1692, when public opinion had turned against the trials and just before the governor closed the court, Parris preached a sermon of reconciliation with the Village, whose support he still needed. His sermon theme was taken from Canticles 1:2: "Let him kiss me with the kisses of his mouth." Parris explained that Christ's kisses were symbolic of reconciliation and affection. Speaking as Christ's ambassador to the community, he begged his congregation, "Oh, be reconciled to me, & give me a kiss of Reconcilia-tion." But it was too little too late. Emphasizing that Christ's kisses "testify true Reconciliation," Parris never apologized for his advocacy role in the witch trials. He referred only in an oblique way to "some jars and differ-ences" among "true friends" and to "seeming breach and estrangedness." In his arrogance, he may have assumed that his offer of reconciliation, cast in the rhetoric of Christ's love for his followers, would be enough to retain Vil-lage support, but it was not.[18]

In November 1694, eighteen months after the last of the accused was acquitted, Parris's opponents submitted a list of ten grievances. The com-plaint spoke for eighty others, some of them church members, who would later vote to remove Parris. The complaint accused him of "Sundry unsafe, if sound points of doctrine delivered in his preaching, which we esteem not warrantable, if Christian" and of "so frequent and positive preaching up some principles and practices," and it stated pointedly that "the dark and dismall mizeries of inequity washing among us was not profitable but of-fencive."[19] Some of the charges are general and might refer to anything, but

Samuel Parris, "the Beginner and Procurer" { 149 }

given the central role of the sermon in Puritan communities, Parris's sermons about Satan's threats to the community played a significant role, as the editors of Parris's sermons point out, in influencing the congregation's reaction to the girls' afflictions.[20] For a frightened congregation that believed Parris had foretold a satanic opposition to the newly founded congregation, his sermons provided a persuasive framework to interpret the meaning of the girls' traumatic behavior. Subsequent sermons served to motivate church members to continue making accusations against new suspects. Unlike Lawson, whose sermon in the Village preached renewed faith through prayer and repentance as the means to stop God's providential unleashing of Satan, Parris had forecast a state of continuous war against the devils in the Village. At the end of March, following the accusations of Cory and Nurse, Parris declared, "Christ knows how many devils there are among us." He estimated there might be as many as twenty, thus encouraging more suspicion and more witch-hunting.[21]

Parris authored and submitted to the court more than two dozen depositions and testimonies on behalf of the accusers. He wrote them during the early phase of the crisis, from March through May 1692, almost all of them against residents of Salem Village. Significantly, Attorney General Thomas Newton judged most of Parris's depositions substantial enough to be used at the grand jury hearings and later at the trials. Parris wrote testimonies on behalf of Abigail Williams against eighteen defendants, eleven of whom were convicted.

Parris was also charged with asking the Village accusers to name people whose specters they saw were causing illnesses in others and with telling others to seek out the accusers for the same purpose. He was charged in particular with "going to Mary Walcott or Abigail Williams, and directing others to them, to know who afflicted the people in their illnesses." Parris acknowledged the charge in the following manner: "The improving [i.e., using] of one afflicted to inquire by who afflicts ye others, I fear may be, & has been unlawfully used to Satan's great advantage."[22] This was a flat-out admission that he had encouraged the accusers to cry out against specific people.

To give one example: in preparation for the grand jury hearing of Rebecca Nurse, Parris wrote a deposition on behalf of Abigail Williams against Nurse and her sister Sarah Cloyce. The deposition, based on spectral evidence, accused Nurse of murdering several people who had recently died. Abigail Williams swore to the truth of this deposition at Rebecca Nurse's grand jury hearing.[23]

Moreover, several court records indicate that Parris had kept detailed lists of dates when Abigail Williams and other girls were afflicted in order to use these dates in later depositions for grand jury hearings and trials. In May, Parris provided the court with three lists of dates in March and April when Abigail Williams and Mary Walcott were afflicted by the specters of John and Elizabeth Procter, Sarah Cloyce, Rebecca Nurse, Martha Cory, Sarah Good, and Dorothy Good. Parris's records of the precise dates were such as only a literate adult could provide. For example:

> The Testimony of Abigail Williams witnesseth & saith that divers times in the month of March last past, particularly on the .14. 21. & .29. dayes of the same month, & also divers times in the month of April last past, particularly, on the 2. & .13. dayes, she the said Abigail hath been greivously vexed with the apparition of Eliz: Proctor the wife of John Proctor of Salem, by which apparition she has been greivously pinched, had also her bowels almost pulled out, by this together with the apparition of Rebekah Nurse, & by the aforesd apparition of Elizabeth Proctor has been tempted by the offer of fine things to subscribe to a book the said apparition tendered her the said Abigail Williams.[24]

Parris submitted this account on May 31 in anticipation of the grand jury hearings of Elizabeth Procter, John Procter, and Rebecca Nurse, which he knew were scheduled in June for the court's first session.

Parris's opponents also charged him with swearing falsely, offering an "unsafe & unaccountable Oath given by him against sundry of thee Accused." The records show that Parris swore to fourteen depositions at grand jury hearings. He responded evasively, saying, "As to my Oath, I never meant it, nor do I know how it can be otherwise construed, than as vulgarly & [by] everyone understood; yea, and upon inquiry it may be found to be worded also." Parris meant that he swore to the truth of the charges in his depositions based on the evidence. The evidence in each case was spectral and invisible, and his opponents claimed that he should have known better. They accused him of differing "from the opinion of the generality of the Orthodox Ministers of the whole country," an indirect reference to the Boston ministers who endorsed Increase Mather's *Cases of Conscience,* which rejected spectral evidence and the touch test. The charge referred specifically to depositions "wherein he swears that the prisoners with their looks knock down those pretended suffers." Parris, for example, swore to his deposition that Elizabeth Hubbard had been knocked down by the "look" of John Willard at Willard's examination. Parris was also accused of perjury, that he "did Swear positively against the lives of such as he could not have any knowledge but they might be innocent."[25] In other words, Parris swore to depositions based on false evidence, presumably referring to his claims that defendants' specters had caused the accusers to fall down during a touch test.[26]

At the request of the Salem magistrates, Parris served as one of the court recorders of the preliminary examinations that occurred initially in Salem Village and later in Salem Town. Parris's handwriting is clear and legible. He was apparently also adept at taking shorthand notes from which he wrote up his accounts.[27] Of the 107 examination records that survive, including fragments and accounts by third parties, Parris authored twenty-one. They record the hearings of twenty-three defendants during March, April, and May. Fourteen of the defendants were condemned, and thirteen were executed.

Parris was accused of making errors in recording these examinations. The men making this charge were members of the Nurse family. Rebecca Nurse was executed on July 19, 1692, and it was Parris who recorded her examination. He also recorded the examinations of Nurse's sisters, Sarah Cloyce and Mary Esty. The Nurse family was given copies of Rebecca's full set of twenty court records, which included her examination of March 24, 1692.[28] We can assume that they attended her examination, and those of her sisters, and would have known all that was said at the time. They charged Parris with "not rendering to ye world so fair if true an account of what he wrote on Examination of ye accused."[29]

Initially, Parris tried to evade this charge by saying that his role as one of the court recorders "was put upon me by authority; and therein have I been very careful to avoid wronging of any." This response did not sit well with the Council of Elders, and they made him amend it. He added the following admission: "I fear that in and through the throng of many things written by me, in the late confusions, there has not been a due exactness always used; and as I now see the inconveniency of my writing so much on those difficult occasions, so I would lament every error of such writings."[30] This was a meager concession, admitting only that his records of the examinations lacked a certain "exactness" and might have contained "errors." It is quite likely that he only recorded information that could prove useful to the prosecution and left out some of what Nurse and her sisters might have said in their defense.

In fairness to Parris, it should be noted that all the court-appointed recorders were working for the prosecution and were hostile to the defendants. Nevertheless, for the members of the Nurse family who were present at the examinations, Parris's account would have appeared biased and far from being a fair representation.

In summing up their grievances, Parris's opponents concluded "that Mr. Parris by these practices and principles, has been the beginner and procurer of the sorest afflictions, not of this village only, but to this whole country, that ever did befall them." He was the "instrument of our miseries." Parris saw it otherwise. He countered by claiming that he was "abundantly persuaded that God . . . has suffered ye evil Angels to delude us on both hands; but how far on ye one side and how far on ye other, is much above me to say." In other words, neither side to the dispute knew the true answer. He went on to say, "I do most heartily, fervently, and humbly beseech pardon of the merciful God . . . of all my mistakes and trespasses in so weighty a matter." But he then undercut this genuine plea by saying that he did what "I apprehended was duty."[31]

He did admit to his error concerning the key theological point about the validity of spectral evidence: he conceded that the devil can "afflict in the Shape of not only Innocent but pious Persons." But he maintained that the Salem crisis was God's will and that the whole affair was "so dark and perplexed" that there could be no agreement about it. With this blanket statement, he sought to mitigate his responsibility.[32]

The council of ministers finally requested the inhabitants of Salem Village to vote on whether Parris should remain or leave his post. Of the people who signed the petition, a majority of 105—52 of whom were church members—voted in favor of keeping him. The anti-Parris minority consisted of 84 votes, 17 of whom were church members. The total number, "more than four score," the council noted, was substantial enough for the council to advise the Village church that Parris's removal was necessary. The council did him the favor of finding a new post for him in Suffield, Massachusetts.[33] But Parris rejected the council's advice and appealed to his congregation for support, which they dutifully gave. The debate over his departure continued to rankle for another year until the church members finally became frustrated with Parris's obstinacy and joined the opposition. The Village reached a financial settlement about Parris's back salary and forced him to deed over the parsonage and additional acres of property to the Village. Parris left the Village in the summer of 1697. He was forty-four years old.

Parris moved first to Stow, Massachusetts, where he had originally served as a part-time minister, and then moved on to five other communities. He became alternately a part-time preacher, schoolteacher, and owner of several retail shops. He died in 1720 in the town of Sudbury.[34]

In 1697, Parris's successor in Salem Village, twenty-two-year-old Reverend Joseph Green, was installed as the new minister. He immediately instituted the Halfway Covenant, which opened the doors to a flock of new church members, and he began to baptize their children. For the first time in its history, Salem Village warmly embraced its minister. The socially outgoing Green established a more liberal church, which became the unifying center of the community that it was originally intended to be.[35]

BLAME AND SHAME

Some were thought by many persons to be Innocent.
— *Governor Sir William Phips, 1693*

[He] Desires to take the Blame and Shame of it.
— *Samuel Sewall (referring to himself), 1697*

I believe the whole Country lies under a Curse to this day.
— *Reverend Michael Wigglesworth, 1704*

I desire to lye in ye dust & earnestly begg fforgiveness of God.
— *Ann Putnam Jr., 1706*

*Accusers and Witnesses . . . [were] persons of profligate
and vicious Conversation.*
— *General Court, 1711*

In 1630, the Puritans of Massachusetts Bay Colony believed they had founded a utopian society that would be
a "city upon a hill," a shining example of Christian society to the rest of the world, and especially to Puritan England. In the fall of 1692, the government and ministers in
Boston realized that the Salem court had caused a legal
and religious debacle and tainted their noble experiment.
Boston's ministers called on Increase Mather to explain
in the most definite terms what was wrong theologically
with the court's procedures, and the government needed
to face up to closing the runaway Court of Oyer and Terminer. The government also needed to justify its actions
to the general public in Massachusetts and to the Crown
in London. Equally important, there had to be an apology to God. As it turned out, it was easy to close the spe-

cial court, but justifying the misguided witch trials involved a considerable amount of cover-up and self-deception. The apology to God was even more difficult and had to be put off until the right words could be found.

How could a deeply religious society shed its feelings of guilt after realizing that it was responsible for killing innocent people in the name of God? Leading ministers in Boston had already raised their voices in criticism, having initially supported the trials, and more outcries would come. Judges, juries, local ministers, accusers, and confessors alike had to reckon with their Christian consciences. As for the families of the executed and condemned, it would take several years before the government would think of compensating them for seizures of property, jail fees incurred, and reputations ruined.

Only one judge stood up publicly and took the "blame and shame" of the trials, and only one young accuser "begged forgiveness of God." The jurors, for their part, confessed that they were "sadly deluded and mistaken." Several who confessed to acts of witchcraft under the pressure of aggressive interrogation and threats said they had "belied" themselves. Samuel Parris belatedly confessed that "God was spitting in my face" and admitted "all of my mistakes," but added that he did what he "apprehended was [my] duty."[1] At first, the government justified the trials in the strongest possible terms. Nineteen years later, it would reverse its position and declare that the court had been in error and would blame the tragedy on the "profligate and vicious" young accusers. The General Court of Massachusetts took its time about clearing the names of the condemned and executed and about giving compensation to their families. Most of the names were cleared and families compensated in 1711. Two hundred and forty-six years later, in 1957, one more name was cleared from the record. The last five victims were exonerated in October 2001, ironically and inappropriately, on Halloween.

By early October 1692, Increase Mather had finally finished writing the lengthy treatise that he had started in early August. As requested by the Boston ministers, his book would explain the errors of the procedures used by the special Court of Oyer and Terminer. It was titled *Cases of Conscience Concerning Evil Spirits Personating Men* and would be published in November. Mather's first criticism of the court's methods appeared prominently on the first page of chapter 1. Mather posed the question: "Whether it is not Possible for the Devil to impose on the Imaginations of Persons Bewitched, and to cause them to Believe that an Innocent, yea that a Pious person does torment them." The answer, he said, "must be Affirmative," that is, the devil was capable of appearing in the shape of an innocent person. Thus the court could no longer give any weight to an accuser's claim to have seen or felt someone's "likeness" or "appearance" hurting the accuser or anybody else. Mather's second proposition negated the two other forms of evidence on which the court had relied, the bewitching "look" of a defendant in the dock and the so-called "touch test." The touch test, which was frequently resorted to in the examinations, required the afflicted person to touch the hand of the defendant in order to recover from a "fit," thereby supposedly returning the demonic power to the witch, thus providing evidence of the defendant's guilt. Such a procedure was obviously manipulable. Mather rejected it entirely, saying "as for . . . the Bewitched Persons being recovered out of their Agonies by the Touch of the suspected Party, it is various and fallible." Mather also rejected the evidence of the evil eye. "Falling down by the cast of an Eye," he said, "proceeds not from a natural, but an arbitrary Cause; not from any Poyson in the Eye of the Witch, but from the Agency of some Daemon."[2]

Boston's ministers were in total agreement. Samuel Willard wrote the preface on behalf of thirteen ministers. Willard made a point of explicitly rejecting "*Spectre Evidence*, and a certain sort of *Ordeal* or trial by the sight and touch." Mather ended his book with the sweeping and laudable conclusion: "It were better that ten suspected Witches should escape, than that one innocent Person should be Condemned."[3]

Had Mather said nothing more than these noble words, history would remember him as the wise elder statesmen who exposed the errors of the court (though rather belatedly) and helped Massachusetts recover from a self-made tragedy. But he did not. In September, Governor Phips and Deputy Governor Stoughton told Cotton Mather to write a defense of the court in anticipation of its closure. Cotton titled his defense *Wonders of the Invisible World,* and it was published in mid-October 1692. When Increase finished the manuscript of *Cases of Conscience* in early October, Cotton asked his father to add a postscript that would endorse his defense. His father did so. He said he was gratified that his son's book would show that more than specter evidence was involved in the court's decisions and that the judges had made no mistake.[4] The book with its postscript was not published until November.

In the postscript, Increase also emphasized that he himself had attended the trial of George Burroughs and that "had I been one of his Judges, I could not have acquitted him." He went on to exonerate the Salem magistrates: "They are wise and good Men," he wrote, "and have acted with all Fidelity according to their Light, and have out of tenderness declined the doing of some things, which in our own Judgments they were satisfied about: Having therefore so arduous a Case before them, Pitty and Prayers rather than Censures are their due."[5] The witch trials were a political embarrassment, and the senior Mather had to tuck them safely away. Despite the court's flawed procedures, the judges had not committed any injustice, and there was no disagreement between himself and his son on this matter. Thus there would appear two books, one supported by the ministers, the other supported by the government, with Increase Mather awkwardly trying to reconcile both. It was a replay of the rift that had surfaced in June after Bridget Bishop's trial, when the judges ignored the ministers' caution.

Increase Mather's postscript was too much for Samuel Willard. Willard had written the preface for *Cases of Conscience* before Increase added his postscript approving the judges' procdeures. Willard's response was to write a tract of his own. He titled it *Some Miscellany Observations on Our Present Debates Respecting Witchcrafts, in a Dialogue between S. & B. by P. E. and J. A.* Willard's essay was composed as a dialogue between two figures, one referred to as "B," which stood for the views of the Boston ministers, the other referred to as "S," which stood for the Salem ministers and magistrates. Willard identified the tract's authors by their initials, "P. E.," presumably for Philip English, and "J. A." for John Alden. Both were prominent men who had been accused and sent to jail for trial but eventually escaped from prison to the safety of New York. Both would be completely exonerated. Willard, obviously annoyed at having been betrayed by Increase Mather, published this essay despite Governor Phips's ban on publications about the witch trials in 1692. To get around the ban, the imprint falsely stated that the essay was printed in Philadelphia by a William Bradford, even though it was printed in Boston by Benjamin Harris.[6]

The Salem judges had claimed that they followed legal guidelines for the trials written by the Puritan divines William Perkins and Richard Bernard. According to Willard, however, the judges had "either not read them or mistake them." Willard points out that both authors "rightly distinguish between Presumption and Conviction; and tell us that some Presumptions [such as special evidence], are stronger than others; some only sufficient for Examination, others enough for Commitment: but they confidently aver, that all presumptions . . . are short of being Conviction." Willard's other telling point concerned the inherent contradiction of accepting evidence given by confessors: "the persons confessing are Witches by their own confession and have therefore abjured God and Christ, and given themselves up to the Devil, the Father of Lies; and what Credit is to be given to the Testimony of such against the Lives of others?"[7]

In defending the trials, Cotton Mather's task was not to become embroiled in such arguments. His purpose was to make clear that the Court of Oyer and Terminer had saved Massachusetts from a satanic plot. In typical fashion, he found himself to be of two minds. He had disagreed with the court's focus on spectral evidence and had warned two of the judges against relying upon it. He therefore had little enthusiasm for the job of defending the whole mess, saying that he had been "forced to produce these Undeserved Lines,"[8] as indeed he had by his friends Phips and Stoughton.

He would justify the trials on the basis of a few selected cases that were the easiest to defend, and he would include all the evidence, spectral and otherwise. Amid the now widespread criticism of the trials, Mather would present vividly detailed cases that showed Satan's real and present threat. He assured Stoughton that, given the public dissent over the witch trials, his book would "help very much to flatten that fury which we now so much turn upon one another."[9] Mather said he would write a defense that would "countermine the whole PLOT of the Devil against New-England."[10] His father's criticism of the court's methods would be published a month later in November, and Cotton needed to make his justification of the trials as strong as possible.

Mather set himself a large task. While waiting for Stephen Sewall, clerk of the Court of Oyer and Terminer, to send copies of the court records so he could summarize them, Mather composed a large theological and historical framework based on biblical and theological justifications, and he drew upon accounts of witch trials in England and Sweden as examples. *Wonders of the Invisible World* was published in Boston in mid-October 1692, two weeks before Phips closed the court.

Phips decided to terminate the Court of Oyer and Terminer after a close vote in the legislative assembly that advised consultation with Boston's Convocation of Ministers about continuing the witch trials. Knowing that the Boston ministers had already rejected the court's procedures, Phips told chief magistrate Stoughton not to convene the next meeting of the Court of Oyer and Terminer and subsequently declared that the court "must fall."[11]

In *Wonders of the Invisible World,* Mather chose to summarize five cases that were amply documented. The first was that of George Burroughs, the alleged ringleader, whom Mather dubbed "King of Satan's Kingdom." The second was the case of Bridget Bishop, an abused spouse who had been previously accused of witchcraft and had frightened men with spectral visits to their bedrooms. Third was the trial of Susannah Martin of Amesbury, whom Mather called "one of the most Impudent, Scurrilous, wicked creatures in the world." Fourth was the trial of Elizabeth Howe of Ipswich, who had been denied admission to her church. Last was the case of Martha Carrier of Andover, who was suspected of carrying smallpox to the Andover community and making her children witches. Mather called her a "Rampant Hag" and "Queen of Hell," thus making her Burroughs's evil consort.

Mather's summaries of the legal records were detailed and accurate. He argued that each case involved not only spectral torment of the Salem Village girls and a few adults but also numerous other evidences of personal injuries, unexplained illnesses, suspected murders, and preternatural events. From the point of view of English common law, the evidence against the accused was devastating. There was only one problem: the indictments were based on the sole charge of spectral affliction, which his father had shown to be unreliable. Mather preferred to ignore this glaring fault. His ultimate justification of the trials was to wrap them up in covenant theology: God had let loose the Devil upon the chosen people of New England and raised up witches as punishment for their sins. Mather's firm belief in millennialism also played a role. The extraordinary onslaught of Satan's witches on Essex County was proof that the devil's demise was near. "The Devil's whole-time," he asserted in his preface, "cannot but be very near its End."[12]

In this way, Mather justified the court's murderous work and protected the new government, barely six months old, from its dissenters within and criticism from England. The new charter had given the Mathers and their friends significant control of the government, and it could not be jeopardized by the scandal of a mismanaged witch-hunt.

Altogether different from Increase Mather's and Samuel Willard's theological arguments was the biting Enlightenment criticism of Thomas Brattle. He was a wealthy merchant and a distinguished mathematician who would become a Fellow of the Royal Society of London. So trenchant was Brattle's criticism of the court's blunders that he used the format of the private letter addressed to an unnamed clergyman to communicate his views in order to protect himself from possible government reprisal. He also signed the letter only with the initials "T. B."

Among other points, Brattle offered a devastating critique of the judges' acceptance of spectral evidence, which he expressed in impeccable logic: "That the afflicted do own and assert, and the Justices do grant, that the Devill does inform and tell the afflicted the names of those persons that are thus unknown unto them. Now these two things being duly considered, I think it will appear evident to any one, that the Devill's information is the fundamental testimony that is gone upon in the apprehending of the aforesaid people." Brattle concluded this paragraph with biting sarcasm: "I cannot but admire that the Justices, whom I think to be well-meaning men, should so far give ear to the Devill." Brattle even accused the court of superstition. "How it comes about," he observed, "that if these apprehended persons are witches, and, by a look of the eye, do cast the afflicted into their fitts by poisoning them . . . I think it rather deserves the name of Salem superstition and sorcery, and it is not fitt to be named in a land of such light as New-England is."

But Brattle aimed his principal argument at the court's privileging of spectral evidence. How could the Salem judges, or "Salem Gentlemen," as he called them, maintain that the defendants were convicted on other kinds of evidence when the indictments specified only the spectral afflictions of their accusers? He acknowledged that there were many depositions claiming that all sorts of people and animals had died for unknown reasons, and various strange wonders had appeared that the accusers witnessed. "But," Brattle exclaimed, "what if there were ten thousand evidences of this nature; how do they prove the matter of indictment!"

Brattle also put his case in plain political terms and named several important political leaders who had expressed opposition to the court. "There are several about the Bay, men for understanding, Judgment, and Piety, inferiour to few (if any) in N[ew] E[ngland], that do utterly condemn the said proceedings, and do freely deliver their Judgment in the case to be this." Brattle mentioned former governor Simon Bradstreet and former deputy governor Thomas Danforth, as well as Boston's two most influential ministers, Increase Mather and Samuel Willard. He concluded by pointing out that the respected political leader Nathaniel Saltonstall, who was one of the original judges on the Court of Oyer and Terminer, had left the court after the first trial "very much dissatisfyed with the proceedings of it." His last political dig was to indicate that "some of the Boston Justices, were resolved rather to throw up their commissions [on the Court of Oyer and Terminer] than be active in disturbing the liberty of their Majesties' subjects, merely on the accusations of these afflicted, possessed children." Brattle did not name any of the prominent men he had in mind, but everyone knew who they were.

Brattle wrote his letter in early October, and it was aimed at his friends in the legislature and on the Governor's Council, which would likely take up the question of continuing the Court of Oyer and Terminer. He knew that the letter would carry little political weight. Indeed, it was not a factor in Governor Phips's decision to close the court. The effective work had already been done by Increase Mather and the Boston ministers. Brattle most likely composed his letter as a statement of conscience. He would write it as an enlightened manifesto on behalf of himself and his liberal Boston friends. As such, it represented an original point of view and was formulated in a completely new kind of language about witchcraft in New England, that of empirical observation, and was devoid of theological terms.[13]

In early October, Phips wrote the first of two letters reporting the embarrassing debacle of the witch trials to his superiors in London. He explained that when he arrived in Boston in May he found the province "miserably harrassed with a most Horrible witchcraft or Possession of Devills," and he found the "prisons full of people." He explained that he had set up a Court of Oyer and Terminer to investigate the charges but then had left Boston to pursue "their Majesties service" and fight the French in Canada. Phips's expedition against the French, which unfortunately for him ended in disaster, was something the Crown had appointed him to do. When he returned to Boston, he said, he found the trials had been bungled and that there was a great "ferment of dissatisfaction." He went on to blame unnamed hotheads "that blew up the flame." He stopped short of admitting that innocent people had been executed and said only that he believed that the devil had taken the shape of some innocent persons. He explained that he had put a temporary stop to the trials and awaited "their Majesties' pleasure." He did not mention that the court was scheduled to resume the following month in early November. He knew there would not be enough time to receive a reply from England, and that he would have to make the decision to close the court himself.

Phips also explained, in his own defense, that some of the magistrates had been overly zealous in prosecution and complained that "my enemies are seeking to turn it all upon me." To avoid inflaming the situation, he said that he had summarily forbidden publications on the subject "one way or the other."[14] He did not mention that he had in fact authorized publication of both Cotton Mather's and Increase Mather's books, which appeared in Boston in October and November 1692, respectively, with the publication imprints postdated to 1693.

Phips's letter to London was both a self-defense and a cover-up. He was less than truthful in saying that he was away from Boston for "almost the whole" time of the trials. The minutes of the Governor's Council show that he was in Boston from June through mid-August, when twelve trials took place, all of which ended in execution.[15] He was also present at meetings of the Council, most of whose members were judges on the Court of Oyer and Terminer. It is inconceivable that on these occasions he did not discuss the trials with these same men who were sitting on the bench in Salem. Indeed, when the Reverend William Milborne had petitioned the General Assembly after Bishop's trial in June, saying that it had relied too much on spectral evidence, Phips himself had signed the order to have Milborne arrested for writing "Seditious and Scandalous Papers or writings."[16] Milborne was told that he could choose to go to prison or pay a severely punitive fine of two hundred pounds. In censoring Milborne, Phips implicitly defended the use of spectral evidence, which was critical to the prosecution of the trials throughout the summer and early fall.

Phips's second letter to London, written in February 1693, explained that when he returned from the eastern frontier he stopped the trials, which "threatened this Province with destruction," because of the number of people executed and the illegal seizure of their property. He emphasized that his deputy governor, William Stoughton, chief magistrate of the Court of Oyer and Terminer, had proceeded "vigorously" with spectral evidence "to the great dissatisfaction and disturbance of the people." He pointed out that Increase Mather had shown that the devil could take the shape of an innocent person, contrary to the court's assumptions. After closing the Court of Oyer and Terminer and ordering new trials to proceed under a different court (the newly instituted Superior Court of Judicature), without relying upon questionable spectral evidence, he reported that Stoughton had become "enraged and filled with passionate anger and refused to sit upon the bench" and conduct the trials. Indeed, when Stoughton learned that Phips had reprieved seven of the death warrants he had signed, he allegedly declared, "We were in a way to have cleared the Land of these [witches], etc., who it is that obstructs the cause of justice, I know not: the Lord be merciful to the country!"[17] Stoughton left the bench temporarily, and another magistrate took over. After the jails were cleared of most defendants, Phips reassured his superiors that there were "no new complaints, but peoples minds before divided and distracted by different opinions concerning this matter are now well composed."[18] Phips thus represented himself as the savior of the Crown's colony from a disaster created by a court run amok by a zealous deputy governor.

The Crown's response expressed complete approval. The queen acknowledged that some individuals of "known and good Reputation" had been convicted, which led to "a great dissatisfaction among Our good Subjects." The queen also commended Phips for showing "care and Circumspection." In the future he was advised to show "the greatest Moderation and all due circumspection," something the Governor's Council duly noted.[19]

In the meantime, the government hastened to clarify its own laws against witchcraft so that spectral afflictions could not cause another debacle. The General Court quickly passed an "Act Against Conjuration" in December 1692. The act affirmed the reality of witchcraft and the penalty of death for invoking and covenanting with evil spirits or using charms "whereby any person shall be killed, destroyed, wasted, consumed, pined or lamed."[20] But the act conspicuously omitted any reference to "spectre evidence," that is, claims of affliction by other people's shapes.

Then came the government's reckoning with God. In keeping with Cotton Mather's framing of the trials in terms of the covenant theology of human sin and God's retribution, the government passed a bill calling for a public Day of Prayer and Fasting to be held in late December 1692. Its purpose was to ask God's forgiveness, not for the court's mistakes but rather, more generally, for the many sins of New England that caused the "Various Awful Judgments of God . . . by permitting Witchcrafts and Evil Angels to Rage amongst his People." It is uncertain whether a public fast day, proposed for December 29, 1692, was actually held because no record of a public proclamation survives. The bill, while admitting that society's sinfulness caused God to loose the devil upon it, nevertheless affirmed that

"Witchcrafts and Evil Angels" did in fact "Rage" against New England. It was therefore an implicit affirmation of the trials and not an admission of guilt for killing the innocent.[21]

Four years later, however, there was growing pressure by Boston ministers to hold a fast day in recognition of the injustice and mistakes of the trials. The immediate context for the government's change of mind was the undertaking of a large military expedition against the French in Nova Scotia in September 1696. The expedition was in retaliation for the capture and destruction of Fort William Henry at Pemaquid, Maine, by the French in August of that year. The Reverend Samuel Willard in Boston took the occasion of an official day of prayer for the new expedition to raise his voice about the government's long failure to make a "public confession of the guilt incurred in the witch trials."[22] Willard's point was clear: the loss of the fort was a sign of God's wrath for the tragedy of the witch trials. The success of the new expedition depended upon asking for God's forgiveness. Willard was Samuel Sewall's minister, and Sewall, who was sympathetic to the need for a public fast day, wrote a note in his diary. Willard, he said, "Spake smartly at last about the Salem witchcrafts, and that no order had been suffer'd to come forth by Authority to ask God's pardon."[23]

The House of Representatives delegated Cotton Mather to write the text of a bill for the proclamation of a fast day in December 1696. The bill, however, was rejected by the Governor's Council. The Council apparently did not like Mather's long list of New England's moral failings in which he had placed the subject of the witch trials, nor apparently did it agree with his blaming the court for executing innocent people. Some of the Salem judges were members of the Council, and they refused to admit that mistakes had been made. Mather had referred too directly to "Errors, whereby Great Hardships were brought upon innocent persons, and we fear Guilt incurred."[24] The Council then turned to Samuel Sewall, one of its members and a former Salem judge, and asked him to draft a shorter and more tactfully worded apology. Sewall found the right words, and the bill was passed.

Sewall's bill became the proclamation for a Day of General Fasting and Prayer, dated January 14, 1697. The proclamation included this key statement, which ducked any specific responsibility: "Especially, that whatever Mistakes, have fallen into either by the Body of His people [the General Court] or by any Orders of Men [that is, judges and ministers], referring to the late Tragedie raised among us by Satan and his Instruments, through the awful Judgment of God; He would humble us therefore, and pardon all the Errors of his Servants and People that desire to Love his Name; and be attoned to His Land." The wording is deliberately vague. It mentions only generalized "Mistakes" that were "fallen into" in regard to "the late Tragedie" caused by "Satan and his Instruments." Although Sewall's statement recognizes the need for pardon and atonement for "Errors," the blame is spread out among everyone: the government, ministers, and the general public; and the whole affair is attributed to Satan and ultimately to God's "awful Judgment."[25]

Sewall himself was preparing to make his own public apology on the appointed fast day. Historians agree that Samuel Sewall's statement is the most direct and unqualified admission of personal responsibility to come from any of the authorities. Nearly two hundred and fifty years later, in 1942, the Massachusetts House of Representatives placed a large mural on the wall of the House chamber in the State House, titled *Dawn of Tolerance in Massachusetts. Public Repentance of Judge Samuel Sewall for His Action in the Witchcraft Trials*. The painting shows Sewall standing in his pew in the South Meeting House of Boston with his head bowed, while the Reverend Samuel Willard reads aloud his statement of repentance for his role as a judge on the Court of Oyer and Terminer.

Sewall's apology says, in part: "Samuel Sewall sensible of the reiterated strokes of God upon himself and family; and being sensible, that as to the Guilt contracted, upon the opening of the late Commission of Oyer and Terminer at Salem (to which the order of this Day related) he is, upon many accounts, more concerned than any he knows of, Desires to take the Blame and Shame of it." Sewall did what others who offered apologies did not. He framed it in terms of his family's personal losses, referring to what everyone knew, namely, that two of his children had recently died. He feared that these losses were God's judgment against him for his role as a judge in the trials. By serving on the court, he believed he had "contracted Guilt," an oblique reference to the execution of innocent people. In saying that he was "more concerned than any he knows of," he was also drawing attention to the silence of the other judges who said nothing about their role in the court's injustices.[26] Two of his fellow judges were members of the Third Church and were undoubtedly present in the congregation when Sewall stood up during the fast day service to take the "Blame and Shame" of the trials. Sewall's apology was a personal statement of conscience, a condemnation of the injustice of the trials, and a cry from the heart for God's mercy in the face of his family's losses.[27]

It is said that when Chief Magistrate William Stoughton heard of Sewall's apology, he "remarked upon it, that for himself, when he sat in judgment he had the fear of God before his eyes, and gave his opinion according to the best of his understanding, and although it might appear afterwards that he had been in an error, he saw no necessity of a public acknowledgment of it."[28] If this statement accurately represents what Stoughton said, it is in keeping with his imperious manner. The statement was also a rebuke to Sewall for making what Stoughton considered a prideful act of public display. Ironically, as William Phips's successor to the governorship in 1697, Stoughton signed the Fast Bill into law.[29] Perhaps he regarded the bill as sufficient acknowledgment of the flawed proceedings.

Another apology delivered on the fast day of January 14, 1697, was written by Thomas Fisk, who had been the foreman of the jury of the Court of Oyer and Terminer. Fisk's statement, signed by eleven jurors, is a carefully worded admission of the jury's failings. It is also an indirect criticism of the magistrates. Fisk starts by saying that the jurors were faced with the "mysterious delusions of the Powers of Darkness, and the Prince of the Air." The "delusions" were those of the afflicted accusers whose spectral afflictions and testimony the jury was required to judge. The statement admits that the jurors lacked the "knowledge in ourselves" to deal with this sort of evidence. It goes on to say that they could have been given "better Information from others" and were "prevailed [upon] to take up with such Evidence against the Accused." Although stated indirectly, the apology implies that the jurors were poorly informed about the nature of spectral evidence and how to evaluate it. Under the circumstances, the jurors said they were "sadly deluded and mistaken." On the other hand, during the course of the trials, Stephen Sewall, as clerk of the court, had emphasized to Cotton Mather "the awe which is upon the hearts of your juries with respect unto the validity of the spectral evidences."[30] The jury was completely taken by the accusers' performances, which the jury members later came to believe was a mistake. Fisk's statement concludes by asking forgiveness from God and from "you all, whom we have justly offended."[31]

A day later, on January 15, Cotton Mather, perhaps hearing of Sewall's public apology and the concern for his family, confided to his diary that he himself might not have done enough to prevent the trials. He was mindful of the possibility of God's retribution "for my not appearing with *Vigor* enough to stop the proceedings of the Judges, when the Inextricable Storm from the Invisible World assaulted the Countrey."[32] But unlike Sewall, Mather believed he had received God's "assurance" that his judgment would not fall on his family. How Mather knew he had assurance from God he does not say. But, not having been a judge in the trials and having warned the court against relying so heavily on spectral evidence, Mather clearly felt free from any guilt.

Two years earlier, when Samuel Parris had his back against the wall, he tried to mollify his opponents by making an apology of sorts to the "dissenting brethren" in his congregation who were trying to expel him from Salem Village. He admitted that "the Lord ordered the late horrid tragedy . . . to break out first in my family," which he took as "a very strong rebuke." He went on to point out that "God . . . has suffered the evil angels to delude us on both hands; but to know how far, on one side or the other, is above me to say." That is, to put it bluntly, it was impossible for anyone to say who was to blame. Nevertheless, he asked God's pardon and forgiveness "for all my mistakes," and he asked his opponents for "all your forgiveness of every offence," saying that he did only what he "apprehended was duty—through weekness, ignorance, &c." Parris ended up by claiming that it was all the fault of "Satan, the devil, the roaring lion, the old dragon," who exploited "our envy and strifes." Distributing the responsibility for the trials among the Village's "envy and strifes" was hardly taking the blame.[33]

A year after Parris left the Village, the ministers of Beverly and Salem, John Hale and Nicholas Noyes, conducted a day of fasting and prayer for the reconciliation of the Village community. Later, the churches in Salem Village and Salem Town realized that they, too, shared in the guilt. The Salem Village congregation had excommunicated Martha Cory in 1692 on the day she was convicted, and the First Church had also excommunicated Giles Cory.

In 1701, Parris's successor as the Village minister, Reverend Joseph Green, and the Village leaders took steps to move the community toward reconciliation. The Village voted to dispense with the meetinghouse where Parris had preached and where the examinations were held. The meetinghouse was to be sold and its pulpit disposed of. Several committees were selected from families of the accusers and the accused to oversee the building of a new meetinghouse on a new location, across the road on the site of the old guard house. The Village also voted to reject the seating plan of the old meeting-house and reorganize the seating of the new building, sometimes putting families of accusers and the accused next to each other.[34]

In 1702, Green urged the congregation, now augmented by many new members, to ask God's forgiveness for excommunicating Martha Cory and to restore her name to the record as a full church member. The first vote failed, but a second produced a larger majority. The motion read: "we desire that this may be entered in our Church book, to take off that odium that is cast on her name and that so God may forgive our sin, & may be atoned for the land." The congregation wished to atone for the sin of casting out one of their own. Some, undoubtedly Parris loyalists, chose not to agree.[35]

It took the church in Salem eleven more years before it could do the same for Martha Cory's husband, Giles. Giles's case was different. He had been indicted for witchcraft but had refused to enter a plea and stand trial, and was therefore never convicted. He died under torture because he refused to put himself at the mercy of "God and country." To force him to enter a plea, he was slowly crushed by the weight of heavy rocks placed on his body as he lay stretched out on the ground. At the time, the church in Salem had concluded that Cory was guilty as charged or had committed suicide by "throwing himself upon sudden and certain death." In 1711, the government decided to clear his name and award his family restitution. Two years later, the church in Salem took up the matter and cleared his name, saying that the church had "testimony that before his death he did bitterly repent of his obstinate refusal to plead in defense of his life."[36] The source of this testimony was not named.

At the same time, the Salem church rescinded the excommunication of Rebecca Nurse. In her case, the church admitted that "in that hour of darkness and temptation" it had committed a sin. The church voted that "Nurse's Excommunication be accordingly erased and blotted out" of the church records, "humbly requesting that the merciful God would pardon, whatsoever Sin, Error or Mistake, was in the Application of that Censure and of that whole affair."[37]

Besides Samuel Sewall's apology, the most famous admission of guilt in the Salem affair was that of twenty-six-year-old Ann Putnam Jr. Her confession is often interpreted as a denial of responsibility. But it is seldom examined in its full context. It was written in the church record book by Joseph Green and signed by Ann herself. Green's note at the bottom says: "The confession was read before the congregation together with her relation Aug: 28, 1706. & she acknowledged it." Green most likely read out the confession to the congregation while Ann stood up to acknowledge that the apology was hers. The occasion was Ann's application to become a full member of the congregation. The confession was followed by her own relation, which undoubtedly told of her experience of God's grace acting in her life. In Ann's case, both her apology and her statement of faith were necessary for her acceptance by the congregation.

The stylistic sophistication of Ann's apology and its theological complexity suggest that it was composed by Green himself. Its first sentence is carefully punctuated and theologically complex. It opens with the following statement: "I desire to be humbled before God for yt sad and humbling providence, that befell my fathers family in the year about '92; I then being in my childhood should by such providence of God be made an instrument for that accusing of several persons of a greivous crime." The opening phrase points to Putnam's family as the object of God's intervention and reminds the congregation that Ann was only a child (twelve years old) at the time. The implication is that because of her youth, Ann's actions need to be understood in the wider context of her family, especially her zealous father and emotionally distraught mother, upon which God was acting. In this context, she was "made an instrument" for the accusation of several innocent persons.

For the Puritans there were two ultimate sources of right and wrong behavior: God and Satan. God in his providence sometimes used Satan to accomplish his purposes, such as the punishment of the sins of both individuals and communities. Ann's confession indicates that God was using her family for his providential purposes, which included making her an "instrument" for the accusation of innocent people. She readily admits that the people she accused were innocent. The next statement clarifies and amplifies what she has said up to this point: "it was a great delusion of Satan yt deceived me in that sad time, whereby I justly fear I have been instrumental with others tho' ignorantly and unwittingly to bring upon myself & this land the guilt of innocent blood." This statement repeats the prevailing theological interpretation expressed in the 1697 Fast Day, which attributed the witch trials to "Satan and his Instruments, through the awful Judgment of God." Anne was not one of Satan's instruments but one of God's.

The crux of the confession comes in the next two sentences. The first states that she did not act out of anger or intent: "what was said or done by me against any person I can truly and uprightly say before God & man I did it not out of any anger malice or ill will to any person for I had no such thing against [any]one of them; but what I did was ignorantly being deluded by Satan." As we have seen, the Puritan understanding was that personal anger and feelings of malice toward someone could easily lead to collusion with the devil and result in a curse. Instead, Ann was "ignorantly deluded" by the Devil and did not act out of her own conscious intent.

Her second and concluding statement is equally crucial. Since she would subsequently be asking for membership as a full communicant, she needed to ask for forgiveness from members of the Nurse family, who were long-standing full church members. She had accused all three Towne sisters, Rebecca Nurse, Sarah Cloyce, and Mary Esty. Nurse and Esty had been tried and executed, and Sara Cloyce had been jailed but not brought to trial. Without receiving forgiveness from the powerful Nurse family, whose vote for acceptance into the congregation was necessary, her request for full membership would fail. Her statement acknowledges her guilt and more. "I was a chief instrument of accuseing of Goodwife Nurse and her two sisters I desire to lye in the dust & to be humbled for it in that I was a cause with others of so sad a calamity to them & their families, for which cause I desire to lye in ye dust & earnestly begg fforgiveness of God." Here she takes full blame for the accusation of the three Towne sisters, even though other people had also accused them. Her admission is unambiguous. Charles Upham tells us that before Ann's apology was presented in church, Samuel Nurse was consulted, as the representative of the Nurse family, and he found the text satisfactory. Upham also relates that a large audience, coming from Salem and other places, assembled in the Village meetinghouse to hear the apology.[38]

Ann concludes her confession by acknowledging the role she also played in the accusation and execution of so many others, a number amounting to more than fifty. She begs forgiveness "from all those unto whom I have given just cause of sorrow & offence, whose relations were taken away or accused."[39]

Through Joseph Green's carefully chosen words, Ann Putnam was able to speak her conscience to the congregation. At twenty-six years old, she was taking as much responsibility as she could for the actions of her childhood.

Her confession did not deal directly with the question of fakery or fraud. Her denial of acting consciously or with malice, however, implies that she did not fake her afflictions.

———————

In 1696, forty-nine-year-old Elizabeth Procter submitted the first petition for financial restitution. She had been tried and condemned, but her execution was postponed because of pregnancy. When the court was closed in late October, she survived, "through gods great goodness," as she later put it. In late January 1693, she had given birth to a son, whom she named John, after her husband.[40] After the closure of the court, Elizabeth was still under attainder, which nullified her legal status and that of her children as heirs and purchasers of property. Her husband's property had been deeded over to another person, who, she said, had "contrived" to have her husband sign it before he was executed. She petitioned the government to reverse the attainder for herself and her family so she and her children could regain legal status and lead a normal life.

In her petition, she characterized her accusers as "som evill disposed or strangly Influenced persons."[41] Hers was the first of many petitions that placed the blame for the witch trials not on the government but on the young accusers, as possessed and deluded by the devil. Her petition was read before the Governor's Council, but the Council did not act at that time.

Four years later, in 1700, forty-eight-year-old Abigail Faulkner Sr., the daughter of the Reverend Francis Dane, submitted her petition to the government. She said that she had been accused by "the afflicted who pretended to see me by theire spectrall sight (not with theire bodily Eyes) and [said] that I afflicted them." She was convicted and condemned on September 17 but not executed because of her pregnancy. She petitioned the General Court to clear her name owing to the severe social stigma and vulnerability caused by the fact that she remained under attainder. She wrote that she had lived for years "as a Malefactor Convict upon record of ye Most henious Crimes," which was causing "utter Ruining and Defacing my Reputacion." She was exposed "to Iminent Danger by New accusations" and "a perpetuall brand of Infamy upon my family."[42] No action was taken.

Three years later, in 1703, twenty-one family members from Andover, Salem Village, Topsfield, Salem Farms, and Ipswich petitioned for the reversal of attainders of eight individuals executed or condemned "of whose Innocency those that knew them are well Satisfyed." The petitioners characterized the accusers as "certain possessed persons" and pointed to "Errors & mistakes in those tryalls." Now, having "Suffered in their persons and Estates their Names are Exposed to Infamy and reproach."[43] The petition was read out to the House of Representatives.

At this time, the government chose to clear the names only of Elizabeth Procter and Abigail Faulkner Sr. and took no further action. In March, Andover, Salem, and Topsfield petitioners characterized the afflicted accusers as "possessed persons" and asked that "Something may be Publickly done to take off the Infamy for the Names and memory of those who have suffered . . . [and] that none of their Surviving Relations, nor their Posterity may Suffer reproach upon that account." In July, twelve ministers from different towns in Essex County petitioned to clear the names of their neighbors who had been executed or condemned. The petition stated flatly that the young accusers were "under diabolical molestations" and that innocent people had "suffered." The ministers pointedly observed that "Errors and mistakes" had been made in the trials, and that unless legal steps were taken to clear the names of the victims, "God may have controversy with the land upon that account."[44] Again, no action was taken.

When the Reverend Michael Wigglesworth, a highly respected Fellow of Harvard College and the minister of the church in Malden, learned of the continuing misery of the families of those executed and condemned, he sent a letter to Increase Mather, deploring the suffering of the families and appealing to Mather's conscience that he might persuade the government. He suggested that "the whole Country lies under a Curse to this day, and will do, till some effectual course be taken by our honored Govenour & Generall Court to make them some amends and reparations.[45]

Seven more years passed before the government could bring itself to act on the backlog of petitions. The precipitating actions appear to have been two petitions that were submitted in May 1709. One was organized by the Salem merchant Philip English and twenty-one other men from Salem, Salem Village, Topsfield, and Andover; and the second was signed by five other men from these same towns on behalf of the same families. Written tactfully, these petitions did not cast judgment upon the court, "whom we hope and Believe Did that which they thought was Right in that hour of Darknes." The petitioners emphasized the plight of the families of the executed, whom they believed to have been innocent and whose reputations and estates had been "blasted." They asked the government to "Restore the

Reputations to the Posterity of the suffurars and Remunerate them as to what they have been Damnified in their Estates." They felt duty bound "in Consience and Duty to god and to our selves, Relatives and posterity and Country Humbly to make this Motion praying God to Direct You in this."[46]

A year later, in 1710, the government finally set up a committee to act on petitions to remove the attainders and to pay compensation for jail fees and seizures of property. The 1711 Act to Reverse the Attainders of George Burroughs and Others was a sweeping one. It cleared the "Judgments and attainders" against twenty-one people, thirteen who had been executed and eight who had been condemned but not executed, as well as Giles Cory, who had been crushed to death, "as if no such convictions, Judgements or Attainders had ever been had or given." The government absolved itself by pointing to "The Influence and Energy of the Evil Spirits so great at that time acting in and upon those who were the principal Accusers and Witnesses proceeding so far as to cause a Prosecution to be had of persons of known and good Reputation." In view of the fast day statement of 1697, this act was a total reversal. Acknowledging no sense of blame and making no apology to God, the government placed the guilt entirely upon the accusers. The accusers, the government said, were "persons of profligate and vicious Conversation" who, under the influence of "Evil Spirits," caused the "Prosecution" of innocent people. The act of 1711 exonerated those who had been found guilty in 1692.[47]

The act was a determined attempt to right the government's wrongs. Whether the act was motivated by the outrageous injustice of the punitive attainders or a lingering sense of guilt before God, or was simply the result of the passage of time, the government decided to put the ugly past behind it. Admissions of guilt and apologies to God were no longer needed. Gone was the theological framework of New England's special covenant relationship with God and the need to repent. Governor Joseph Dudley, who had presided over the court that executed Goody Glover for witchcraft in 1688, signed the act reversing the attainders in 1711.

The Dudley government, however, wished to protect itself and the authorities from future legal claims. Thus the act stated in conclusion that neither the local officials nor the state could be sued for damages: "no penalties or forfeitures . . . shall be Liable to any prosecution in the Law for any thing they then Legally did in the Execution of their Respective Offices."[48]

Having gone this far to protect itself morally and legally, the government took the next step and started to make compensation for the financial losses incurred by prison fees and confiscations of property. But there was to be no compensation for lives lost.

John Moulton, one of the sons-in-law of Giles Cory, petitioned on behalf of his family for restitution of the money extorted by Sheriff Corwin. Corwin had threatened to seize Cory's estate unless he was paid in cash: "wee Complied with him and paid him Eleaven pound six shillings in monie by all which wee haue been greatly damnified & impovershed."[49] Giles Cory's estate had in fact been legally deeded to Moulton in July before Cory died, which Moulton no doubt told Corwin. But the aggressive Corwin must have brushed this aside and grabbed the money.[50]

Several families had to endure the confiscation of their property in addition to the execution of their relatives and the defaming of their names. Robert Calef describes the plundering of John Procter's estate after he and his wife were imprisoned:

> The Sheriff [George Corwin] came to his House and seized all the Goods, Provisions, and Cattle that he could come at, and sold some of the Cattle at half price, and killed others, and put them up for the West-Indies; threw out the Beer out of a Barrel, and carried away the Barrel . . . and left nothing in the House for the support of the Children.[51]

Edward and Sarah Bishop were also victims of Sheriff Corwin's predations after the Bishops were sent to prison. In 1711, Edward Bishop petitioned for recompense of the money spent to redeem his property. "In my absanc the shrefe wente too my hous and and tok away so mutch of my housall goods as afterwards I payed tene pounds for to haue It again." Bishop listed six cows, a number of pigs, and forty sheep "whitch I neuer had eney againe."[52]

Such seizures were not legal in England or New England, except in cases of treason. Governor Phips explicitly denied having authorized Corwin's confiscation of property, saying that the seizures had been done "without my knowledge or consent." He blamed Stoughton, who by "his warrant hath caused the estates, goods and chattles of the executed to be seized and disposed of."[53] Phips's accusation indicates that there was no accounting for the proceeds from Corwin's confiscations, which, if authorized, should have reverted to the Crown, but which ended up in Corwin's pocket. Later, Phips told Corwin to provide a list of the items taken from the home of Philip English, Salem's wealthiest merchant, who had been accused and imprisoned together with his wife.

It has sometimes been supposed that the taking of property was one of the motives for the witch trials or at least for some of the accusations. Few confiscations are documented, however, and there is no indication that Corwin's powerful relatives on the court (Bartholomew Gedney, Jonathan Corwin, and Wait Winthrop) knew about it or profited. There is evidence, however, that Corwin himself benefited. The money obtained from the sale and repurchase of the goods and livestock confiscated by Corwin ended up in his possession. According to Philip English, the provisions taken from his estate were also "used to subsist ye numerous Company of prisoners" in 1692. Governor Phips later charged Corwin with taking property from English's home and warehouses, and Phips demanded repayment, which Corwin promised to do.[54]

During the trials, Philip and Mary English had fled from prison in Boston to the safety of New York, where they became guests of the governor. When the Englishes returned, their names were cleared, but their home in Salem had been looted and Philip English's warehouses stripped of goods. English accused Corwin of seizing the property. But William Stoughton, who by this time had become chief justice of the Superior Court, came to Corwin's rescue and ordered that he be acquitted of "all manner of sum or sums of money, goods or chattels levied, received, or seized, and of all debts, duties, and demands which are or may be charged in his, the said Corwin's accounts . . . by reason of the sheriff's office."[55]

Though Sheriff Corwin was only twenty-six years old at the time of the trials, he died suddenly four years later in 1696. Stoughton's court order protecting him notwithstanding, Philip English was able to compel Corwin's executors to pay for some of English's losses. According to English's granddaughter Susannah Hathorne, English's claim against Corwin's estate temporarily held up the burial of George Corwin's body until the debt had been paid. Corwin's widow was forced to give over some of the family silver plate and linens as payment. Corwin's estate was small and considerably indebted when he died, which suggests that he did spend what money he gained from the confiscations.[56]

Philip English submitted his claim for full restitution of his losses, which he set at 1,183 pounds, a very large amount of money. In 1719, the state awarded him only 200 pounds "in full satisfaction" of his claim.[57] English and his wife had escaped confinement in Boston (the wealthy were generally given daytime privileges outside of jail) and had never been put on trial. Because he had not been convicted, he did not qualify for compensation. The state's award of the small sum of 200 pounds angered English, and he refused to accept it. After his death, the money was given to his heirs.

The financial compensation paid to the families of those who had been convicted covered only the jail fees and other expenses that were claimed. William Good, husband of the impoverished Sarah Good, left it to the committee to determine compensation for the jail fees and expenses incurred during the "destruction of my poor family." His wife, Sarah, had been executed, their infant child died in prison, and their five-year-old daughter, Dorothy, who had been chained in jail like some of the other defendants, became mentally disabled by her long imprisonment. The committee awarded William Good 30 pounds, far more than the prison fees alone. Thomas Carrier requested compensation of 7 pounds for his wife's prison fees and those of his four children, who had been imprisoned for several months. Eighty-two-year-old Isaac Esty, whose wife, Mary, had been executed, stated that "I can not but think my charge in time & mony might amount to twenty pounds besides my trouble & sorrow of heart in being deprived of her after such a manner which this world can never make me any compensation." The Nurse family did not request any specific amount of money for Rebecca Nurse's five months in jail. As for the wrongful taking of Nurse's life, the petition stated that "we know not how to express our loss of such a Mother in such a way; so we know not how to compute our charge." The Nurse family received 25 pounds to cover their expenses. The highest compensation of 150 pounds was paid to the family of John Procter Jr., for the benefit of his widowed mother, Elizabeth, and her children, who had lost all legal rights to John Procter's estate. The property had been forfeited to someone else, which had reduced the Procter family to poverty.

The last compensation on record was paid in 1724 to Thomas Rich, the son of Martha Cory by her first husband. Rich asked the General Court to pay him 60 pounds that his father had left him but that had been taken at the time of his mother's arrest by Sheriff George Corwin. The court awarded Rich a payment of 50 pounds.[58]

In 1957, the General Court passed a bill clearing the names of Ann Pudeator and "certain others," which had been sponsored by Pudeator's descendants. In 2001, the General Court passed a bill clearing the last five of those unnamed "others" mentioned in the act of 1957. The bill had been sponsored by descendants of the five victims and signed by the acting governor, Jane Swift. Swift thought it fitting to sign the bill into law on October 31, thus continuing Salem's long tradition of associating the tragedy of the witch trials with the celebration of Halloween.[59]

The acts of 1711, 1957, and 2001 never acknowledged the government's responsibility for the deaths of four adults who died in jail because of intolerable conditions from May 1692 to March 1693. Nor did the government acknowledge the death of the infant child of Sarah Good while her mother was in the Boston prison awaiting trial and execution.

12

MAPPING THE SALEM
WITCH TRIALS

*[Y]e late horrid calamity (wch afterwards, Plague-like), spread
in many other places.*
— Samuel Parris, 1694

*We [should] build the memorial column on the height which our
fathers made sacred with their blood.*
— Nathaniel Hawthorne

Samuel Parris, in attempting to defend himself from the
charge of being the "beginner and procurer" of the witch
trials crisis, portrayed it as a "plague-like" act of God, a
vast and inescapable unfolding of divine judgment. His
exact words were: "the Lord ordered ye late horrid calamity (wch afterwards, Plague-like), spread in many other
places to break out first in my own family."[1] Parris used
the plague analogy to suggest that such a widespread
and devastating experience resembled the spread of a
biological epidemic—in extent, severity, and unpredict-
ability. In other words, Parris attempted to minimize the
role of human agency behind the witch trials. His only
admission of responsibility, if we can call it that, was to
acknowledge that the afflictions and accusations started
in his own family. In Puritan thought, only the hand of the
Almighty could cause such a devastating event, sent as a
punishment for the sins of the people.

Six years later, the Boston merchant Robert Calef, the
trials' most trenchant contemporary critic, published a
detailed exposé, which he titled *More Wonders of the In-*

visible World. Near the beginning of the book, Calef employed the plague analogy to characterize the disaster. He styled the witch-hunt as a tragedy caused by "possessed Wenches" who had let loose the all-too-natural "Devils of Envy, Hatred, Pride, Cruelty, and Malice against each other." God was not involved. After listing the many cruelties and sufferings of the trials, Calef concluded: "all which Tragedies, tho begun in one Town, or rather by one Parish, has Plague-like spread more than through that Country. And by its Eccho giving a brand of Infamy to the whole Country, throughout the World."[2] For Calef, the witch trials were a self-inflicted calamity caused by personal jealousies and conflicts that resulted in New England's shame before the world.

Parris and Calef perceived the witch trials from different interpretive perspectives and from different geographic and social vantage points. The minister stood at the heart of the affair in Salem Village and saw it as a judgment of God. The merchant stood at the periphery in Boston and saw it as a human tragedy caused by "possessed" young girls. But both compared the rapid spread of the witchcraft accusations across communities in Essex County to a deadly epidemic ravaging New England.

The accusations spread rapidly over a large area, from the eastern coastal community of Gloucester to the western communities of Billerica and Woburn, southward to Charlestown and Boston, and up to the northern communities of Piscatagua and Great Island, New Hampshire. Wells, Maine, was its northernmost extent, where George Burroughs was arrested while serving as the minister. Referring to the remarkably large geographic reach of the accusations, Mary Beth Norton has rightly observed that the Salem witch trials might better be known as the "Essex County witchcraft crisis."[3] Salem Town, of course, was its legal center, where the Court of Oyer and Terminer held its four sessions from June 2 through September 17. But for the first two months, the Salem Village meetinghouse served as the courtroom for most of the examinations, and it was here that the relentless legal momentum and social turmoil began.

If the accusations seemed to spread "plague-like" over Essex County, it was, as Richard Latner has shown, an epidemic that progressed in two major phases, separated by a three-week hiatus. The first phase began in Salem Village in March and spread to thirteen towns during April and May, and involved 68 cases. The second phase, which eventually centered in Andover and neighboring communities, began in late June, after a three-week interruption, and ended in mid-September with the court's last session. This phase involved 83 new cases in seven different communities. Altogether, the surviving records show that 152 cases of witchcraft were brought to court.[4]

Given the intensity and duration of these events, the three-week break in June between the two major phases stands out. The pause in the accusations between the first and last weeks of June was not due to any hesitation on the part of the accusers. The break in the proceedings was most likely due to the governor's request to the Boston ministers for their opinion concerning the court's first trial, that of Bridget Bishop, who had been executed on June 10. The court suspended its examinations, grand jury hearings, and trials until the ministers gave their judgment on June 15 in a document called "Return of Several Ministers." If the ministers had spoken strongly against the court's use of spectral evidence—indeed, if they had outright condemned its use, as they would later—the trials might have ended at this point. But the ministers spoke ambiguously, and the court ignored their caution. In retrospect, the break in accusations and the review by the Boston ministers was a critical opportunity that was lost. Taking away spectral evidence from the legal process would have stymied the young afflicted accusers on whom the court relied, as later happened when the governor banned it at the end of October. The legal process resumed on June 28 and 29 with the trial of Sarah Good, and accelerated in mid-July around the Andover hub.[5]

The two phases of the witch-hunt were centered primarily in two different communities, Salem (Village and Town) and Andover, which accounted for thirty-nine and forty-six accusations respectively. Most of the other communities involved two to four accusations, and one had nine. Once ended, accusations did not resume in any of these communities. In Salem Village and Town, the accusations were intense but short-lived and did not recur. In Andover, the accusations lasted for two months. As Latner points out in summary: "Salem witchcraft was not a continuous, yearlong event but, rather, took place in two distinct phases, each associated with different communities. Within most communities, the witch-hunt passed quickly, erupting for only a brief period, then fading away, not to return."[6]

Latner concludes that the whole seven-month episode does not justify the frequently used tropes of "panic," "contagion," "epidemic," and "hysteria," commonplace descriptions of a society out of control. He would rather portray these events in a "more complex perspective that tempers the pervasive concept of Salem as bedlam."[7] Nevertheless, as September wore on and as Boston's ministers called the court's procedures into question, the first two weeks of September turned out to be the most active period for accusations, hearings, trials, and executions before the court went into recess on September 22. Although "bedlam" is too strong a characterization of the events of the first two weeks of September, the nineteen grand jury hearings, eleven trials, and eight executions that occurred during this period mark it as the culmination of a deadly crescendo that Chief Magistrate William Stoughton drove relentlessly and methodically forward.

The inexorable legal activity during the seven-month period from March through September affected twenty-five different communities. "All history is spatial" is a catchphrase among today's mapmaking historians that emphasizes the fact that geospatial conditions play an enormous role in shaping history. A dynamic geographical display of the accusations helps us visualize the witch-hunt's "plague-like" spread as it played out on the ground. Using the chronological, geographic, and social information contained in the court records, it is possible to create a dynamic geographic display of the diffusion of the accusations across Essex County and surrounding areas.

―――――――――

Historians have traditionally used maps to illustrate geographic information contained in textual sources. Only recently have researchers created maps to help reveal otherwise indiscernible patterns. Such patterns are not always perceived by the participants themselves, and for historians the patterns may not be evident in the textual form of the sources. Digital maps can represent geographical information about the same place at different times by displaying separate visual layers that represent different time periods over the same geographic space, in order to answer questions about spatial patterns over time. The several phases of an event can also be presented in the form of a continuous movie, showing an event's geographic development over time as it moves across a landscape. For example, the stages of a military battle or the progress of a drought or a biological epidemic can be represented in this way.[8]

The court records specify the dates of complaints and arrests, the names of the accused individuals, and the towns in which they lived. These data can be entered into a table that is interpreted in a geographic display of the accusations as they progressed chronologically in the eastern part of the

Bay Province in 1692. On the Regional Accusations Map (http://salem.lib
.virginia.edu/maps/accusationMaps/regionmap/regionmap.swf), clicking the
"Play" button drives the display and shows the territorial range, chronological sequence, and number of accusations in each town. The accusations
started in Salem Village and moved through eastern Essex County as new
communities became involved. The map shows the widening spread and
the increasing numbers of accused individuals across twenty-five different
communities. The display appears to replicate Parris's and Calef's on-the-
ground characterization of the Salem crisis as a plague-like event, something
that started small and over time became a widening phenomenon affecting
an increasing number of people.

The digital display shows that in little more than a month the number of
complaints and arrests tripled and began to spread beyond Salem Village's
boundaries. The accusations spilled over the Village's borders in early April
and rapidly progressed outward into neighboring communities. In contrast
to Salem Village and Town, where the witch-hunt started, the accusations
in most other communities involved very few people and lasted a short time
before burgeoning into the exceptionally large number of accusations in the
town of Andover, Salem Village's western neighbor.

From start to finish, the legal process brought most of the accused into
the courtroom, first in Salem Village and then in Salem Town, to stand
before the magistrates and the afflicted accusers. What the map does not
show is how the activity in the Salem courtroom fed into witchcraft fears in
outlying towns, which generated new accusations against local neighbors,
largely based on old conflicts and grudges. These accusations led to arrests
and brought new suspects into the Salem courtroom to be examined before
the magistrates and the afflicted accusers.

In *The Tipping Point: How Little Things Can Make a Big Difference,* Malcolm Gladwell observes that seemingly irrational social phenomena, such as
fashion crazes and crime waves, can be illuminated by noting their parallels
to epidemics of disease. Gladwell's contribution to understanding such social epidemics is the framework he identifies for understanding the power
of social messages streaming through a social network. Like biological dis-
eases, social epidemics start small, spread rapidly through contagious behavior, generally among neighboring communities, and cover a geographic
area many times larger than their point of origin. The most important phase
is the dramatic moment when a local, small-scale problem is suddenly trans-

formed into a widespread and amplified crisis. Gladwell calls this the tipping point, "the moment of critical mass, the threshold, the boiling point," when sudden change brings about unexpected results.[9]

In the Salem episode, a critical escalation occurred shortly after it began, not initially in the courtroom but in the imaginations of Tituba and the young accusers. The four Village girls accused three people of witchcraft on February 29. A day later, Tituba said she saw the signatures of nine people who had made their marks in the devil's book, "Some [who live] in & Boston & Some here in this Towne," that is, in Salem Village. Barely three weeks later, on March 21, the Reverend Deodat Lawson reported that the girls had witnessed the specters of a "company of about 23 or 24" witches "mustering" outside the Village meetinghouse during Martha Cory's examination. This was consistent with Tituba's claim that the witchcraft torments in Salem Village were the result of an organized assault by witches from the outside converging on the Village. Three weeks later, on April 11, Abigail Williams reported seeing forty witches holding a devil's sacrament next to Parris's house.[10] This was more than four times the number initially reported by Tituba on March 1. Neither Lawson nor the magistrates raised any question about the sizable number of specters seen at Cory's mid-March examination, nor did Hathorne and Corwin question Abigail Williams's startling claim in the courtroom that she saw twice this number attending a satanic mass in Parris's pasture. The escalation in the minds of the young accusers primed the authorities, as well as the local community, for the torrent of formal complaints and accusations that was to come, initially from their own mouths.

Incredibly, the authorities appear to have unquestioningly accepted the young accusers' reports of increasingly large satanic events. When Lawson left Salem Village on April 5, eight people had been arrested. But the girls, perhaps influenced by the gossip of anxious adults and their own fearful imaginations, had already expanded the scope to three times that number; and there is every indication that local authorities and the general public accepted it. Judging from Parris's sermon on March 27, when he estimated that there might be as many as twenty devils "among us," he, too, had no doubt that the Village harbored many more witches. Expectation, fear, and an overriding sense of urgency, centered on the perceived threat to the Salem Village ministry, appear to have propelled the initial accusations forward, first in the community's fevered imaginations and then in the courtroom.

Once the court hearings started, long-held suspicions originating in other neighboring communities were communicated to the accusers, who became afflicted by specters of people they had never known, who were then hauled into court. The Regional Accusations Map shows the resultant legal process in a chronological and geographical display.

By April 21, the number of accusations had reached twenty-three, which matched the number of specters that the girls had seen two and a half weeks earlier. The legal process had caught up with the girls' imaginations. The number of accused was almost triple the number in Hartford, Connecticut, the site of New England's largest witch-hunt up to that point. This was the tipping point in the legal process. The Salem witch-hunt had far exceeded a critical mass, intensified by three new confessions and bolstered by the identification of the Reverend George Burroughs as Satan's agent. There was no turning back. After he arrived in mid-May, Governor Phips noted with some urgency that the Boston area's jails (in Boston, Charleston, Salem, and Ipswich) were "thronging" with prisoners who were sweltering "at this hot season of the year." Trials would have to be held.[11]

As in cases of biological epidemics, most of the key factors that cause a tipping point were present at the beginning in Salem Village. The immediate context included Parris's inflammatory sermons about the devil attacking the Village church; the failure of three to six weeks of prayer for the afflicted girls' relief; a local doctor's witchcraft diagnosis; the decision by the local magistrates to prosecute the accused; the dramatic behavior of imaginative and fearful girls; Salem Village's intense division over its minister; and individuals in nearby communities eager to settle old scores by accusing their neighbors of witchcraft. Taken together, these factors stimulated a fear of satanic activity in Salem Village and neighboring communities.

Helping to spread the news of the witchcraft outbreak were the Reverend Deodat Lawson's vividly described scenes of the girls' afflictions, which he published in Boston in early April, barely five weeks after the first accusations, thereby adding to Salem Village's growing notoriety as the center of an escalating witch-hunt.

Although social networks both inside and outside Salem Village supplied the Village accusers with malicious gossip about likely suspects, the magistrates' decision to act was crucial. One of the ways in which biological epidemics succeed in human communities is by circumventing or compromising the body's protective immune system. The Salem authorities ignored basic legal safeguards, as well as a thirty-year precedent of caution exercised to prevent an unchecked prosecution of people suspected of witchcraft. Magistrates failed to require the Village complainants to post the usual monetary bond for prosecution. The lack of a requirement to post a bond facilitated the filing of multiple complaints on behalf of a dozen people in the first five weeks. A single complaint might also carry the names of as many as nine or ten people. Unprecedented in New England, the targeting of such large groups also showed the efficiency of the rumor networks in channeling names of suspects to the afflicted accusers and their families.

As Gladwell points out, the attempt to identify a tipping point in a social epidemic that happened in the distant past usually means looking at the past as a world fundamentally different from our own. It can be difficult to believe that people could inhabit such a world; hence, social epidemics in the past often appear irrational and mysterious. The Salem witch trials have been frequently characterized as a historical "mystery" and a kind of social "hysteria" characterized by irrational acts and unexplained circumstances. Television programs and popular websites thrive on the apparent inexplicability of the events in Salem, attributing the witch-hunt to rampant superstition and social irrationality, and even to toxic grain. But in the world of social epidemics, as Gladwell notes, very small beginnings can quickly produce very large effects that seem all out of proportion to their initial causes.[12] Focusing on Salem's tipping point enables us to track the links in a chain of causation back to the critical factors at the beginning in Salem Village and the escalation that occurred in connection with the accusation of the Reverend Burroughs.

Although the dynamic digital map provides a useful geographical representation of the legal process as it unfolded over Essex County, it cannot represent one important factor that drove the accusations forward. The girls' repeated performances in the Salem courtroom served to attract accusations from people living in communities at the periphery. As long as the government in Boston kept the Salem court in session, accusations among neighbors in outlying communities would continue to pour in to the court for the accusers, aided by dozens of confessors, to support with their fits.

Like the famous Broad Street well pump in mid-nineteenth-century Soho, London, that gushed out water containing cholera bacteria—causing a severe cholera epidemic to spread out over a widening area—the Salem courtroom gushed out spectral evidence to validate old and new suspicions, enlivening fears throughout Essex County and thus sustaining a growing geographic involvement.[13]

Only when the Boston ministers found their voice in early September was there sufficient countervailing force to stop the special court's deadly proceedings. The trials were deemed to have gone completely awry, killing people who were "doubtless innocent," as Governor Phips put it. He stepped in, closed the court, and forbade the use of spectral evidence, and thus, in his words, "dissipated the black cloud that threatened this Province with destruccion."[14]

Taking Gladwell's analysis of social epidemics as a guide, it is possible to see the Salem tragedy as the result of the interaction of individuals within and between four basic social networks: (1) the two communities of Salem Village and Salem Town and their principal actors—Samuel Parris, the Village church members, the afflicted girls, Thomas Putnam, the other local ministers, and the examining magistrates—whose actions started off and accelerated the legal process; (2) Increase Mather, Cotton Mather, and the ministers in Boston (among them the liberal-minded Samuel Willard), who initially approved of the trials despite their heavy reliance on spectral evidence; (3) the governor and his Council in Boston, whose members served as the judges on the Court of Oyer and Terminer, led by the zealous deputy governor William Stoughton, who drove the trials forward; and (4) the town of Andover, which became the center of the explosive second phase of witchcraft accusations and of numerous confessions, which propelled the Salem trials to even greater heights. It was the interaction between these networks, and the leading individuals within them, that created the Salem calamity.

Previous historians have wondered whether the outbreak's geographic characteristics could explain the occurrence of accusations in Salem Village. Charles Upham, a local Salem minister and author of the now classic nineteenth-century, two-volume work *Salem Witchcraft*, indicated that several accusations, all stemming from various Putnams, had to do with disputes over property boundaries between the Putnam family of Salem Village and the Towne family of neighboring Topsfield. The protracted dispute lasted more than twenty years, and the Putnams believed themselves to be the aggrieved party. The conflict was still alive in 1692.

Scholars usually attribute the accusations by Putnam family members against three Towne sisters—Rebecca Towne Nurse, Sarah Towne Cloyce, and Mary Towne Esty—to acrimony and suspicion caused by this unresolved boundary dispute.[15] These accusations, however, were the only ones that clearly related to conflicts over property. Nothing, in fact, was said about land disputes in any of the court records.

Paul Boyer and Stephen Nissenbaum have also investigated the geographic relationship between accusers and accused in Salem Village. In their important book *Salem Possessed,* they created a map of Salem Village that showed the locations of the houses of the accusers and the accused in 1692. Their conclusion was that the map showed that "accusers and accused lived on opposite sides of the village."

Published in 1974, this map was based on a rudimentary collection of court records published in the mid-nineteenth century by W. Elliot Woodward. A considerably larger and more complete collection of records was organized and transcribed in 1938 by the Works Progress Administration (WPA). Boyer and Nissenbaum published the WPA typescript in 1977, under the title *The Salem Witchcraft Papers.* The map in *Salem Possessed,* however, remained unchanged.[16]

The most complete collection of records to date is the recent scholarly edition *Records of the Salem Witch-Hunt* (Bernard Rosenthal, general editor), published in 2009. Using this edition, it is possible to create a more complete map based on the geographic and social data contained in the records. Map 1 is based on the new edition, which contains all of the known records of the accusations by people in Salem Village and its environs. It shows the locations of a total of fifteen people who were accused in Salem Village and fifty-seven Village residents who were their accusers.[17]

This map, which shows Boyer and Nissenbaum's east–west demarcation line, makes it clear that Salem Village was not geographically divided east–west, with accusers and accused on different sides of the Village. There were twenty-five accusers in the east and thirty-two in the west, a fairly symmetrical number. The vast majority of the accused in Salem Village lived on the eastern side of the Village, but so did half of their accusers. There was therefore no real east–west division between accusers and accused.[18]

There was, however, a clear social division over Samuel Parris within the Salem Village community. The Village aligned itself along not geographic

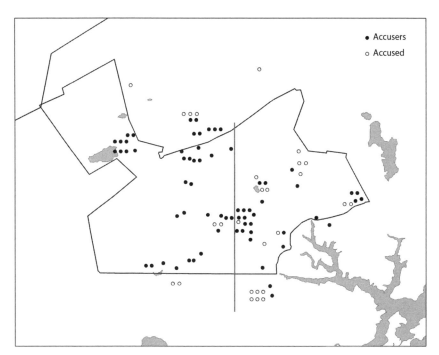

MAP 1. *Geography of accusations in Salem Village.*

but religious lines. This division was instrumental to the initiation and spread of the accusations.

Given Parris's ongoing sermons about "devils" and "assistants of Satan" in Salem Village, it is not surprising that 65 percent of the Village accusers (41 out of 65) belonged to the households of church members or supporters of Parris. More telling is the fact that 76 percent of the Village men (13 out of 17) who signed the original Village covenant either initiated witchcraft complaints, the sine qua non of the legal process, or testified against at least one person. Equally significant is the fact that 76 percent (13 out of 17) of the most active Village accusers (those who accused more than three people) belonged to church member families. Of this group, the most active accusers belonged to the large Putnam family, whose members were involved in the accusations against all fifteen Village residents arrested for witchcraft.

The witchcraft accusations in Salem Village sprang from the heart of an embattled congregation, whose members initially directed their fears against those who were not full members—the unregenerate non-members living among them—a classic opposition between "us" and "them" within a bounded community. A large proportion of those accused in the Village were not members of the Village church or churches elsewhere, 71 percent (10 out of 14 accused adults). If we narrow down the group of accused in the Village to those who were not full members of the Village church, the ratio is even stronger: 86 percent of those accused (12 out of 14). Although Rebecca Nurse was a church member in Salem Town and Sarah Buckley a member elsewhere, neither had transferred her membership to the Village church, and they had not been formally "received" by Samuel Parris into the Village covenant.[19]

Although the conflict between Samuel Parris and his opponents precipitated fears of witchcraft, that was not the sole motivating force for the accusations. Only two out of the five opposition leaders were touched by the accusations. Whatever grudges the accusers harbored against their neighbors, they were far more likely to finger individuals who were not members of the congregation. Thus, more than any other single factor, geographic or economic, one's status within or without the Village covenant became the distinguishing characteristic of the accusers and the accused within the Village community.

Although no one in Salem Village is recorded as having noticed the correlation between the unbaptized and non-church members and those accused of witchcraft, Cotton Mather, whose own congregation had rejected the Halfway Covenant, attributed the woeful episode in Salem Village to the large number of unbaptized inhabitants of the Village. In mid-December 1692, he wrote to John Richards, a witch trials judge and leading member of his congregation, who was opposed to Mather's wish to establish the Halfway Covenant in his church: "I have seen that the Divels have been Baptising so many of our miserable Neighbours, in that horrible Witchcraft. . . . I cannot be well at Ease, until the Nursery of Initiated Beleevers . . . [have] been duely Watered, with Baptism. . . . I would mark [with baptism] as many as I should, that the Destroying Angels may have less claim to them."[20] Mather apparently believed the accused in the Salem affair had succumbed to the very thing that he feared might claim the unbaptized in his own church community: outside the Christian community, they had been tempted to "sign the Devil's book" and thus join Satan's covenant. Was this a comment

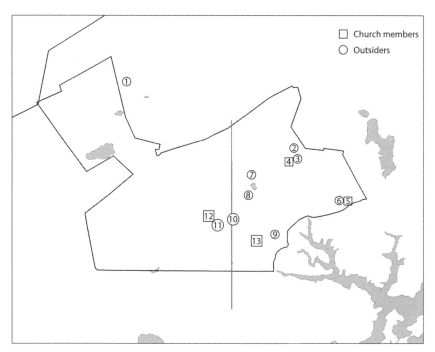

MAP 2. *Proportion of church members among individuals accused of witchcraft in Salem Village.*

Names of accused (not in sequence of accusations) are noted below by inset numbers:

1. John Willard	6. Edward Bishop	10. Tituba
2. Daniel Andrews	7. Sarah Osborne	11. Mary Witherdge
3. Rebecca and George Jacobs	8. Sarah and Dorothy Good	12. Sarah Buckley
4. Sarah Cloyce	9. Mary Black	13. Rebecca Nurse
5 Sarah Bishop		

against Salem Village's rejection of the Halfway Covenant, which had prevented more baptisms in Salem Village, where it all started? For Mather, at least, it made a good argument for adopting the halfway solution in his own church.

_____

The tall, sloping promontory called Gallows Hill is located on the western side of Salem and is familiar to everyone in the town. For visitors, Gallows Hill is easily identified by the large water tower that stands on top. The tower bears the city's name as well as the black silhouette of a witch flying on a broomstick. Witchcraft Heights Elementary School is located on the flat crest of the hill. It stands near streets named Gallows Hill Road, Witch Way, and Witchcraft Road.

Today, no one knows exactly where on Gallows Hill the nineteen witch-hunt victims were executed and buried, although recent research has located the general area. The execution warrants refer only to "the place of execution" without further specification.[21] In the eighteenth century, the site was apparently well known. John Adams visited Gallows Hill, which was then called Witch Hill, in August 1766, while staying in Salem at the home of his brother-in-law Richard Cranch. He noted that locust trees were planted "over the graves" as memorial markers, but his account does not give the location. Nathaniel Hawthorne, who lived in Salem, visited the area sometime in the mid-1800s and made it the setting of his haunting tale "Alice Doane's Appeal." From Hawthorne's description, it is clear that the usual path to ascend the hill was approached from the northeast side, along the Boston Road via the bridge over the North River, which was just beyond the "outskirts of the town." Hawthorne's narrator speaks of "turning aside from a street of tanners and curriers" (in an area that is still known as "Blubber Hollow") that was then called the Boston Road, and proceeding to the left and upward along the gradual slope of the hill. From this side, he says, "it was less steep than its aspect threatened." Even today, ascent from the south and west sides of the hill is difficult; it would have been impossible for an ox-drawn cart carrying the prisoners in 1692.

Gallows Hill was still kept as common land in Hawthorne's time and was known then as the Great Pasture. Hawthorne thought that the execution site was located at the top "on the long broad ridge." Here, he wrote, "the eminence formed part of an extensive tract of pasture land, and was traversed by cow paths in various directions." Hawthorne does not mention seeing the locust trees, which had likely disappeared by this time. He refers only to the decayed stumps of two trees, perhaps ones he believed were the symbolic locusts. Although Hawthorne's narrator imagines that he might stumble anytime "into the hollow of a witch's grave," he recognizes that all vestiges of the execution site had vanished. With the disappearance of the locust trees in the mid-nineteenth century and the sale of the common land for residential plots in the twentieth century, the location of the execution site became lost to local memory.

In the 1860s, the most knowledgeable local historian of the time, Charles

Upham, believed like Hawthorne that the executions took place at the top of the hill not far from where the water tower stands today. But this was clearly not the site once marked by the locust trees that the locals had known. In the 1920s, the local historian Sidney Perley gathered references from published sources and local family tradition and made the case for a site on the hill's lower flank known as Proctor's Ledge, which lies on the northeastern side, between today's Pope Street and Proctor Street. Here, Perley believed, the locust trees once stood, and he created his own maps to show his findings.

Perley's research was corroborated in the 1980s by the local historian Marilynne Roach. Roach brought to light an overlooked reference in the court records that confirms Perley's findings.[22] Rebecca Eames's examination record, dated August 19, says that she was asked in court if she was "at the execution" that took place earlier that day. She had been taken by guard from Boxford to Salem for her court appearance that day, and she would have traveled to Salem along the Boston Road. Her guards may have stopped at one of the houses along the road to view the executions on the nearby hill. Eames said that she was "at the house below the hill," and that she "saw a few folk," referring to people who were at the site at the time of the execution.[23] The execution of five people took place a short time before Eames appeared in the Salem courtroom later that morning. There were only a few houses on that section of the road at the time Eames and her guards paused to observe the executions. According to Perley, all these houses had a view of Proctor's Ledge on the hill above.

One question raised by Perley's work is whether his hand-drawn maps are accurate. Another is whether the topography of the area is such that it was possible to see Proctor's Ledge from the houses on Boston Street, as Perley claimed, and as the Eames record suggests. Still another is whether the top of the hill was or was not visible from the Boston Road where Eames passed by and hence whether it was the possible location.

The accuracy of Perley's hand-drawn maps can be checked by overlaying digital copies onto aerial photographs and topographical maps to examine their geographic fit. Perley's maps turn out to be remarkably accurate. They indicate the area of Proctor's Ledge where Perley believed the sources placed the gallows and burials. Inspection of this area, now bordered by houses along Proctor Street and Pope Street, shows the rock formations of ledges and crevices that Perley photographed and indicated on his maps.

Topographical analysis of the sight lines from the houses below the hill Perley mentions confirms that people standing at or near the houses would have had an unobstructed view to Proctor's Ledge. The top of the hill where Upham and Hawthorne believed the executions occurred is not visible from the houses in this area. One of the likely houses stood at 19 Boston Street and was owned by John McCarter; on the other side of the road was the Joshua Buffum house; farther away was the John Symond house, located at the site of what was later the Upham School and is now the North Street Shell Service Station at 111 North Street. Although the view toward Gallows Hill is obscured today by other buildings and tall trees, a viewshed analysis of the topography shows that Proctor's Ledge would have been clearly visible from each of these houses in the seventeenth century.[24]

The final question concerns the pathway taken by the procession of prisoners and spectators as they moved from the Salem prison to Proctor's Ledge. Perley rightly indicates that the prisoners were taken by oxcart from the jail on Prison Street (now St. Peter's Street). It took the prisoners along Main Street (now Essex Street), then turned north onto Bridge Street, and downward toward the Town Bridge and crossed over the North River.

In 1852, Nathaniel Hawthorne imagined this somber procession as it passed along Main Street. He portrayed the Reverend George Burroughs among the forlorn group of condemned:

> Who would not say, while we see him offering comfort to the weak and aged partners of his horrible crime,—while we hear his ejaculations of prayer, that seem to bubble up out of the depths of his heart, and fly heavenward, unawares,—while we behold a radiance brightening on his features as from the other world, which is but a few steps off,—who would not say, that, over the dusty track of the Main-street, a Christian saint is now going to a martyr's death?[25]

The road over Town Bridge was the only way to get to where it was possible to ascend the slope of Gallows Hill. The pasture was common land, outside the Town's residential area, and lacked any houses. In some parts, the sides of the hill are fairly steep and craggy, and would have caused the sort of difficulties for the oxcart carrying the prisoners that were described in a contemporary account. Since no one owned the property, this uninhabited area was suitable for the execution and burial of individuals whose presence was considered an abomination. The execution site was probably selected by George Corwin of Salem, the high sheriff of Essex County. The execution warrants were addressed to him, and he wrote his report on the back, confirming that the executions had been carried out at "the place provided."

After crossing the bridge, the oxcart would have turned left and proceeded up the northeastern slope, following the cow and sheep paths. Topographical analysis suggests that the easiest route lay near today's Pope Street, along the edge of a body of water then known as Bickford's Pond, which is now filled in, and up the slope to the area of Proctor's Ledge. The final progress to the top of the ledge outcrop was steep. Robert Calef's contemporary account mentions that a wheel of the oxcart carrying the prisoners became stuck on the rocky surface. The promontory had a view over the North River and Salem to the west. Whether George Corwin intended to execute the witches in a place that was visible from the town, thus creating a spectacle of "triumph" over Satan, as Upham suggested, is unknown. Proctor's Ledge, however, is quite possibly the place he chose. It was on the lower side of the common land of Great Pasture hillside, but high enough to be visible from the town, and it was at some distance from the property owners on the Boston Road.

There exist several contemporary reports of the scene of the executions. There is also the unrecorded but legendary exchange between Sarah Good and the Reverend Nicholas Noyes at the time of Good's execution as she stood on the ladder from which she would be pushed: "Mr. Noyes urged Sarah Good to Confess, and told her she was a witch, and she knew she was a Witch, to which she replied, 'you are a lier; I am no more a Witch than you are a Wizard, and if you take away my Life, God will give you Blood to drink.'" According to local tradition, Noyes died twenty-five years later while choking on his own blood, an incident that Hawthorne adapted for *The House of the Seven Gables.*

Robert Calef reported that the crowd witnessing the executions mocked the prisoners. On September 22, when the oxcart with its heavy load of eight prisoners became stuck going up the hill, "the afflicted and others said, that the Devil hindred it." On the same day, Samuel Wardwell spoke to the crowd and attempted to declare his innocence. He choked on smoke from the executioner's pipe, and the "accusers said, the Devil hindered him with smoke." Nicholas Noyes was heard to say, "what a sad thing it is to see Eight Firebrands of Hell hanging there."

Thomas Brattle summarized what he saw or was told about the behavior of the prisoners at the time of their executions on August 19:

> They protested their innocency as in the presence of the great God, whom forthwith they were to appear before: they wished, and declared their wish, that their blood might be the last innocent blood shed upon that account. With great affection they intreated Mr. C[otton]. M[ather]. to pray with them: they prayed that God would discover what witchcrafts were among us; they forgave their accusers; they spake without reflection on Jury and Judges, for bringing them in guilty, and condemning them: they prayed earnestly for pardon for all other sins, and for an interest in the precious blood of our dear Redeemer; and seemed to be very sincere, upright, and sensible of their circumstances on all accounts; especially Proctor and Willard, whose whole management of themselves, from the Goal [*sic*] to the Gallows, and whilst at the Gallows, was very affecting and melting to the hearts of some considerable Spectatours, whom I could mention to you:—but they are executed, and so I leave them.[26]

Calef related that "when she [Mary Esty] took her last farewell of her Husband, Children and Friends, [she] was, as is reported by them present, as Serious, Religious, Distinct, and Affectionate as could well be exprest, drawing Tears from the Eyes of almost all present."[27]

Nathaniel Hawthorne was the first to write about the placement of a memorial on Gallows Hill. Hawthorne wanted there to be two monuments at the top: "We [should] build the memorial column on the height which our fathers made sacred with their blood, poured out in a holy cause. And here in dark, funereal stone, should rise another monument, sadly commemorative of the errors of an earlier race, and not to be cast down, while the human heart has one infirmity that may result in crime."[28] At this time, there is still no memorial on Gallows Hill for the victims who died there, and the silhouette of a witch remains painted on the water tower at the top.

13

INDIANS, AFRICANS, GENDER, AND THE "BLACK MAN"

[S]hee saw a thing like an indian all black.
— *Sarah Osborne*

[T]he Devil, in the shape of [a] Black man whispering in her ear.
— *Salem Village accusers*

Satan is setting upon these [women] rather then on men, since his unhappy onset and prevailing with Eve.
— *Richard Bernard*

Ethnicity and gender played important roles in the Salem witch trials, and historians have only recently been able to clarify their significance. As previously indicated, the court records consistently refer to Tituba and her husband, John, as ethnically Indian. It is likely that the renewed fear of Indians that occurred at the start of King William's War, or the Second Indian War, in 1688 made Tituba appear to be a possible suspect in the Parris household. She had admitted to carrying out what Parris called the "diabolical" witch-cake procedure, she was a woman, and the girls said they were tormented by her specter. The question is whether the Second Indian War was a significant factor in the escalation of the Salem witch trials. Later generations would change Tituba's ethnicity from Indian to part-African and part-Indian, and finally to fully African.

Another matter of ethnicity, which has gone almost unnoticed by historians, is the fact that two African slaves, who were presumably among the most vulnerable ethnic group, were accused by the court's star witnesses but never put on trial, even though they were made to incriminate themselves in court and appeared to cause the usual damning afflictions among the Village girls. Why did the court choose to overlook them?

Gender also played a determinative role in the Salem episode as it did in all New England witchcraft cases. In Puritan New England, as well as Protestant and Catholic Europe, women accounted for about 80 percent of those accused of witchcraft, and they were understood to be repeating the biblical Eve's temptation by Satan. Never before, however, were girls and young unmarried women the principal accusers in the courtroom, as in Salem.

From 1688 to 1697, the Indian raids on the settler communities in the Maine frontier revived the fears of Indian terrorism associated with the devastating King Philip's War of 1675–78. King Philip's War, also called the First Indian War, was the greatest single calamity to befall seventeenth-century New England. In little more than a year, twelve of the region's towns were entirely destroyed and many more damaged, the colony's economy was nearly ruined, and much of its population was killed, including one-tenth of all men available for military service. Proportionately, it was one of the bloodiest and costliest wars in the history of North America. The memories of this war and especially its atrocities to men, women, and children lingered on. From the Puritan point of view, God had unleashed the devil-worshiping Indians and created the First Indian War as punishment for New England's sins.

The devil was also, of course, behind the witchcraft attacks of 1692. As Mary Beth Norton has pointed out, in 1692 the new government of Massachusetts was fighting the devil on two fronts—against the Indians in the visible world, and against the witches in the invisible world. The battles were occurring simultaneously, but they were spoken of separately. The Indian attacks are barely mentioned in Salem court records; and very few individuals involved in the Salem trials had any connection with the Maine frontier and the Indian wars. The individual with the most prominent connection was the Reverend George Burroughs, but as we have seen, the charges against him stemmed from his failure as pastor of Salem Village and from his unorthodox practices and suspicions of spousal abuse.

The historical documents tell parallel stories about the aggression by the French and Indians, and the witchcraft attacks, the former being the larger and more preoccupying issue for the government. The two stories converged in the office of the governor and his Council in Boston, where decisions were made about repulsing the Indians and prosecuting the witches. In only two instances did the stories converge in the Salem courtroom, both times when the magistrates referred to the militia soldiers who were fighting the Indians in Maine. Both instances were in connection with George Burroughs, who was said to have bewitched the soldiers, thus causing their defeat. The ministers in Boston spoke of the Indian wars and the witch trials separately, and Samuel Sewall, the major diarist of the period, who was directly involved in both episodes, wrote about them separately. For Sewall, the two events were apparently parallel but not intrinsically connected.

The most active accuser among the refugees of the Indian wars in Maine was seventeen-year-old Mercy Lewis. She lost her paternal grandparents and several uncles and cousins during King Philip's War in 1676, when she was a child living in Falmouth, Maine. Her family fled to Salem Town but returned to Falmouth in the early 1680s. At age fifteen, Mercy worked in Falmouth for a time as a maid in the house of George Burroughs. Later, when she and her family returned to Salem, she became a maid in the household of Thomas Putnam. Mercy was orphaned in 1689, when her parents were killed in Falmouth, possibly in the Indian attack that year.[1] As Norton suggests, Ann Putnam Jr., no doubt responding to gossip about George Burroughs told her by Lewis, accused Burroughs of bewitching "a great many" English soldiers "at the eastward," thus helping the Indians in their raids. No other accuser mentioned this kind of treachery, even Lewis, and Ann spoke of it only once in her two depositions against Burroughs; nor does Cotton Mather's detailed summary of Burroughs's trial refer to the matter.

Another connection between the Salem accusers and the Maine frontier occurred in the case of the highly respected mariner John Alden of Boston. Alden was a sea captain who was often in the government's service, supplying local militias' needs on the frontier and dealing with the Indians. According to Alden's account of his examination, one of the young Salem Village accusers cried out that Alden "sells Powder and Shot to the Indians and French, and lies with the Indian Squaes, and has Indian Papooses." When Alden was told by Justice Bartholomew Gedney to look at his accusers, he reported that "they fell down." Alden challenged Gedney about this behavior. He asked why his (Alden's) looking directly at Gedney did not strike him down, but he received no answer.[2]

Particularly damning from Alden's point of view was not the charge about his dealings with the Indians but magistrate Gedney's belief in the evil eye, the witch's harmful "look." Gedney told Alden that "he had known Aldin many Years, and had been at Sea with him, and always look'd upon him to be an honest Man, but now he did see cause to alter his judgment." The girls were then brought to Alden and made to touch him, upon which they recovered, though not immediately. Alden then told Gedney "that he could assure him that there was a lying Spirit in them, for I can assure you that there is not a word of truth in all these say of me." Alden's challenge to Gedney went unanswered. Thomas Brattle, who described the same encounter between Alden and Gedney, expressed surprise at Gedney's gullibility. Brattle had observed that when the girls did not recover immediately upon touching Alden's hand, the magistrates told them to "grasp hard" until the desired effect happened.[3] Despite the gossip about illicit trade with the Indians, the issue at Alden's examination appears to have been the evidence of the touch test. Alden eventually decided to take the advice of his friends and escaped from the prison in Boston to the safety of New York. Alden returned when the trials were over and was acquitted by proclamation.

Eighteen-year-old Susannah Sheldon was a 1688 refugee from Black Point, Maine, whose family had settled in Salem Village. Susannah had lost her uncle in an Indian raid on Black Point in 1675 and her brother more recently in the Indian attack on Falmouth in 1690. She joined in the accusations against Philip English, a French Huguenot who had settled in Salem. English was a wealthy merchant and shipowner, and his ships traded regularly along the Maine coast and in French Canada. There is no record indicating what triggered Sheldon's charge against English except that she saw his specter in the Village meetinghouse during a worship service. English had been named together with five other individuals in a complaint by Jonathan Walcott and Thomas Putnam on April 30 for bewitching the Village girls, including Sheldon, but the basis of Sheldon's complaint is not mentioned. Like most men accused in Salem whose wives had been accused of witchcraft, English may have emerged as a suspect because of his wife's accusation, which occurred a week before his own. A local Marblehead man also accused English of witchcraft in August 1692—after English and his wife had fled from jail in Boston—because of his sharp business practices. As a wealthy French-speaking merchant trading with the hated French in a time of war,

English was undoubtedly open to suspicion. But nothing of his connections with the Maine frontier or the French is mentioned in the court records.

In the few cases, then, where it did occur, the connection between the Indian wars, the Maine frontier, and witchcraft accusations was slight. It appears to have served as a point of gossip that the magistrates followed up but without any legal impact. As Cotton Mather pointed out, New England was in great turmoil from the devil on two fronts, from the Indians and from witchcraft, but in the courtroom, the records indicate that the evidence for witchcraft was understood to be strictly personal and local.

When Samuel Parris and his family arrived in Salem Village, he brought with him two adult Indian slaves, Tituba and her husband, John Indian. The ownership of slaves in seventeenth-century New England was not unusual, but it was rare for clergymen to own them. In 1692, the fates of the two Indians were very different from those of others accused at Salem. Tituba was accused and confessed. She was not accused for making the witch cake, to which she admitted, but, as the depositions show, for tormenting the girls in Parris's house in spectral form. As an ethnic Indian, she could be suspected of worshiping the devil and of treachery against her master. John Indian sometimes worked as a servant in Nathaniel Ingersoll's tavern next door to the parsonage.[4] A month after Tituba's accusation, John joined the "afflicted" as an accuser, perhaps to avoid his wife's fate. He appeared in court as an afflicted witness, never as a defendant.

The court records and contemporary accounts consistently identify Tituba as "Indian" twenty-six times and never as "Negro," the term used for people of African descent. The origins of Tituba's alleged Negro ethnicity are to be found in embellished literary accounts dating from the late nineteenth century, after the Civil War, when the institution of slavery and African American ethnicity became closely identified. From the moment Henry Wadsworth Longfellow changed Tituba's ethnic identity from Indian to half-Indian, half-Negro in his play *Giles Corey of the Salem Farms*, popular historians and writers adopted the change. In Longfellow's play, Mary Walcott looks into Tituba's divination glass of vaporous liquid and sees the image of Tituba's father. She says he looks like "a man all black and fierce." Tituba tells Walcott that her father was "an Obi man, and taught me magic." Looking into the divination glass again, Walcott sees Tituba's father melting a waxen figure of a woman in a fire, and then she sees the woman herself, "wasted and worn away," in the language of the Salem indictments.[5]

From 1868 to the 1950s, Tituba remained a "half breed Negro." It was Arthur Miller who took the final step in Tituba's ethnic evolution. He removed the last trace of her actual race, making her a "Negro slave." Miller also followed earlier tradition and made Tituba the performer of magical rituals before the girls in the Parris household. In *The Crucible*, Tituba stirs a witches' bubbling caldron and sacrifices toads. Miller had spent several days in the Salem courthouse reading the original court records, where he would have found no references to Tituba performing rituals of any kind. He relied, however, on Charles Upham's *Salem Witchcraft*, which said that Tituba practiced magic rites, learned from somewhere in the Caribbean, with the girls looking on. Miller's Tituba is thus a double fiction, a "Negro slave" and an expert at "conjuring."

Two African slaves, Mary Black of Salem Village and Candy of Salem Town, both referred to in the court records as "negro," were accused on April 21 and July 1, respectively. Like dozens of other defendants, Mary and Candy were never brought to trial by the Court of Oyer and Terminer. They were tried and cleared of all charges during the General Jail Delivery of 1693. The interesting question is why these two seemingly vulnerable African slaves, who had been compelled by the magistrates to give incriminating evidence in the courtroom, were not indicted and brought to trial, despite the Salem Village girls' performance of fits in their presence. Such evidence was produced against nearly all the defendants, and for more than two dozen, it led to formal trials and conviction. Why were the accusations against these two African slaves never taken seriously, despite the magistrates' and accusers' best efforts at their hearings?

Mary Black is identified in a complaint dated April 21, 1692, as "a Negro woman of Lieut. Nathaniel Putnam's." The complaint, issued by Thomas Putnam and John Buxton of Salem Village, accused a large number of people—six women and three men—of afflicting Ann Putnam Jr. and Mercy Lewis. Nathaniel Putnam, Mary Black's master, was the seventy-three-year-old church member and elder of the Putnam clan known by the informal honorific title of "Landlord Putnam."[6] He was a respected leader in the Village who had served as a deputy to the General Court in Boston and had been a selectman for Salem Town. But unlike most of his Putnam kinsmen,

Nathaniel was skeptical of the witchcraft excitement around him and did not join his relatives in their accusations. Indeed, he defended the innocence of his longtime neighbor Rebecca Nurse. It must have annoyed him that one of the complainants against Mary was his eager nephew Thomas and that two of the accusers were his grandnieces Ann Putnam Jr. and Mary Walcott, who had also accused Rebecca Nurse.[7] Nathaniel stood by Rebecca Nurse in the face of accusations by other Putnams and wrote a petition defending her innocence.

During Mary Black's preliminary examination, Magistrate Hathorne pressed her to admit that she was a witch. As a slave facing the court, she was surprisingly uncooperative in the face of Hathorne's aggressive interrogation. Her reluctance suggests that she may have been coached by Putnam to hold firm and deny everything: "Mary, you are accused of sundry acts of witchcraft: Tell me be you a Witch?—Silent. How long have you been a Witch? I cannot tell. But have you been a Witch? I cannot tell you. Why do you hurt these folks? I hurt no body. Who doth? I do not know." The judges turned to Benjamin Putnam, Nathaniel's son, who told the court that about a year earlier his father had said that "a man" had sat down with Mary. This may have been a reference to an encounter with a stranger or, perhaps, some sort of vision that Mary had experienced and reported to her master. When one of the magistrates asked Mary about it, she told him that the man did not say anything to her. Hathorne then turned to Mary's young accusers, Ann Putnam Jr., Mary Walcott, and Mercy Lewis, all of whom had accused Rebecca Nurse: "Doth this Negro hurt you? Several of them said yes." When one of the justices noticed that Mary was nervously clutching her neck scarf, he asked, "Do you prick sticks?," implying that she was using the pins in her scarf to "prick" the girls. "No, I pin my neck cloth," said Mary. Then came the justices' attempt to make Mary incriminate herself: "Well take out a pin, & pin it again." When Mary did this, "several of the afflicted [girls] cried out that they were pricked. Mary Walcott was pricked in the arm till the blood came, Abigail Williams was pricked in the stomach & Mercy Lewes was pricked in the foot." It was Parris who recorded Mary's examination.[8] On the basis of this evidence, Mary was sent to jail in Boston, but she was not brought to trial in 1692.

Why was she accused in the first place, the slave of the venerable Nathaniel Putnam? A month earlier, Ann Putnam Jr. and Mary Walcott had accused Rebecca Nurse, and, in light of Nathaniel Putnam's later defense of Nurse, it seems likely that he let his skepticism be known. His skepticism may have aroused Ann's and Mary's desire to retaliate by accusing his slave Mary.[9] Nathaniel himself never made any charges against her, and no one else in the Village supported the girls' accusations against her. Despite the aggressive efforts by the magistrates and her accusers, who had helped to condemn so many others, no one came forward with stories of affliction. The much-respected Nathaniel Putnam was apparently too powerful a protector. When Mary was put on trial by the Superior Court of Judicature in January 1693 for the purpose of clearing the jails, nobody appeared against her, and she was "Cleer'd by proclamacon."

Candy was the name of a slave of Margaret Hawkes of Salem Town, formerly of Barbados. Both Candy and Hawkes were accused on July 1, 1692, two months after the accusations were made against Mary Black. Candy was accused by Thomas Putnam and his nephew John Putnam Jr. Unlike Mary Black, Candy readily confessed. Her examination in court began with the usual question: "Candy! are you a witch?" Candy replied, "Candy no witch in her country. Candy's mother no witch. Candy no witch, [in] Barbados." She went on to explain that her mistress had made her a witch. Intrigued, the justices asked, "What did your mistress do to make you a witch?" The record continues: "A[nswer]: Mistress bring book and pen and ink, make Candy write in it. Q[uestion]: What did you write in it?—She took a pen and ink and upon a book or paper made a mark." Here, Candy was making use of the concept of "signing the devil's book," making a pact with the Devil, thereby gaining demonic powers. Wanting to know more, the justices asked her how she afflicted her victims. The usual means was to use a poppet, or doll-like effigy, to represent the witch's intended victim. "How did you afflict or hurt these folks, where are the puppets you did it with?—She [Candy] asked to go out of the room and she would show or tell . . . and she presently brought in two clouts [cloths], one with two knots tied in it [to represent a poppet]." As soon as Candy's accusers saw them, "they were greatly affrighted and fell into violent fits." The accusers said they saw the specters of the black man together with Mrs. Hawkes and Candy pinching the poppets, and they were afflicted. The magistrates and the Reverend Nicholas Noyes, who was present in the courtroom, then experimented with the poppets to confirm their effect. The record states that "a bit of one of the rags being set on fire, the afflicted all said they were burned, and cried out dreadfully." Another piece of the rag was put into water, "and two of the forenamed persons were in dreadful fits almost choked, and the other was violently running down to the river, but was stopped."[10] The evidence of witchcraft must have been clear to everyone in the courtroom. And yet Attorney General Thomas Newton decided that it was not strong enough to bring Candy before the grand jury. Why not?

As in Mary Black's case, no one besides the afflicted girls came forward to accuse Candy, despite the young accusers' best courtroom performances. Nor is there any record indicating that Candy's mistress, Margaret Hawkes, was apprehended in response to the girls' accusations. Candy's attempt to place the blame on her mistress may not have been taken seriously, coming as it did from a slave, but another explanation for the court's lack of interest in prosecuting Hawkes may lie in the honorific "Mrs." that was used with her name. The title indicates that Margaret Hawkes was someone of high social status, a woman, now a widow, who had been married to an important member of the community. Although Margaret Hawkes was named in the same complaint as Candy, apparently her social status protected her. The court appears to have been more interested in ascertaining the power of Candy's poppets than in pursuing Candy's case any further. On January 6, 1693, the Superior Court of Judicature found Candy "not guilty."

Historians have noted that about 80 percent of the people who were accused of witchcraft in New England were women, and that most were older women (over the age of forty) and of lower social class. Men who were accused were less likely to be tried and convicted, and their penalties were less severe. In Salem, the ratio of accused women to men was about four to one.

In early colonial New England, witchcraft accusations were used to control and punish people, especially women, for what was regarded as socially deviant behavior, usually quarreling and cursing their neighbors. As David Hall reminds us, the term "witch-hunting" is preferable to "witchcraft" because there were actually no witches worshiping the devil and signing the devil's book—although many people confessed to doing so to save themselves—but there were witch-hunts. The term "witch" was also applied to women who did not conform to the restrictive norms of a patriarchal society.[11] Carol Karlsen points out a number of cases in which women who inherited wealth, either as single women or widows, were charged with witchcraft by men, usually relatives, attempting to take their money. Wealth was usually held by men, including a married woman's money and property, and a single woman with money and property gained through inheritance and with no male heirs represented a disruption of the normal transfer of wealth.[12]

The New England accusers came from all ranks of society. Most were adults between twenty and fifty years old, and most were male. In Salem, as we have seen, the most active accusers were girls and young women twenty years old and younger. Not until recently have scholars pursued the general question of why women in Puritan society (as well as Catholic and Protestant Europe) were the major targets of witchcraft accusations.

Mary Beth Norton has pointed to some of the telling passages in the Puritan divine Richard Bernard's *Guide to Grand-Jury Men,* which the ministers and Salem magistrates read and followed. For Bernard, the susceptibility of women to initiate acts of witchcraft goes back to the biblical Eve. Although Bernard indicates that witches can be of either gender, he states they are more likely to be women because "Satan is setting upon these [women] rather then on men, since his unhappy onset and prevailing with *Eve.*" Because of Eve, Bernard says, Satan preferred to deal with women; they were "more credulous" and "more malicious" when displeased, and "more apt to bitter cursing, and far more revengeful" than men. Thus he concluded that women were "more fit instruments of the Devil."[13]

This does not mean that Puritans believed that women were naturally more sinful. Women, in fact, made up the majority of church members, New England's Elect of God. Women, however, were deemed to be more vulnerable to Satan's temptations, like the biblical Eve. The historian Elizabeth Reis explains that New England Puritans, like their European Catholic and Protestant counterparts, believed that because women's bodies were physically weaker than men's, "the weaker bodies of women rendered their souls more accessible to Satan."[14] Carol Karlsen points out that the much-respected Samuel Willard, minister of Boston's Third Church, defined Eve as Satan's "willing agent" in the Garden of Eden because she acted "upon deliberation and was voluntary in what she did."[15] Commenting on Genesis, Willard stated that "the last instrumental cause of the Transgression, was the Woman"; that is, in the chain of causation from Satan's temptation of Eve to Eve's temptation of Adam, Eve was the final cause of original sin, the Fall of humanity from God's grace. Thus women, forever inherently tainted by Eve's weakness, were deemed more likely to give in to Satan's temptations and turn to witchcraft, which was his sphere. By contrast, Samuel Willard saw Adam, as the first human being God created, to be imprinted with God's moral rectitude and goodness. The view that women were the conduit of the devil is as old as the early church fathers. The second-century Tertullian put it most strongly: "*You* are the *devil's* gateway: *you* are the unsealer of that (forbidden) tree: *you* are the first deserter of the divine law: *you* are she who persuaded him whom the *devil* was not valiant enough to attack. *You* destroyed so easily God's image, man."[16] Karlsen concludes, "Eve was in Puritan culture the main symbol of woman-as-evil. She was in many ways the archetypal witch."[17]

Witchcraft was also understood to be motivated by feelings of pride, discontent, envy, jealousy, and malicious thoughts. These, said Willard, are the very sins that made human beings act like devils and turn to Satan. As Elizabeth Reis points out, some of the women who confessed to witchcraft said they had harbored feelings of depravity and believed that they were probably guilty of witchcraft, although unaware of it.[18] Forty women confessed in the Salem courtroom, compared to only four men.

The Salem court records frequently mention one type of witchcraft—the sticking of pins or thorns into dolls, called poppets, representing the victims. Association with the making of dolls (poppets were made from rags) is women's craft, and sewing pins and needles are women's tools.

From the point of view of the ministers, accusers, and judges, the primary instigator of the Salem story was the devil. He appeared first to Tituba, who said he looked like a "man" dressed in black clothes. The devil revealed himself to Tituba in Samuel Parris's house, together with Sarah Good and Sarah Osborne and two unknown female witches that he had brought along with him. One of the witches wore a black silk hood; the other wore a white hood. The devil had not appeared to the young accusers before Tituba saw him, but afterward he appeared to them in the form of the "black man." He became the girls' constant tormentor and the tormentor of the confessed witches. Tituba also said that the devil sometimes appeared to her as a hog or a great black dog. But his appearance as "the black man" was the one appropriated by the Salem Village girls, and the term "black man" occurs more than one hundred times in the court records, from the first to the last of the proceedings.

The black man made his first spectral appearance in the courtroom on March 21, during the hearing of Martha Cory, who was the next to be examined after Tituba. During her interrogation, Mary Walcott and Abigail Williams said they saw "a Black man whispering in her [Cory's] ear," presumably telling her to deny that she was a witch.[19] The girls said the same thing three days later at Rebecca Nurse's examination, when Ann Putnam Sr. claimed that in a fit she saw Nurse with the "black man" in spectral form. A month later, he was seen by Abigail Hobbs and then by Abigail's stepmother, Deliverance Hobbs. He was subsequently seen by all the afflicted accusers both inside and outside the courtroom. The last reference to him in court was on September 16, when eleven-year-old Johanna Tyler of Andover told of his attempt to make her "sett my hand to his book."[20] Dozens of depositions from March through September told of the "black man" torturing the afflicted girls and confessing women.

Mary Toothaker's vision of the devil in the shape of a "tawny man" who promised to protect her from the Indians was influenced by her fear of Indian attacks. She was the only witness during the Salem trials to say that the devil appeared in shape of an Indian. Indians could be seen as black. According to Sarah Osborne's testimony, she "saw a thing like an indian all black which did pinch her." Cotton Mather also noted that although people referred to the devil as a "black man," they "generally say that he resembles an Indian."[21] Seeing the devil as an Indian is understandable from the seventeenth-century New England perspective, when Indians annihilated so many settlements during King Philip's War, but the Salem court records' consistent reference to his blackness, without any ethnic identity, indicates that the devil's color transcended ethnic categories. New Englanders saw the devil as black because he was the personification of the absolute darkness of evil.

A Note on Court Records, Dates, and Names

Seventeenth-century English law required written records of cases that were brought to court. As they concerned a capital crime, witchcraft cases necessitated a full set of records, from the first stage of complaints, arrest warrants, and preliminary hearings, through the second stage of indictments and grand jury hearings, and the final stage of trials and verdicts. There are nearly 950 extant court records pertaining to the witch trials of 1692. Some are dated well beyond 1692 and relate to the lengthy legal aftermath through 1750. As the defendants' cases moved through the legal process, more documents accumulated, and additional incriminating information was sometimes added to records from earlier stages. More than 1,400 different names appear in the records, including those of accusers and accused (and family members of both), ministers, magistrates, sheriffs, constables, jurors, deponents, witnesses, defenders of the accused, scribes of some records, attorneys general, jail keepers, and even the blacksmiths who made the iron shackles. The Salem Witch Trials Documentary Archive enables users to search for all the names, regardless of variant spellings.

The records of the preliminary hearings are the products of the best literate hands available in and around Salem at the time. But in the few cases in which two independent records of the same examination exist, comparison reveals that they are not verbatim transcriptions of the dialogue in the courtroom. The court-appointed recorders were well-educated local men using quill pens that had to be dipped frequently in ink. They attempted to record fast-paced dialogue delivered in an emotionally charged setting. To keep up with the flow of dialogue in the courtroom, recorders may have used shorthand-like characters from which they later reconstructed their accounts, but no such notes are known to exist. Corrections to the examination records were also made after they were written, and sometimes additional information was added.[1] During the hearings, the recorders—who were biased observers in full agreement with the prosecution—selected the elements of dialogue that they deemed important. Whatever was said in court that the recorders did not consider relevant was not written down and is lost from the official record.

There are a few third-party eyewitness accounts of examinations written from a perspective that is favorable to the defendant, and these reveal different information, such as Nathaniel Cary's account of his wife Elizabeth's examination, John Alden's account of his own examination, and Lawson's accounts of the Cary and Nurse examainations. The most objective description we have of certain aspects of the examinations comes from Thomas Brattle. For example, Brattle tried to expose the magistrates' mistaken assumptions about the effects of the touch test and the defendants' "look" upon the accusers by describing only what he saw, not what he believed he saw. In Brattle's words: "The Justices order the apprehended to look upon the said children, which accordingly they do; and at the time of that look, (I dare not say by that look, as the Salem Gentlemen do) the afflicted are cast into a fitt."[2]

The accuracy of the depositions is also questionable. Depositions were written outside the court by third parties, friends of the deponents, paid scribes, court clerks, or the deponents themselves. The depositions often use stock phrases, and in cases where they were written down by someone other than the deponent, they state what the writer understood to be the main points, perhaps using words and phrases that were not the deponents' own. It is also likely that most deponents could not read the cursive script of their depositions to check their accuracy. Nevertheless, the depositions that the attorneys general selected for use as evidence in the trials were always read back to the deponents in court, and the deponents then swore to their accuracy, putting their signatures or marks at the bottom of the depositions. Stephen Sewall, the clerk of the special Court of Oyer and Terminer, confirmed the sworn oaths by writing *Jurat in Curia* (swears in court) on such depositions.

It is estimated that a large number of people (more than 250) took part in writing the records (examinations, depositions, warrants, and indictments) that survive. Thus there was a large scope for error and bias. The presence of an indeterminate amount of inaccuracy and bias in the court records, especially the examination records, has not, however, proved paralyzing for historians. The records used in the hearings and trials constituted the substance of the legal process and were used to condemn the defendants. Magistrates and witnesses attested to them, and so did the confessors who signed their own confessions, even though they knew they were patently false.

Granted, the problem of inaccuracy is always relevant. But this question does not obscure the fact that what mattered in the court's decisions were the words and behavior that were recorded, described, and attested to in the court records. The magistrates, juries, witnesses, and defendants acted on the proceedings and events that they witnessed in court and were described in the court records, and they were the basis for the legal actions taken.

There is a significant gap, however, in the body of surviving records. The records of the trials of the special Court of Oyer and Terminer from June through September 1692 do not survive. By contrast, the summary record of the subsequent trials conducted by the newly created Superior Court of Judicature from January through May 1693 do survive and have been bound into a single volume. What happened to the records of the proceedings of the 1692 trials is not known. References to such records occur in the petitions to the General Court in 1710 for restitution to the families of several of those executed in 1692.[3]

In 1867, Charles Upham noted the absence of these records and suggested that they were deliberately destroyed in order to blot out the shameful memory of the tragedy. More recently, Mary Beth Norton has proposed the same interpretation. Public opinion having turned against the trials, the Salem magistrates or their descendants, Norton suggests, might have destroyed the records so that the magistrates' role would not reflect badly upon them.[4]

Nevertheless, although the summary record of the trials of 1692 does not exist (or has not yet been found), most of the records that were selected for use in the trials do exist, in addition to the large number of documents that were not selected for use. Judging from the brief summary record of the trials by the Superior Court of Judicature of 1693, which disposed of the backlog of witchcraft cases from 1692, the 1692 record of the trials of the Court of Oyer and Terminer may have been little more than a brief summary of the indictments, with references to "evidences and examinations" presented in court, and a statement of the verdicts.[5] Given the fact that most of the records used at the Salem trials do exist in addition to other contemporary accounts, scholars are fully confident that a substantive historical account can be written.

The transcriptions presented in the *Salem Witchcraft Papers* (*SWP*) modernize archaic spelling conventions and abbreviations for ease of reading. See the online *SWP* for further explanation. For the purposes of scholarly research, the transcriptions in the *RSWH* should be taken as authoritative.

Until 1752, the English calendar began the new year on March 25, and the period from January 1 to March 24 belonged to the previous year. But by the 1670s, the English had begun to combine the two calendars. Thus, March 24, 1691, was often written as March 24, 1691/2, which is March 24, 1692, by our present-day calendar. The court records of the Salem witch trials, as well as various record books, generally use the combined dating convention, for example, 1691/2.

_____

The surnames of Cory and Procter (as well as others) are spelled in various ways in the source records. In keeping with other scholarship, I have standardized these names in my own text.

NOTES

Abbreviations
"Church Record Book"
  "Church Record Book Belonging to Salem Village," 1689–1717, First Church
  of Danvers Congregational, United Church of Christ, deposited in the Danvers
  Archival Center, Danvers, Mass.
RSWH
  Records of the Salem Witch-Hunt, Bernard Rosenthal, general editor (Cambridge:
  Cambridge University Press, 2009)
SVW
  *Salem-Village Witchcraft: A Documentary Record of Local Conflict in Colonial
  England,* edited by Paul Boyer and Stephen Nissenbaum (Boston: Northeastern
  University Press, 1993; originally published 1972)
SWP
  The Salem Witchcraft Papers, http://salem.lib.virginia.edu/texts/tei/swp
"Village Record Book"
  "A Book of Record of the Severall Publique Transactions of the Inhabitants of
  Salem Village Vulgarly Called the Farmes 1672–1713," Danvers Archival Center,
  Peabody Institute Library, Danvers, Mass., http://salem.lib.virginia.edu/texts/tei
  /SalVRec

Introduction
  Epigraph from Brattle, "Letter."
 1 Brattle, "Letter," 182.
 2 Phips, "Letters of Governor Phips," 201; the introduction draws on material in
    Ray, "Salem Witch Mania."
 3 Boyer and Nissenbaum, *Salem Possessed,* 33–35.
 4 See Rosenthal, *Salem Story,* 29–30; and Norton, *In the Devil's Snare,* 40–41.
 5 Boyer and Nissenbaum, *Salem Possessed,* 35.
 6 Norton, *In the Devil's Snare,* 300.
 7 Caporael, "Ergotism: The Satan Loosed in Salem?"; Spanos and Gottlieb, "Er-
    gotism and the Salem Village Witch Trials"; Woolf, "Witchcraft or Mycotoxin?";
    Carlson, *A Fever in Salem.*
 8 Rosenthal, *Salem Story,* 19–20ff.; Rosenthal, "General Introduction," 21–35. Nor-
    ton suggests a more nuanced view: that at the beginning, the girls' torments were

psychologically genuine but later sometimes deliberately faked, and that, for some, PTSD may have been involved (*In the Devil's Snare*, 307–8).

9 For the argument that there was witchcraft in Salem, see Hansen, *Witchcraft at Salem*. As Bernard Rosenthal points out, Hansen's argument is based entirely on the testimony of people who confessed to save themselves from trial and gave evidence against others in order to validate their confessions (see Rosenthal, *Salem Story*, 78–82).

10 Brattle, "Letter," 190.

1. Samuel Parris and the New Covenant

First epigraph from Parris, *Sermon Notebook;* second epigraph from Lawson, *Christ's Fidelity*.

1 *SVW*, 171.

2 See Latner, "Here Are No Newters," 92–122.

3 Gragg, *Quest for Security*, chap. 1.

4 D. Hall, *Faithful Shepherd*, chap. 8.

5 Gragg, *Quest for Security*, 49; cf. *SVW*, 349.

6 *Records of the First Church in Salem*, 169.

7 Ibid., 169–70.

8 Parris, *Sermon Notebook*, 38.

9 *Records of the First Church in Salem*, 170.

10 Stout, *New England Soul*, 89.

11 For the issues facing second-generation preachers and their responses to these issues, see D. Hall, *Faithful Shepherd*.

12 Parris, *Sermon Notebook*, 44, 49.

13 Gragg, *Quest for Security*, 51.

14 Parris, *Sermon Notebook*, 44, 48–49, 51.

15 Ibid., 190, 50. In the context of the New Testament, the distinction between "clean" and "unclean" relates to the betrayal of Christ. The words appear in the Gospel of John 13, which relates the story of the Last Supper and Jesus's washing of the feet of his disciples. In John 13:11, Jesus distinguishes between the disciples who are "clean" and the one disciple who will betray him: "For he knew who should betray him; therefore said he, Ye are not all cleane" (KJV). Parris would soon be accusing his opponents of acting like Judas and betraying him. For more on the Reverend John Oxenbridge and the First Church of Boston, see Hill, *History of the Old South Church*, 2:40–49.

16 Brown and Hall, "Family Strategies and Religious Practice," 42; see also Gerbner, "Beyond the 'Halfway Covenant.'"

17 "Church Record Book," 3; *SVW*, 270.

18 "Church Record Book," 4; *SVW*, 271.

19 The church in Salem went even further and allowed halfway members to partake of communion (Pope, *The Half-Way Covenant*, 140–45, 193).

20 Oxenbridge, *New England Freemen Warned*, 44; Simmons, "Founding of the Third Church," 250.

21 Cf. Gragg, *Quest for Security*, 68.

22 Parris's list of birth records in the "Church Record Book" shows a strong correlation between the men and women who joined the new congregation as full members and the children born to them soon after Parris's arrival. (For birth records recorded by Parris, see Roach, "Records of the Rev. Samuel Parris, Salem Village," 6–30.)

23 *SVW*, 350–51; cf. Gragg, *Quest for Security*, 87.

24 Cf. Cooper and Minkema, introduction to Parris, *Sermon Notebook*, 27n36.

25 Parris, *Sermon Notebook*, 126, 147–48.

26 Ibid., 148.

27 Ibid., 65; Eusden, introduction to Ames, *Marrow of Theology*, 28.

28 Parris, *Sermon Notebook*, 64.

29 Ibid., 83, 182, 194.

30 Latner, "Here Are No Newters," 95.

31 The newly elected committee members were Joseph Porter, Joseph Hutchinson, Joseph Putnam, Daniel Andrew, and Francis Nurse. They would remain opposed to Parris from this point onward.

32 Parris took note of what the new committee had done in the "Church Record Book" and listed the names of the members. He immediately called a meeting of church elders to tell the new committee to raise the funds for his salary and resume supplying his firewood ("Church Record Book," 10; *SVW*, 276–77).

33 Boyer and Nissenbaum, *Salem Possessed*, 68.

34 *SVW*, 277.

35 Cooper and Minkema, introduction to Parris, *Sermon Notebook*, 20.

36 Parris, *Sermon Notebook*, 184.

37 On the calculation of this date, see the note about seventeenth-century English calendar dates on page 212 of this volume.

38 Calef, *More Wonders*, 341–42.

39 Hale, *Modest Inquiry*, 414.

40 Ibid.

41 Norton, *In the Devil's Snare*, 19.

42 Patton, *Doctor's Dilemma*, 13; Norton, *In the Devil's Snare*, 19. Rachel Hubbard Griggs was admitted to membership in the First Church in 1659. Parris's wife, Elizabeth Eldridge, was admitted in 1671, and Parris was admitted two years later in 1672 (*Records of the First Church in Boston*, 58, 68, 87, 335).

43 Perley, *History of Salem*, 3:256. In 1695, when two petitions appeared—one petition for Parris's remaining as the Village minister, the other against—Griggs signed the petition supporting his continuation.

44 Hale, *Modest Inquiry*, 413.

45 Parris, *Sermon Notebook*, 188, 191.

46 For an explanation of the witch-cake procedure, see Calef, *More Wonders*, 342, and Hale, *Modest Inquiry*, 413.

47 *SVW*, 278.

48 Hale, *Modest Inquiry*, 414.

49 Members of the Rebecca Nurse family also reported that Parris initially allowed the girls to enact their torments during church services ("Church Record Book," 23; *SVW*, 296).

50 Gragg, *Quest for Security*, 125; Cotton Mather, *Diary*, 1:151–52.

51 Cooper and Minkema, introduction to Parris, *Sermon Notebook*, 6.

52 *RSWH* No. 3/*SWP* No. 63.3.

53 Hale, *Modest Inquiry*, 411. On the concept of "refuser's guilt," see Briggs, *Witches and Neighbors*, 140–41.

54 *RSWH* No. 5/*SWP* No. 63.6.

55 *RSWH* No. 345/*SWP* No. 63.7.

56 "Sarah Osburn Her Examination," *RSWH* No. 4/*SWP* No. 95.1.

57 Sarah Osborne's first husband was Robert Prince, brother of Rebecca Prince, who was the wife of John Putnam, one of the most influential men in Salem Village.

58 *RSWH* No. 3/*SWP* No. 95.2.

2. *Tituba's Confession*

Epigraph from *RSWH* No. 3/*SWP* No. 125.4.

1 See Rosenthal, *Salem Story*, chap. 1, and Rosenthal, "Tituba's Story," 190–203. Historians have also dismissed Tituba's African and African American identity for lack of evidence (see Hansen, "The Metamorphosis of Tituba"; and Rosenthal, *Salem Story*, 13).

2 Norton, *In the Devil's Snare*, 21.

3 See also Rosenthal, *Salem Story*, chap. 1; Breslaw, "Tituba's Confession."

4 Tituba was present in the meetinghouse during Good's and Osborne's examinations (see *RSWH* No. 3/*SWP* No. 125.4).

5 A witch cake was made by mixing rye meal and the bewitched person's urine (see Calef, *More Wonders*, 342, for an explanation of the procedure).

6 Calef, *More Wonders*, 343. "The account she since gives of it is, that her Master did beat her and otherways abuse her, to make her confess and accuse (such as he call'd) her Sister-Witches, and that whatsoever she said by way of confessing or

accusing others, was the effect of such usage; her Master refused to pay her Fees, unless she would stand to what she had said."

7 "Being searched by a Woman, she was found to have upon her body the marks of the Devils wounding of her" (Hale, *Modest Inquiry*, 415).

8 *RSWH* No. 345/*SWP* No. 63.7.

9 *RSWH* No. 6/*SWP* No. 125.5.

10 Perkins, *A Discourse of the Damned Art of Witchcraft*. Sanderson was appointed deacon in 1665 at the time when the controversy over the Halfway Covenant in the First Church reached its crisis and would have been a strong supporter of Parris. (Gragg, *A Quest for Security*, 128–29; Hill, *History of the Old South Church*, 1:40–49).

11 *RSWH* No. 345/*SWP* No. 63.7.

12 The king's attorney general in Boston, Thomas Newton, who oversaw the initial prosecutions for the trials, wrote a summary of Tituba's evidence against Sarah Good that shows he regarded Tituba as a reliable witness. Hathorne's list of dates of examinations of Good, Osborne, and Tituba, written on March 7, indicates that Tituba was examined on four different occasions (on March 1, 2, 3, and 5), so vital was her testimony about the nature and extent of Satan's plot against the Village (*RSWH* No. 4/*SWP* No. 125.3). The only records of Tituba's examinations that survive are those of March 1 and 2.

13 Joseph Putnam's name does not turn up as the recorder of any other surviving court record.

14 As Peter Grund has shown, none of the records of the preliminary examinations can be taken as verbatim accounts of what was said in court, even though the accounts are often written as direct speech and appear to be verbatim transcriptions of courtroom dialogue (see Grund, "From Tongue to Text").

15 The main elements of Tituba's first two examinations are corroborated by Attorney General Thomas Newton's summary of Tituba's evidence against Sarah Good (*RSWH* No. 345/*SWP* No. 63.7).

16 *RSWH* No. 3/*SWP* No. 125.4.

17 *RSWH* No. 6/*SWP* No. 125.5.

18 *RSWH* No. 6/*SWP* No. 125.5.

19 *RSWH* No. 3/*SWP* No. 125.4; *Vital Records of Salem, Massachusetts, Births* (vol. 1); cf. Roach, "Biographical Notes," 936.

20 *RSWH* No. 6/*SWP* Nos. 125.5, 125.6.

21 *RSWH* No. 6/*SWP* Nos. 125.5, 125.6. For convenience, I have converted the old calendar dates to the modern calendar in this account; please see page 212 for a note on old-style calendar dating.

22 Parris, *Sermon Notebook*, 188.

23 *RSWH* No. 6/*SWP* Nos. 125.5, 125.6.

24 On the subject of Parris's sermons and religious discord in the Village, see Gragg, *Quest for Security;* Cooper and Minkema, introduction to Parris, *Sermon Notebook;* Latner, "Here Are No Newters"; and Ray, "Satan's War."

25 Hale also noted that during her examination in prison Tituba was "herself afflicted and complained of her fellow Witches tormenting of her, for her confession, and accusing them" (*Modest Inquiry*, 415). Breslaw also suggests that "Tituba's credibility to her Salem audience was enhanced by her identity as an American Indian whose culture had long been associated with demonic power" ("Tituba's Confession," 536).

26 Lawson, *Christ's Fidelity,* 93–94.

27 Bernard, *Guide to Grand-Jury Men,* chap. 1.

28 Lawson, *Christ's Fidelity,* 94, 102, 104.

29 Parris, *Sermon Notebook,* 194–95.

30 Ibid., 194–97.

31 Ibid., 198.

32 *RSWH* No. 844/*SWP* No. 125.7.

33 Calef, *More Wonders,* 343. The account submitted by Salem's jail keeper, William Dounton, says: "for Tetabe Indan [Tituba Indian] A whole year and 10 month" (*RSWH* No. 857). If this account is correct, Tituba would have left jail sometime in December 1693.

3. *The Village Girls Who Cried "Witch!"*

First epigraph from *RSWH* No. 3/*SWP* No. 63.3; second epigraph from Lawson, *Brief and True Narrative.*

1 Hale, *Modest Inquiry,* 413–14.

2 Calef, *More Wonders,* 342.

3 Cotton Mather, *Memorable Providences,* 4.

4 *SVW,* 278.

5 *RSWH* No. 185/*SWP* No. 137.36. Sarah's death occurred on December 17, 1689 (*New England Historic Genealogical Society* 36 [1862]: 88).

6 *RSWH* No. 6/*SWP* No. 125.5.

7 Her great-aunt Rachel Hubbard Griggs was in fact named by young Benjamin Gould on April 11, but this accusation was not followed up, given the social standing of Dr. Griggs in the Salem community (*RSWH* No. 49/*SWP* No. 106.4).

8 *RSWH* No. 345/*SWP* No. 63.7.

9 *RSWH* No. 3/*SWP* No. 63.3.

10 Cotton Mather, *Memorable Providences,* 8.

11 See Nathaniel Cary's account of his wife's examination, *RSWH* No. 203/*SWP* No. 29.2.

12 Lawson, *Brief and True Narrative*, 153–54.

13 Cotton Mather reported similar behavior in his account of the Goodwin case: "They would *fly* like *Geese;* and be carried with an incredible *Swiftness* thro the *air,* having, but just their *Toes* now and then upon the ground, and their *Arms* waved like the Wings" (Cotton Mather, *Memorable Providences,* 14).

14 Lawson, *Brief and True Narrative,* 153–54.

15 Ibid., 154.

16 Lawson, *Christ's Fidelity,* 80.

17 Lawson, *Brief and True Narrative,* 156.

18 Norton, *In the Devil's Snare,* 48–50.

19 *RSWH* No. 18/*SWP* No. 38.12.

20 *RSWH* No. 16/*SWP* No. 38.3.

21 Ibid.

22 Brattle, "Letter," 187. Brattle's critical observation about the girls' behavior also applies to today's biomedical interpretations. For critical comment on the ergot theory and similar biomedical interpretations, with references, see Spanos and Gottlieb, "Ergotism and the Salem Village Witch Trials"; Spanos, "Ergotism and the Salem Panic"; and Woolf, "Witchcraft or Mycotoxin?" For a diagnosis of cerebral meningitis, see Carlson, *A Fever in Salem.*

23 Some historians attribute the accusation of Martha Cory to the Village's disapproval of her having an illegitimate mulatto son (Boyer and Nissenbaum, *Salem Possessed,* 146n25; Norton, *In the Devil's Snare,* 47). A document in the Massachusetts Registry of Deeds, Southern Essex County, Historic Records, Book 13:208, refers to one of the wives of Giles Cory, an "English woman," as having a "mulatto son" who was named Benoni, which means, "child of my sorrow," born in 1677. But Giles Corey had three wives, and the document does not give the name of the wife in question.

24 Boyer and Nissenbaum, *Salem Possessed,* 149.

25 *RSWH* Nos. 267, 362/*SWP* Nos. 94.24, 94.25.

26 *RSWH* No. 35/*SWP* No. 94.27. Rebecca's two other sisters were accused and arrested. Sarah Cloyce, wife of Peter Cloyce of Salem Village, was arrested but not tried; Mary Esty, wife of Isaac Esty of Topsfield, was tried, convicted, and executed.

27 *RSWH* No. 28/*SWP* Nos. 94.2, 94.3. I owe this insight into Nurse's confusion to Richard Latner (personal communication, 2013).

28 Lawson, *Brief and True Narrative,* 161.

29 *RSWH* Nos. 501, 46, 58/*SWP* Nos. 107.8, 106.2, 106.3, 107.7.

30 *RSWH* No. 262/*SWP* No. 135.5. In a separate deposition, Mary English confirmed the Bishops' as well as Mary Esty's doubts about the afflicted girls being "dis-

tracted," that is, "confused or troubled in the mind" (*Oxford English Dictionary*) (*RSWH* No. 263/*SWP* 135.6).

31 *RSWH* No. 75/*SWP* No. 135.1; Lawson, *Brief and True Narrative*, 162. Burr's note is mistaken: the "Mary W." in Lawson's account refers to Mary Warren, not Mary Walcott.

32 This account of the Esty case is put together from the following records: *RSWH* Nos. 79, 86, 191, 192, 204, 206, 362, 601/*SWP* Nos. 136.1, 45.3, 45.12, 45.11, 45.19, 45.16, 94.25, 45.21.

33 *RSWH* Nos. 240, 244, 245/*SWP* Nos. 38.8, 94.17, 106.13; cf. Norton, *In the Devil's Snare*, 56.

34 *RSWH* No. 457/*SWP* No. 22.18.

35 *RSWH* Nos. 310, 235, 80/*SWP* Nos. 75.3, 24.3, 135.3.

36 *RSWH* No. 86/*SWP* No. 45.3.

37 *RSWH* Nos. 133, 540/*SWP* Nos. 78.3, 98.4.

38 *RSWH* No. 17; Lawson, *Brief and True Narrative*, 156.

39 Calef, *More Wonders*, 359.

40 See Rosenthal's note to *RSWH* No. 245; *RSWH* No. 371/*SWP* No. 138.

41 *RSWH* Nos. 293, 364, 365, 366, 367, 368/*SWP* Nos. 73.1, 12.2, 12.3, 12.5, 12.1, 73.2.

42 Brattle, "Letter," 184.

43 Ibid., 170.

44 Calef, *More Wonders*, 160.

45 Cotton Mather, *Wonders*, 223.

4. The Magistrates

Epigraph from Brattle, "Letter."

1 Phips, "Letters of Governor Phips," 196; *RSWH* No. 220.

2 Boyer and Nissenbaum, *Salem Possessed*, 6.

3 Rosenthal, *Salem Story*, 29–30.

4 Sewall, *Diary*, 1:287–88.

5 The list of Governor's Council members was agreed upon by Sir Henry Ashurst and Increase Mather in England on September 18, 1691 (see Moody and Simmons, *Glorious Revolution in Massachusetts*, 598).

6 On the legal aspects of the intercharter period and its bearing on the witchcraft outbreak in Salem Village, see Konig, *Law and Society*, 169ff.

7 *SVW*, 276.

8 Young George Corwin was the magistrate's only surviving son. His four other sons died at an early age (*Vital Records of Salem, Massachusetts, Births*, 1:209, *Deaths*, 6:177; cf. Roach, "Biographical Notes," 936).

9 Phips, "Letters of Governor Phips," 196.

10 Hale, *Modest Inquiry*, 415; cf. Norton, *In the Devil's Snare*, 22.

11 John Hale, *Modest Inquiry*, 415–16, lists the several law books consulted by the magistrates: Richard Bernard, *Guide to Grand-Jury Men;* Joseph Glanvill, *Collection of Sundry Tryals in England and Ireland (1658);* Mathew Hale, *Tryal of Witches* (London, 1682); William Perkins, *A Discourse of the Damned Art of Witchcraft;* Joseph Keble, *An Assistance to Justices of the Peace* (London, 1683); in addition to Cotton Mather's *Memorable Providences Relating to Witchcrafts* (Boston, 1689).

12 Hale, *Modest Inquiry*, 413–14.

13 Rosenthal, "General Introduction," 18ff.

14 Ibid., 6.

15 Bernard, *Guide to Grand-Jury Men,* chap. 19, "Of the Manner of Examining Witches," 228.

16 Hale, *Modest Inquiry*, 415.

17 *RSWH* No. 17; Lawson, *Brief and True Narrative*, 155.

18 Lawson, *Brief and True Narrative*, 162.

19 Ibid., 148.

20 See McCarl, "Spreading the News," 39–61.

21 Increase Mather, *Illustrious Providences;* Cotton Mather, *Memorable Providences*.

22 In addition to William Griggs, four other local doctors are mentioned in the court records as endorsing witchcraft diagnoses in various cases.

23 *RSWH* No. 220.

24 Murrin, "Coming to Terms," 336.

25 *RSWH* No. 693/Phips, "Letters of Governor Phips," October 12, 1692.

26 See *RSWH* No. 836/Phips, "Letters of Governor Phips," February 21, 1693. The Crown's reply to Phips restates Phips's point that the court was set up to determine whether there was witchcraft or possession by the devil (*RSWH* No. 854).

27 John Demos, "A Diabolical Distemper," chap. 4 of Demos, *Entertaining Satan*.

28 Other Governor's Council members included Samuel Sewall and Thomas Danforth, the former deputy governor, who conducted George Burroughs's examination on May 9.

29 See Rosenthal's note to *RSWH* No. 186.

30 The nine magistrates were: John Richards (Boston), Peter Sargent (Boston), Wait Winthrop (Boston), William Stoughton (Dorchester), Nathaniel Saltonstall (Haverhill; later resigned), Samuel Sewall (Boston), John Hathorne (Salem), Jonathan Corwin (Salem), and Bartholomew Gedney (Salem).

31 Norton, *In the Devil's Snare*, 198.

32 Upham, *Salem Witchcraft*, 2:250.

33 Stoughton, "Letter," in Cotton Mather, *Wonders*, 212.

34 Hutchinson, "Witchcraft Delusion," 413.

35 Calef, *More Wonders,* 382.

36 Brattle, "Letter," 187–88; Calef, *More Wonders,* 387.

37 *RSWH* No. 313/*SWP* No. 13.22.

38 See Rosenthal, *Salem Story,* 69; and *RSWH* Nos. 273, 274, 275, 276, 313/*SWP* Nos. 13.3, 13.4, 13.5, 13.6, 13.22.

39 Rosen, *Witchcraft in England,* 57–58.

40 Cotton Mather, "Return of Several Ministers."

41 As in the notorious witchcraft trial at Bury St. Edmunds (see Murdock, *Increase Mather,* 294).

42 Bernard, *Guide to Grand-Jury Men,* 217–18.

43 Cotton Mather, "Return of Several Ministers."

44 Ibid.

45 Indeed, it would appear that the court could not have given primacy to spectral evidence without the approval of the Crown's attorneys, Newton and Checkley, who oversaw the prosecution of the Salem trials.

46 Trask, "Legal Procedures Used during the Salem Witch Trials," 49ff.; Rosenthal, "General Introduction," 21.

47 Stoughton, "Letter," in Cotton Mather, *Wonders,* A2.

48 *RSWH* Nos. 319, 320. Cf. Norton, *In the Devil's Snare,* 216.

49 Samuel Sewall, Wait Winthrop, and Peter Sergeant.

50 Peterson, "Ordinary Preaching," 99.

51 Calef, *More Wonders,* 360.

52 Cotton Mather to John Richards, in *Selected Letters,* 36.

53 Cotton Mather to John Foster, in *Selected Letters,* 41–43.

54 Pike, "Letter from R. P. to Jonathan Corwin," in Upham, *Salem Witchcraft,* 2:538.

55 Upham, *Salem Witchcraft,* 2:541.

5. *Reports of Witches' Meetings*

First epigraph from Lawson, *Brief and True Narrative;* second epigraph from *RSWH* No. 525/*SWP* 9.4.

1 Parts of this chapter appeared in Ray, "They Did Eat Red Bread Like Mans Flesh."

2 Under the 1691 Massachusetts charter, church membership was no longer required to vote in elections or to hold political office. Eligibility was based on financial means, which greatly enlarged the electorate.

3 *RSWH* No. 6/*SWP* No. 125.6.

4 Lawson, *Brief and True Narrative,* 156.

5 Ibid., 160–61.

6 Ibid., 161.

7 Lawson, *Christ's Fidelity*, 94–95.

8 *RSWH* No. 49/*SWP* No. 106.4.

9 *RSWH* No. 77/*SWP* No. 69.3.

10 *RSWH* No. 95/*SWP* No. 70.2.

11 *RSWH* Nos. 168, 145/*SWP* Nos. 21.1, 135.4.

12 *RSWH* No. 255/*SWP* No. 22.29.

13 *RSWH* Nos. 342, 345/*SWP* Nos. 70.3, 63.7.

14 *RSWH* No. 419/*SWP* No. 59.4.

15 *RSWH* Nos. 441, 442/*SWP* Nos. 128.2, 128.4.

16 *RSWH* No. 424/*SWP* Nos. 87.5, 87.7.

17 *RSWH* No. 508/*SWP* No. 83.2.

18 *RSWH* No. 519/*SWP* No. 103.1.

19 *RSWH* No. 525/*SWP* No. 9.4.

20 Brattle, "Letter," 189.

21 Calef, *More Wonders,* 376.

22 Hale, *Modest Inquiry,* 416.

23 Cotton Mather, *Wonders* (1693), 16–19.

6. *Thomas Putnam*

First epigraph from *RSWH* No. 82/*SWP* No. 22.20; second epigraph from *RSWH* No. 11/*SWP* No. 95.4.

1 The documents written by Thomas Putnam are identified in the notes to the transcriptions in *RSWH*.

2 Upham, *Salem Witchcraft,* 2:295. On the extensive role of Thomas Putnam on behalf of the prosecution, see Rosenthal, "General Introduction," 30ff.; and Trask, "Legal Procedures," 46–47.

3 *RSWH* No. 3/*SWP* No. 125.4.

4 *RSWH* No. 30/*SWP* No. 94.29.

5 *RSWH* Nos. 269, 185/*SWP* Nos. 137.18, 137.36.

6 Lawson, *Brief and True Narrative,* 157.

7 *RSWH* No. 30/*SWP* No. 94.29.

8 *RSWH* No. 82/*SWP* No. 22.20.

9 Lawson, *Christ's Fidelity,* 94; Parris, *Sermon Notebook,* 195.

10 *RSWH* No. 49/*SWP* No. 106.4.

11 *RSWH* Nos. 85, 457/*SWP* Nos. 22.28, 22.18.

12 *RSWH* Nos. 125, 126, 457/*SWP* Nos. 22.21 (see frontispiece), 22.34, 22.18.

13 *RSWH* No. 82/*SWP* No. 22.20.

14 *RSWH* No. 122/*SWP* No. 22.26

15 *RSWH* No. 124/*SWP* No. 22.24.

16 *RSWH* No. 866/*SWP* No. 171.2.

17 "Will of Giles Coaree," Massachusetts Registry of Deeds, Southern Essex County, Historic Records, Book 9:46 (July 25, 1692).

18 Sewall, *Diary,* 1:295–96.

19 The amount of the fine is not recorded (*Records and Files of the Quarterly Courts of Essex County,* 6:190–91).

20 *RSWH* No. 673; Cotton Mather, *Wonders,* 250.

21 Sewall, *Diary,* 1:695.

22 *RSWH* No. 673; Cotton Mather, *Wonders,* 250.

23 *SVW,* 267–68.

7. Andover

First epigraph from *RSWH* No. 419/*SWP* No. 59.4; second epigraph from *RSWH* No. 525/*SWP* No. 9.4.

1 Bailey, *Historical Sketches of Andover,* 202.

2 Martha's brother Andrew Allen, in whose house the Carriers stayed, died of small-pox in 1690 (Roach, "Biographical Notes," 927).

3 *RSWH* No. 235; *SWP* No. 24.3.

4 See Rosenthal's note to *RSWH* No. 419.

5 *RSWH* No. 419/*SWP* No. 59.4.

6 *RSWH* No. 424/*SWP* Nos. 87.5, 87.7.

7 *RSWH* No. 428/*SWP* Nos. 87.2, 87.3.

8 *RSWH* No. 428/*SWP* Nos. 87.2, 87.3.

9 *RSWH* No. 503/*SWP* No. 26.1.

10 Calef, *More Wonders,* 372.

11 This chapter is largely based on Richard Latner's excellent analysis in his article "Here Are No Newters." See also Latner's "The Long and Short of Salem Witchcraft." Basic background to the Andover accusations may be found in Bailey, *Historical Sketches of Andover.*

12 Bailey, *Historical Sketches of Andover,* 422.

13 Robinson, *Salem Witchcraft,* 274–75.

14 *RSWH* No. 749/*SWP* No. 172.9

15 Thomas Brattle explained the theory of the touch test in the following way: "The Salem Justices . . . do assert, that the cure of the afflicted persons is a natural effect of this touch. . . . [T]he account they give of it is this; that by this touch, the venemous and malignant particles, that were ejected from the eye, do, by this means, return to the body whence they came, and so leave the afflicted persons pure and whole" ("Letter," 171).

16 *RSWH* No. 749/*SWP* No. 172.9.

17 Latner, "There Are No Newters," 110.

18 Stout, *New England Soul,* 89.

8. Confessions

First epigraph from *RSWH* No. 753/*SWP* No. 80.4; second epigraph from *RSWH* No. 433/*SWP* No. 107.20; third epigraph from Brattle, "Letter"; fourth epigraph from *RSWH* No. 750/*SWP* No. 96.3.

1 D. Hall, *Worlds of Wonder,* 189–90.

2 See page 40 in this volume.

3 *RSWH* Nos. 67, 89/*SWP* Nos. 69.1, 70.1.

4 See Calef, *More Wonders,* 349, 352, 376.

5 *RSWH* Nos. 25, 33; Lawson, *Brief and True Narrative,* 159–60.

6 See Norton, *In the Devil's Snare,* 118–19; *RSWH* Nos. 68, 70, 72/*SWP* Nos. 69.8, 69.9, 69.5.

7 *RSWH* No. 67/*SWP* No. 69.1.

8 *RSWH* Nos. 75, 145/*SWP* Nos. 135.1, 135.4.

9 *RSWH* No. 145/*SWP* No. 135.4.

10 *RSWH* No. 676/*SWP* No. 68.19.

11 Hale, *Modest Inquiry,* 424.

12 P. Miller, "Judgment of the Witches," 197.

13 Hale, *Modest Inquiry,* 424.

14 Cotton Mather to Richards, in *Selected Letters,* 35–40; cf. Murrin, "Coming to Terms," 337–38.

15 *RSWH* Nos. 173, 174/*SWP* No. 137.5, 137.6. See Rosenthal's note to *RSWH* No. 173.

16 *RSWH* No. 425/*SWP* No. 87.5.

17 Brattle, "Letter," 182.

18 *RSWH* Nos. 258, 480, 261/*SWP* Nos. 113.2, 78.11, 30.2. Mercy Lewis later claimed that she had "perswaded hir to confess" at Churchill's examination (*RSWH* No. 134/*SWP* No. 78.16). The record of Churchill's examination is not extant.

19 Ingersoll and Andrews's statement for Sarah Churchill is not formally addressed to the court, but it had become part of the court's records, indicating that it had been received.

20 *RSWH* Nos. 399, 480, 478, 479/*SWP* Nos. 113.3, 78.10, 78.4, 78.5.

21 *RSWH* Nos. 433, 428, 429/*SWP* Nos. 107.20, 87.2, 25.2.

22 In the case of reluctant defendants, Bernard endorsed "threat[s] with imprisonment and death" to make them confess, even the use of torture (*Guide to Grand-Jury Men,* 239–40), as did Perkins (*A Discourse of the Damned Art of Witchcraft,* 204).

23 *RSWH* No. 745/*SWP* No. 167.6.

24 *RSWH* No. 753/*SWP* No. 80.4. There is a notation in a list of witnesses against John Willard that "Willard diswaded from confession Sarah Churchill and Margaret Jacobs" (*RSWH* No. 295/*SWP* No. 137.14). This suggests that while in jail Willard tried to talk Churchill and Jacobs out of confessing or tried to convince them to retract their confessions, which Jacobs did.

25 Hutchinson, *History of the Colony and Province of Massachusetts-Bay*, 30. Jacobs's examination took place on May 11, but the record is not extant.

26 *RSWH* No. 512/*SWP* No. 80.3.

27 Calef, *More Wonders*, 366.

28 *RSWH* No. 712/*SWP* No. 44.6.

29 *RSWH* No. 654/*SWP* No. 45.25.

30 *RSWH* No. 655/*SWP* No. 113.16.

31 *RSWH* No. 745/*SWP* No. 167.6.

32 Brattle, "Letter," 174.

33 Rebecca Eames, Abigail Faulkner Sr., Ann Foster, and Abigail Hobbs were tried and condemned on September 17 but not sent to the gallows.

34 Roach, *Gallows and Graves*, 16.

35 Cotton Mather, *Selected Letters*, 40.

36 The recantations recorded by Increase Mather are those of eight Andover women: Mary Osgood, Eunice Frye, Deliverance Dane, Abigail Barker, Mary Tyler, Sarah Wilson Sr., Mary Bridges Sr., and Mary Marston.

37 Increase Mather, postscript to *Cases of Conscience*.

38 Brattle, "Letter," 189.

39 *RSWH* No. 696/*SWP* No. 167.2.

40 Names and ages of the children who confessed: Dorothy Good, from Salem Village (5), and from Andover, Sarah Phelps (10), Rose Foster (13), Sarah Carrier (8), Thomas Carrier Jr. (10), William Barker Jr. (14), and Mary Bridges Jr. (13).

41 As previously indicated, Mather had successfully negotiated the terms of the new charter for Massachusetts. He also nominated the new governor and the members of the Governor's Council, most of whom were his friends, and several were serving as judges on the Court of Oyer and Terminer.

42 See *RSWH* No. 712/*SWP* No. 44.6. If Brattle and Mather did visit the Salem jail together, their visit occurred sometime between the end of September, when Mather finished *Cases of Conscience*, and October 8, when Brattle wrote his "Letter" revealing that coercion had been used to obtain confessions.

43 *RSWH* No. 699/*SWP* Nos. 139.1, 17.2, 96.2.

44 *RSWH* No. 699/*SWP* No. 131.1.

45 The four confessors were Rebecca Eames, Abigail Faulkner, Abigail Hobbs, and Mary Lacey Sr.

46 Calef, *More Wonders*, 382.

47 P. Miller, "Judgment of the Witches," 197–98.

48 Calef, *More Wonders*, 375–76.

49 Hale, *Modest Inquiry*, 416. Hale completed his manuscript in 1698; it was published posthumously in 1702.

9. The Apparition and Trial of George Burroughs

Epigraph from *RSWH* No. 457/*SWP* No. 22.18.

1 Boyer and Nissenbaum, *Salem Possessed*, 55.

2 Norton, *In the Devil's Snare*, 100, 129–30.

3 Upton, *Devil and George Burroughs*, 38–49.

4 Ibid., 48.

5 *RSWH* No. 519/*SWP* No. 103.1.

6 See Rosenthal, *Salem Story*, chap. 7.

7 See, for example, *RSWH* Nos. 424, 425, 429/*SWP* Nos. 87.5, 87.2, 25.2.

8 *RSWH* No. 126/*SWP* No. 22.34.

9 Norton, *In the Devil's Snare*, chap. 4.

10 The ten accused: Sarah Good, Sarah Osborne, Tituba, Dorothy Good, Martha Cory, Rebecca Nurse, Rachel Clinton, Sarah Cloyce, Elizabeth Procter, and John Procter.

11 Lawson, *Christ's Fidelity*, 94–95; Parris, *Sermon Notebook*, 197.

12 *RSWH* Nos. 85, 122/*SWP* Nos. 22.28, 22.26.

13 *RSWH* Nos. 85, 122/*SWP* Nos. 22.28, 22.26; Cotton Mather, *Wonders*, 219.

14 *RSWH* No. 97/*SWP* No. 22.3.

15 Norton, *In the Devil's Snare*, 141–43.

16 *RSWH* No. 120/*SWP* No. 22.4; Upton, *Devil and George Burroughs*, 42.

17 *RSWH* No. 77/*SWP* No. 69.3.

18 Cotton Mather to John Cotton, dated August 5, in *Selected Letters*, 40–41.

19 *RSWH* Nos. 452, 453, 454, 455/*SWP* Nos. 22.8, 22.6, 22.5, 22.7.

20 Cotton Mather, *Wonders*, 215–22.

21 Mather's words are a paraphrase of Ady's *Candle in the Dark*, 11, as, perhaps, was the passage that Burroughs introduced as his defense in court.

22 Cotton Mather, *Wonders*, 222; see also Burr's note on the same page.

23 Cotton Mather, *Wonders*, 219–20.

24 Calef, *More Wonders*, 360–61.

25 Hale, *Modest Inquiry*, 420–21.

26 *RSWH* Nos. 931, 934/*SWP* Nos. 173.47, 173.48.

10. Samuel Parris, "the Beginner and Procurer"

First epigraph from *SVW*, 299; second epigraph from *SVW*, 308.

1 Upham, *Salem Witchcraft*, 2:502.

2 Boyer and Nissenbaum, *Salem Possessed*, 167.

3 Gragg, *Quest for Security,* xviii.

4 *OED:* "an agent, spokesperson, or advocate"; also "a prime mover; an instigator *of* something."

5 *SVW,* 279.

6 *RSWH* No. 366/*SWP* No. 12.5.

7 Parris, "Church Record Book," 23–24; *SVW,* 296.

8 John Tarbell was married to Rebecca's daughter Sarah Nurse, and Peter Cloyce was married to Rebecca's sister Sarah Towne.

9 Parris, "Church Record Book," 19; *SVW,* 284.

10 "Church Record Book," 17; *SVW,* 282–83.

11 *SVW,* 258.

12 Parris, *Sermon Notebook,* 219, 230, 267, 284, 290, 313.

13 Parris, "Church Record Book," 23; *SVW,* 296.

14 Ibid.

15 For an excellent treatment of this subject, see Winship, *Seers of God,* chap. 6.

16 Parris, *Sermon Notebook,* 201, 203.

17 See M. Hall, *Last American Puritan,* 263.

18 Parris, *Sermon Notebook,* 211.

19 "Church Record Book," 23; *SVW,* 297, 296.

20 Parris, *Sermon Notebook,* 2.

21 Ibid., 197.

22 "Church Record Book," 25; *SVW,* 266, 297, 298.

23 *RSWH* No. 244/*SWP* No. 94.17.

24 *RSWH* No. 245/*SWP* No. 106.13.

25 *SVW,* 297, 298, 296, 266.

26 See *RSWH* No. 109, and following/*SWP* No. 92.27.

27 Grund et al., "Linguistic Introduction," 66.

28 *RSWH* No. 285/*SWP* No. 94.4.

29 "Church Record Book," 24; *SVW,* 297.

30 "Church Record Book," 24; *SVW,* 298.

31 *SVW,* 266, 299.

32 Parris, "Church Record Book," 25; *SVW,* 298–99.

33 Parris, "Church Record Book," 34–36; *SVW,* 308.

34 Roach, "That Child, Betty Parris," 16–21.

35 Latner, "Here Are No Newters," 118–20; Ray, *Satan's War,* 94.

11. Blame and Shame

First epigraph from Phips, "Letters of Governor Phips," February 21, 1693; second epigraph from Sewall, *Diary,* 1:366–67; third epigraph from Wigglesworth, "Letter"; fourth epigraph from "Church Record Book," 47; fifth epigraph from *RSWH* No. 931/*SWP* No. 173.47.

1 "Church Record Book," 25; *SVW,* 298.

2 Increase Mather, *Cases of Conscience,* 1, 41–42.

3 Ibid., A3, 66.

4 *Wonders of the Invisible World* was published in Boston in mid-October 1692; *Cases of Conscience* was published in November 1692. Both books were postdated to 1693 to conform to Governor Phips's ban on publications discussing the witch trials.

5 Increase Mather, postscript to *Cases of Conscience.*

6 McCarl, "Spreading the News," 56–57.

7 Willard, *Some Miscellany Observations,* 4–5, 15.

8 Cotton Mather, *Wonders,* 213.

9 Cotton Mather, *Selected Letters,* 43.

10 Cotton Mather, *Wonders,* 211.

11 Norton, *In the Devil's Snare,* 289. Spectral evidence was thereafter ignored. Even a deposition filed in Ipswich in early November, based on the spectral evidence given by the persistent Elizabeth Hubbard who accused three more women, failed to be taken up by Hathorne, Gedney, and Corwin in Salem (*RSWH* No. 707/*SWP* No. 46.3).

12 Cotton Mather, *Wonders,* 35.

13 See P. Miller, "Judgment of the Witches," 196.

14 Phips, "Letters of Governor Phips," 197, 198.

15 Baker and Reid, *New England Knight,* 155; cf. Norton, *In the Devil's Snare,* 237–38, 269.

16 *RSWH* Nos. 319, 320.

17 Calef, *More Wonders,* 382–83.

18 Phips, "Letters of Governor Phips," 201–2.

19 *RSWH* No. 824.

20 *RSWH* No. 721/*SWP* No. 168.1.

21 Love, *Fast and Thanksgiving Days,* 264; see *RSWH* No. 727.

22 Love, *Fast and Thanksgiving Days,* 265.

23 Sewall, *Diary,* 1:356. The raid, which was successful, took place on September 20–29, 1696.

24 Love, *Fast and Thanksgiving Days,* 265–69; see Sewall, *Diary,* 1:361n23. See also Cotton Mather, *Diary,* 1:211.

25 Love, *Fast and Thanksgiving Days,* 269.

26 Sewall, *Diary,* 1:366–67.

27 One hundred and fifty years later, Nathaniel Hawthorne apologized for the brutal

role of his ancestors William Hathorne and John Hathorne as justices in Salem. William was a renowned persecutor of Quakers, and John the equally renowned persecutor of alleged witches. In the introduction to *The Scarlet Letter,* Hawthorne wrote, "I, the present writer, as their representative, hereby take shame upon myself for their sakes, and pray that any curse incurred by them . . . may be now and henceforth removed" (Hawthorne, "The Customs House: Introductory to 'The Scarlet Letter,'" 10).

28 Hutchinson, "Witchcraft Delusion," 413–14.

29 Phips had died of a fever in London in February 1695.

30 Norton, *In the Devil's Snare,* 279.

31 Calef, *More Wonders,* 387–88.

32 Cotton Mather, *Diary,* 1:216.

33 "Church Record Book," 25; *SVW,* 299.

34 "Village Record Book," entries for the years 1701 and 1702.

35 Green, "Church Record Book," February 14, 1703, 34.

36 *Records of the First Church in Salem,* 173, 219.

37 Ibid., 219.

38 Upham, *Salem Witchcraft,* 2:509–10.

39 Green, "Church Record Book," August 25, 1706, 47. Ann signed her apology as "Anne Putnam."

40 Assuming an average forty-week gestation period, Elizabeth Procter would have conceived her child in late April or early May when she and her husband, John, were in jail together in Boston. Elizabeth was then forty-five years old. Her pregnancy would have been obvious to her by mid-August and presumably known to John before he was executed on August 19. The conception date is based on the birth of her son on January 27, 1693 (Perley, *History of Salem,* 2:23).

41 *RSWH* No. 871/*SWP* No. 172.1.

42 *RSWH* No. 875/*SWP* No. 172.6.

43 *RSWH* No. 876/*SWP* No. 172.5.

44 *RSWH* No. 878/*SWP* No. 172.7.

45 Wigglesworth, "Letter." The letter is dated in the old calendar style, "5 month, 22 day, 1703," which is July 22, 1703, in the modern calendar.

46 *RSWH* Nos. 881, 882/*SWP* Nos. 172.10, 172.11.

47 *RSWH* No. 931/*SWP* No. 173.95. Compensation was granted to Elizabeth Procter on February 19, 1712, the year in which she died (*RSWH* No. 959/*SWP* No. 173.80).

48 *RSWH* No. 931/*SWP* No. 173.95.

49 *RSWH* No. 899/*SWP* No. 173.12.

50 "Will of Gyles Coaree," Massachusetts Registry of Deeds, Southern Essex County, Historic Records, Book 9 (July 25, 1692): 46.

51 Calef, *More Wonders*, 361.

52 *RSWH* No. 884/*SWP* No. 173.5.

53 *RSWH* No. 836/*SWP* No. 163.3. See also Phips, "Letters of Governor Phips," February 21, 1693.

54 *RSWH* Nos. 903, 840/*SWP* No. 173.16.

55 As quoted in Upham, *Salem Witchcraft*, 2:472–73.

56 See Roach, *Salem Witch Trials*, 580–81; see also Upham, *Salem Witchcraft*, 2:470; and Bentley, *Diary*, 2:26.

57 *RSWH* Nos. 902, 973/*SWP* No. 173.17.

58 *RSWH* No. 794.

59 The last names cleared were those of Bridget Bishop, Susannah Martin, Alice Parker, Wilmot Redd, and Margaret Scott. The bill itself never mentioned the executions of 1692 (188th General Court of the Commonwealth of Massachusetts, *Session Laws: Acts of 2001*, "An Act Relative to the Witchcraft Trial of 1692 [House, No. H2752] Approved by the Acting Governor, October 31, 2001").

12. Mapping the Salem Witch Trials

First epigraph from *SVW*, 297; second epigraph from Nathaniel Hawthorne, "Alice Doane's Appeal."

1 *SVW*, 297.

2 Calef, *More Wonders*, 299.

3 Norton, *In the Devil's Snare*, 8.

4 For a full tabulation of the names of the accused, their places of residence, and the names of the accusers, see Latner, The Salem Witchcraft Site, www.tulane.edu/~salem.

5 *RSWH*, "Timeline," p. 923.

6 Latner, "The Long and Short of Salem Witchcraft," 146; Latner, The Salem Witchcraft Site, www.tulane.edu/~salem.

7 Latner, "The Long and Short of Salem Witchcraft," 137.

8 See Knowles, "GIS and History."

9 Gladwell, *Tipping Point*, 12.

10 *RSWH* No. 49/*SWP* No. 106.4.

11 *RSWH* No. 220.

12 Gladwell, *Tipping Point*, 11.

13 Dr. John Snow's map of the cholera outbreak of 1848 in London was the first mapping of the geographic spread of a disease and showed how the epidemic spread

outward from its source at the Broad Street water pump (see Johnson, *The Ghost Map*).

14 *RSWH* No. 693/*SWP* No. 163.1.

15 See Boyer and Nissenbaum, *Salem Possessed*, 149; and Norton, *In the Devil's Snare*, 47.

16 Woodward, *Records of Salem Witchcraft*, 1864–65; Boyer and Nissenbaum, *Salem Possessed*, 34.

17 The location of Sarah and William Good's place of residence in Salem Village at the time of Sarah's accusation is unknown. I have placed two o's, representing Sarah Good and Dorothy Good, at the location of the home of Samuel and Mary Sibley, to the right of the east/west dividing line, where the Good family previously lived (see *RSWH* No. 352/*SWP* No. 63.14).

18 Ray, "Geography of Accusations in 1692 Salem Village."

19 Ray, "Satan's War against the Covenant of Salem Village, 1692." Five-year-old Dorothy Good does not count as one of the accused adults.

20 Cotton Mather, as quoted in Pope, *The Half-Way Covenant*, 197.

21 *RSWH* Nos. 313, 418/*SWP* Nos. 13.22, 63.29.

22 Roach, *Gallows and Graves*, 13–14.

23 *RSWH* No. 511/*SWP* No. 44.2.

24 See Sanborn Salem City maps for 1890, 1906, and 1950.

25 Hawthorne, "Main-Street," 95.

26 Brattle, "Letter," 177.

27 Calef, *More Wonders*, 367–68.

28 Hawthorne, "Alice Doane's Appeal," 280.

13. *Indians, Africans, Gender, and the "Black Man"*

First epigraph from *RSWH* No. 3/*SWP* No. 95.2; second epigraph from *RSWH* No. 17/Lawson, *Brief and True Narrative*, 156; third epigraph from Bernard, *Guide to Grand-Jury Men*.

1 Norton, *In the Devil's Snare*, 48–50.

2 *RSWH* No. 234/*SWP* No. 6.3.

3 Brattle, "Letter," 170–71.

4 Samuel Parris was probably paid for the work of his slave John Indian at Ingersoll's tavern (which was located near the minister's house), which would have supplemented his income.

5 Longfellow, *Giles Corey of the Salem Farms*, act 1, scene 3.

6 Putnam, *History of the Putnam Family*, 24.

7 But Putnam did join his in-law Peter Tufts in a complaint against two women, one in Malden and the other in Charlestown, for afflicting Mercy Lewis and Mary Warren.

8 *RSWH* Nos. 79, 84/*SWP* Nos. 136.1, 15.1.

9 See Rosenthal, *Salem Story,* 91.

10 *RSWH* Nos. 395, 414, 415/*SWP* Nos. 66.1, 23.1, no *SWP* for *RSWH* 415.

11 D. Hall, *Witch-Hunting,* 6.

12 Karlsen, *Devil in the Shape of a Woman,* chaps. 3 and 4.

13 Norton, *In the Devil's Snare,* 32; Bernard, *Guide to Grand-Jury Men,* 92–93.

14 Reis, *Damned Women,* 107.

15 Karlsen, *Devil in the Shape of a Woman,* quoting Willard, 176.

16 Tertullian, "On the Apparel of Women," 4:14.

17 Willard, *Compleat Body of Divinity,* 125, 184; Karlsen, *Devil in the Shape of a Woman,* 177.

18 Reis, *Damned Women,* 124, 151–52.

19 *RSWH* Nos. 17, 20/Lawson, *Brief and True Narrative,* 153–54, *SWP* No. 38.10.

20 *RSWH* No. 658/*SWP* No. 130.1.

21 Cotton Mather, *Wonders,* 219–20.

A Note on Court Records, Dates, and Names

1 See Grund et al., "Linguistic Introduction," 66.

2 Brattle, "Letter," 170.

3 *RSWH* No. 875 and note/*SWP* No. 172.6.

4 Upham, *Salem Witchcraft,* 2:462; Norton, *In the Devil's Snare,* 13.

5 Trask, "Legal Procedures Used during the Salem Witch Trials," 54; Rosenthal, "General Introduction," 40.

BIBLIOGRAPHY

Ames, William. *The Marrow of Theology.* Translated and edited by John Dykstra
Eusden. Boston: Pilgrim, 1968.

Bailey, Sarah Loring. *Historical Sketches of Andover, Comprising the Present Towns of
North Andover and Andover, Massachusetts.* Boston: Houghton Mifflin, 1880.

Baker, Emerson, and James Kenses. "Maine, Indian Land Speculation, and the Essex
County Witchcraft Outbreak of 1692." *Maine History* 40, no. 3 (2001): 159–89.

Baker, Emerson W., and John G. Reid. *The New England Knight: Sir William Phips,
1651–1695.* Toronto: University of Toronto Press, 1998.

Bentley, William. "A Description and History of Salem." *Massachusetts Historical
Society, Collections,* 1st ser., vol. 6 (1799): 212–88.

———. *The Diary of William Bentley, D. D.* Vol. 2. January 1793–December 1802.
Salem, Mass.: Essex Institute, 1907.

Bernard, Richard. *A Guide to Grand-Jury Men.* London: Felix Kingston, 1627.

Boyer, Paul, and Stephen Nissenbaum. *Salem Possessed: The Social Origins of
Witchcraft.* Cambridge: Harvard University Press, 1974.

———, eds. *Salem-Village Witchcraft: A Documentary Record of Local Conflict in
Colonial England.* Boston: Northeastern University Press, [1972] 1993.

Brattle, Thomas. "Letter of Thomas Brattle, F. R. S., 1692." In *Narratives of the New
England Witchcraft Cases, 1648–1706,* edited by George Lincoln Burr, 167–90.
New York: Scribner's Sons, 1914.

Breslaw, Elaine G. "Tituba's Confession: The Multicultural Dimensions of the 1692
Salem Witch-Hunt." *Ethnohistory* 44 (Summer 1997): 535–56.

Briggs, Robin. *Witches and Neighbors: The Social and Cultural Context of European
Witchcraft.* New York: Viking, 1996.

Brown, Anne S., and David D. Hall. "Family Strategies and Religious Practice:
Baptism and the Lord's Supper in Early New England." In *Lived Religion in
America: Toward a History of Practice,* edited by Hall. Princeton: Princeton
University Press, 1997.

Calef, Robert. *More Wonders of the Invisible World, or, the Wonders of the Invisible
World Display'd in Five Parts.* London, 1700. Abridged in *Narratives of the New
England Witchcraft Cases, 1648–1706,* edited by George Lincoln Burr, 289–393.
New York: Scribner's Sons, 1914.

Caporael, Linnda. "Ergotism: The Satan Loosed in Salem?" *Science* 192 (1976): 21–26.

Carlson, Laurie Winn. *A Fever in Salem: A New Interpretation of the New England
Witch Trials.* Chicago: Ivan R. Dee, 1999.

"Church Record Book Belonging to Salem Village," 1689–1717. First Church of Danvers Congregational, United Church of Christ. Deposited in the Danvers Archival Center, Danvers, Mass.

Dalton, Michael. *The Countrey Justice.* London, 1618.

Demos, John. *Entertaining Satan: Witchcraft and the Culture of Early New England.* New York: Oxford University Press, 1982.

Eberle, Paul, and Shirley Eberle. *The Abuse of Innocence: The McMartin Preschool Trial.* Amherst, N.Y.: Prometheus, 1993.

Garven, Sena, James Wood, Roy S. Malpass, and John S. Shaw III. "More Than Suggestion: The Effect of Interviewing Techniques from the McMartin Preschool Case." *Journal of Applied Psychology* 33 (1998): 347–59.

Gerbner, Katherine. "Beyond the 'Halfway Covenant': Church Membership, Extended Baptism, and Outreach in Cambridge, Massachusetts, 1656–1667." *New England Quarterly* 85, no. 2 (June 2012): 281–301.

Gladwell, Malcolm. *The Tipping Point: How Little Things Can Make a Big Difference.* Boston: Little, Brown, 2000.

Godbeer, Richard. *The Devil's Dominion: Magic and Religion in Early New England.* Cambridge: Cambridge University Press, 1992.

Gragg, Larry. *A Quest for Security: The Life of Samuel Parris, 1653–1720.* New York: Greenwood, 1990.

Grund, Peter. "From Tongue to Text: The Transmission of the Salem Examination Witchcraft Records." *American Speech* 82 (2007): 119–50.

Grund, Peter, Risto Hiltunen, Leena Kahlas-Tarkka, Merja Kytö, Matti Peikola, and Matti Rissanen. "Linguistic Introduction." In *Records of the Salem Witch-Hunt,* Bernard Rosenthal, general editor, 64–90. Cambridge: Cambridge University Press, 2009.

Hale, John. *A Modest Enquiry into the Nature of Witchcraft.* Boston: Benjamin Elliot, 1702. Abridged as *A Modest Inquiry into the Nature of Witchcraft* in *Narratives of the New England Witchcraft Cases, 1648–1706,* edited by George Lincoln Burr, 399–432. New York: Scribner's Sons, 1914.

Hall, David D. *The Faithful Shepherd: A History of the New England Ministry in the Seventeenth Century.* Chapel Hill: Published for the Institute of Early American History and Culture, Williamsburg, Va., by University of North Carolina Press, 1972.

——, ed. *Witch-Hunting in Seventeenth-Century New England: A Documentary History, 1638–1693.* 2nd ed. Boston: Northeastern University Press, 1999.

——. *Worlds of Wonder, Days of Judgment: Popular Religious Belief in Early New England.* New York: Knopf, 1989.

Hall, Michael G. *The Last American Puritan: The Life of Increase Mather, 1639–1723.* Middletown, Conn.: Wesleyan University Press, 1988.

Hansen, Chadwick. "The Metamorphosis of Tituba, or Why American Intellectuals Can't Tell an Indian Witch from a Negro." *New England Quarterly* 47, no. 1 (March 1974): 3–12.

———. *Witchcraft at Salem.* New York: George Braziller, 1969.

Hawthorne, Nathaniel. "Alice Doane's Appeal." In *The Centenary Edition of the Works of Nathaniel Hawthorne,* 11:266–80. Columbus: Ohio State University Press, 1974.

———. "The Customs-House: Introductory to 'The Scarlet Letter.'" In *The Scarlet Letter: A Romance.* Boston: Ticknor, Reed, and Fields, 1850.

———. "Main-Street." In *The Snow-Image and Other Twice Told Tales.* Boston: Ticknor, Reed, and Fields, 1852.

Hill, Hamilton Andrews. *History of the Old South Church (Third Church) Boston, 1669–1884.* 2 vols. Cambridge, Mass.: Houghton Mifflin, 1890.

Hutchinson, Thomas. *The History of the Colony and Province of Massachusetts-Bay.* 2nd ed. Vol. 2. Edited by Lawrence Shaw Mayo. Cambridge: Harvard University Press, 1936.

———. "The Witchcraft Delusion of 1692." *New England Historic Genealogical Society* 24 (October 1870): 381–414.

Johnson, Steven. *The Ghost Map.* New York: Riverhead, 2006.

Karlsen, Carol F. *The Devil in the Shape of a Woman: Witchcraft in Colonial New England.* New York: Norton, 1987.

Kences, James E. "Some Unexplored Relationships of Essex County Witchcraft to the Indian Wars of 1675 and 1689." *Essex Institute Historical Collections* 120, no. 3 (1984): 179–212.

Knowles, Anne Kelly. "GIS and History." In *Placing History: How Maps, Spatial Data, and GIS Are Changing Historical Scholarship,* edited by Knowles, 1–25. Redlands, Calif.: ESRI Press, 2008.

Konig, David Thomas. *Law and Society in Puritan Massachusetts: Essex County, 1629–1692.* Chapel Hill: University of North Carolina Press, 1979.

Latner, Richard. "'Here Are No Newters': Witchcraft and Religious Discord in Salem Village and Andover." *New England Quarterly* 79, no. 1 (March 2006): 92–122.

———. "The Long and Short of Salem Witchcraft: Chronology and Collective Violence in 1692." *Journal of Social History* 42, no. 1 (Fall 2008): 137–56.

———. The Salem Witchcraft Site. www.tulane.edu/~salem.

Lawson, Deodat. *A Brief and True Narrative of Some Remarkable Passages Relating to Sundry Persons Afflicted by Witchcraft, at Salem Village: Which Happened from*

the Nineteenth of March, to the Fifth of April, 1692. Boston: Benjamin Harris,
    1692. Reprinted in *Narratives of the New England Witchcraft Cases, 1648–1706*,
    edited by George Lincoln Burr, 152–64. New York: Scribner's Sons, 1914.

———. *Christ's Fidelity the Only Shield Against Satan's Malignity*. Boston, 1693.
    Reprinted in Richard B. Trask, *"The Devil Hath Been Raised": A Documentary
    History of the Salem Village Witchcraft Outbreak of March 1692; Together with a
    Collection of Newly Located and Gathered Witchcraft Documents*, 64–119. Rev. ed.
    Danvers, Mass.: Yeoman, 1997.

Longfellow, Henry Wadsworth. *Giles Corey of the Salem Farms*. 1868. In *The
    Complete Poetical Works of Henry Wadsworth Longfellow*. Boston: Houghton
    Mifflin, 1902.

Love, William De Loss. *The Fast and Thanksgiving Days of New England*. Boston:
    Houghton Mifflin, 1895.

Massachusetts Registry of Deeds. Southern Essex County. Historic Records. Books
    9, 13.

Mather, Cotton. *Diary of Cotton Mather*. Preface by Worthington Chauncey Ford.
    2 vols. 1911. Reprint, New York: Frederick Ungar, n.d.

———. *Memorable Providences Relating to Witchcrafts and Possessions*. Boston: R. P.,
    1689.

———. "The Return of Several Ministers Consulted by His Excellency, and the
    Honourable Council, upon the Present Witchcrafts in Salem Village." Single
    unnumbered page printed at the back of Increase Mather, *Cases of Conscience*.

———. *Selected Letters of Cotton Mather*. Edited by Kenneth Silverman. Baton
    Rouge: Louisiana State University Press, 1971.

———. *The Wonders of the Invisible World*. Boston: Sam. Phillips, 1693.

Mather, Increase. *Cases of Conscience Concerning Evil Spirits Personating Men;
    Witchcrafts, Infallible Proofs of Guilt in Such as Are Accused with That Crime*.
    Boston: Benjamin Harris, 1693.

———. *An Essay for the Recording of Illustrious Providences*. Boston, 1684.

McCarl, Mary Rhinelander. "Spreading the News of Satan's Malignity in Salem:
    Benjamin Harris, Printer and Publisher of the Witchcraft Narratives." *Essex
    Institute Historical Collections* 129, no. 1 (January 1993): 39–61.

Miller, Arthur. *The Crucible: A Play in Four Acts*. New York: Viking, 1953.

Miller, Perry. "Judgment of the Witches." In *The New England Mind: From Colony to
    Province*, 197–98. Cambridge: Belknap Press of Harvard University Press, 1983.
    First published 1953 by Harvard University Press.

Moody, Robert Earle, and Richard Clive Simmons, eds. *The Glorious Revolution
    in Massachusetts: Selected Documents, 1689–1692*. Boston: Colonial Society of
    Massachusetts, 1988.

Murdock, Kenneth Ballard. *Increase Mather: The Foremost American Puritan.* Cambridge: Harvard University Press, 1925.

Murrin, John M. "Coming to Terms with the Salem Witch Trials." In *The Enduring Fascination with Salem Witchcraft,* 309–47. Worcester, Mass.: American Antiquarian Society, 2003.

Norton, Mary Beth. *In the Devil's Snare: The Witchcraft Crisis of 1692.* New York: Knopf, 2002.

Oxenbridge, John. *New England Freemen Warned and Warmed to Be Free Indeed, Having an Eye to God in Their Elections in a Sermon Preached before the Court of Election at Boston on the Last Day of May, 1671.* Cambridge, Mass.: 1673.

The Oxford English Dictionary. www.oed.com/.

Parris, Samuel. *The Sermon Notebook of Samuel Parris, 1689–1694.* Edited by James F. Cooper Jr. and Kenneth P. Minkema. Boston: Colonial Society of Massachusetts, 1993.

Patton, Anthony. *A Doctor's Dilemma: William Griggs and the Salem Witch Trials.* Salem, Mass.: Salem Witch Museum, 1998.

Perkins, William A. *A Discourse of the Damned Art of Witchcraft.* Cambridge: Cantrel Legge, 1610.

Perley, Sidney. *The History of Salem, Massachusetts.* 3 vols. Salem, Mass.: Essex Institute, 1924–28.

Peterson, Mark A. "Ordinary Preaching and the Interpretation of the Salem Witchcraft Crisis by the Boston Clergy." *Essex Institute Historical Collections* 129 (January 1993): 84–102.

Phips, William. "Letters of Governor Phips to the Home Government, 1692–1693." In *Narratives of the New England Witchcraft Cases, 1648–1706,* edited by George Lincoln Burr, 191–202. New York: Scribner's Sons, 1914.

Pope, Robert G. *The Half-Way Covenant: Church Membership in Puritan New England.* Princeton, N.J.: Princeton University Press, 1969.

Putnam, Eben. *A History of the Putnam Family in England and America.* Salem, Mass.: Salem Press, 1891.

Ray, Benjamin C. " 'Candy No Witch': Two African Slaves Caught Up in the Salem Witch Trials of 1692." *Newsletter.* Carter Woodson Institute of African and Afro-American Studies, University of Virginia, April 2, 2009.

———. "Geography of Accusations in 1692 Salem Village." *William and Mary Quarterly,* 3rd ser., vol. 65, no. 3 (July 2008): 449–78.

———. "The Salem Witch Mania: Recent Scholarship and American History Textbooks." *Journal of the American Academy of Religion* 78, no. 1 (2010): 40–64.

———. "Satan's War against the Covenant of Salem Village, 1692." *New England Quarterly* 80, no. 1 (March 2007): 69–95.

————. " 'They Did Eat Red Bread Like Mans Flesh': Reports of Witches' Meetings in Salem Village in 1692." *Common Place* 9, no. 4 (July 2009). www.common -place.org.

Records and Files of the Quarterly Courts of Essex County, Massachusetts. Edited by George Francis Dow. 9 vols. Salem, Mass.: Essex Institute, 1911–75. http://salem .lib.virginia.edu/Essex/index.html.

The Records of the First Church in Boston 1630–1868. Edited by Richard D. Pierce. Vol. 39. Boston: Colonial Society of Massachusetts, 1961.

The Records of the First Church in Salem Massachusetts, 1629–1736. Edited by Richard D. Pierce. Salem, Mass.: Essex Institute, 1974.

Records of the Salem Witch-Hunt. Bernard Rosenthal, general editor. Cambridge: Cambridge University Press, 2009.

Reis, Elizabeth. *Damned Women: Sinners and Witches in Puritan New England.* Ithaca, N.Y.: Cornell University Press, 1997.

Roach, Marilynne K. "Biographical Notes." In *Records of the Salem Witch-Hunt,* Bernard Rosenthal, general editor, 925–64. Cambridge: Cambridge University Press, 2009.

————. *Gallows and Graves: The Search to Locate the Death and Burial Sites of the People Executed for Witchcraft in 1692.* Watertown, Mass.: Sassafras Grove, 1997.

————. "Records of the Rev. Samuel Parris, Salem Village, Massachusetts, 1688– 1696." *New England Historic Genealogical Society* 157 (January 2003): 6–30.

————. *The Salem Witch Trials: A Day-by-Day Chronicle of a Community under Siege.* New York: Cooper Square, 2002.

————. " 'That Child, Betty Parris': Elizabeth (Parris) Barron and the People in Her Life." *Essex Institute Historical Collections* 124 (January 1988): 1–27.

Robinson, Enders A. *Salem Witchcraft and Hawthorne's "House of the Seven Gables."* Bowie, Md.: Heritage, 1992.

Rosen, Barbara. *Witchcraft in England, 1558–1618.* Amherst: University of Massachusetts Press, 1991.

Rosenthal, Bernard. "General Introduction." In *Records of the Salem Witch-Hunt,* Bernard Rosenthal, general editor, 15–43. Cambridge: Cambridge University Press, 2009.

————. *Salem Story: Reading the Witch Trials of 1692.* Cambridge: Cambridge University Press, 1993.

————. "Tituba's Story." *New England Quarterly* 71 (June 1998): 190–203.

The Salem Witchcraft Papers: Verbatim Transcripts of the Legal Documents of the Salem Witchcraft Outbreak of 1692. Edited by Paul Boyer and Stephen Nissenbaum. 3 vols. New York: Da Capo, 1977. Revised, corrected, and augmented by Benjamin C. Ray and Tara S. Wood. http://salem.lib.virginia.edu, 2011.

Sewall, Samuel. *The Diary of Samuel Sewall*. Edited by M. Halsey Thomas. 2 vols. New York: Farrar, Straus and Giroux, 1973.

Simmons, Richard C. "The Founding of the Third Church in Boston." *William and Mary Quarterly*, 3rd ser., vol. 26, no. 2 (April 1969): 241–52.

Spanos, Nicholas P. "Ergotism and the Salem Panic: A Critical Analysis and an Alternative Explanation." *Journal of the History of Behavioral Sciences* 19, no. 4 (1983): 1390–94.

Spanos, Nicholas P., and Jack Gottlieb. "Ergotism and the Salem Village Witch Trials." *Science* 194 (1976): 1390–94.

Stout, Harry S. *The New England Soul: Preaching and Religious Culture in Colonial New England*. New York: Oxford University Press, 1986.

Tertullian. "On the Apparel of Women." Translated by S. Thelwall. In *The Ante-Nicene Fathers*, vol. 4. 1885. Peabody, Mass.: Hendrickson, 2004.

Trask, Richard B. *"The Devil Hath Been Raised": A Documentary History of the Salem Village Witchcraft Outbreak of March 1692; Together with a Collection of Newly Located and Gathered Witchcraft Documents*. Rev. ed. Danvers, Mass.: Yeoman, 1997.

———. "Legal Procedures Used during the Salem Witch Trials and a Brief History of the Published Version of the Records." In *Records of the Salem Witch-Hunt*, Bernard Rosenthal, general editor, 44–63. Cambridge: Cambridge University Press, 2009.

Upham, Charles W. *Salem Witchcraft; With an Account of Salem Village, and a History of Opinions on Witchcraft and Kindred Subjects*. 2 vols. 1867. Reprint, New York: Frederick Unger, 1959.

Upton, Gilbert. *The Devil and George Burroughs: A Study in Seventeenth Century Justice*. London: Wordwright, 1997.

"Village Record Book." "A Book of Record of the Severall Publique Transactions of the Inhabitants of Salem Village Vulgarly Called the Farmes 1672–1713." *The Historical Collections of the Danvers Historical Society*, 1924–31. http://salem.lib .virginia.edu/texts/tei/SalVRec.

Vital Records of Danvers, Massachusetts, to the End of the Year 1849. Salem, Mass: Essex Institute, 1909–10.

Vital Records of Salem, Massachusetts, to the End of the Year 1849. Vols. 1–6. Salem, Mass: Essex Institute, 1916–25.

Wigglesworth, Michael. "Letter." *Collections of the Massachusetts Historical Society*, 4th ser., vol. 8:646.

Willard, Samuel. *A Compleat Body of Divinity*. 1726. Edited by Edward M. Griffin. New York: Johnson Reprint Corporation, 1968.

———. *Some Miscellany Observations on Our Present Debates Respecting Witchcrafts,*

in a Dialogue between S. & B. by P. E. and J. A. Philadelphia: Printed by William
Bradford for Hezekiah Usher, 1692. http://salem.lib.virginia.edu/texts/willard
/index.html.

Winship, Michael P. *Seers of God: Puritan Providentialism in the Restoration and
Early Enlightenment.* Baltimore: Johns Hopkins University Press, 1996.

Woodward, W. Elliot. *Records of Salem Witchcraft, Copied from the Original
Documents.* 2 vols. Roxbury, Mass.: W. Elliot Woodward, 1864.

Woolf, Alan. "Witchcraft or Mycotoxin? The Salem Witch Trials." *Journal of
Toxicology: Clinical Toxicology* 38, no. 4 (June 2000): 457–60.

Young, Christine Alice. *From "Good Order" to Glorious Revolution: Salem,
Massachusetts, 1628–1689.* Ann Arbor, Mich.: UMI Research Press, 1980.

INDEX

historiography: of accusations of witchcraft, 205–7; of geography of witch-hunt, 187–88; of Salem witch-hunt, 2, 3–5; of Tituba, 33, 197, 201–2; and use of court records, 9, 210

Hoar, Dorcas (accused), 118

Hobbs, Abigail (accused): accused Burroughs, 137–38; accused Eames, 125; on Burroughs, 140; confession of, 59, 88–89, 115–16, 120

Hobbs, Deliverance (accused): accused Burroughs, 89, 137–38; accused Sarah Good, 90; confession of, 116–17

Hubbard, Elizabeth: accusations ignored by magistrates, 229n11; accused Burroughs, 101, 137–38; accused Tituba, 35; afflicted, 27, 48; affliction as turning point for witch-hunt, 70–71; attempt to discredit, 63–64; background of, 44–45, 49. *See also* afflicted girls

Hutchinson, Joseph, 63–64

Indian raids, connection to witch-hunt, 3, 37, 53, 86, 134–35, 136, 198–201. *See also* First Indian War; Second Indian War

Ingersoll, Sarah, 121–23

Ireson, Mary (accused), 61–62

Jacobs, George, Sr. (accused), 62, 121–22

Jacobs, Margaret (accused): accused Burroughs, 124; accused George Jacobs Sr., 124; acquittal of, 125; confession and recantation of, 124–25

John Indian, 34; as accuser, 57; afflicted, 201; ethnicity of, 197; hired out to Ingersoll's tavern, 201, 232n4; and witch cake, 28

Johnson, Elizabeth, Jr. (accused), 91; confession of, 123–24

Johnson, Elizabeth, Sr. (accused), confession of, 123–24

judges on Court of Oyer and Terminer. *See* Richards, John (judge); Sewall, Samuel (judge)

justices in Salem who conducted examinations. *See* Corwin, Jonathan (magistrate); Gedney, Bartholomew (magistrate); Hathorne, John (magistrate); Higginson, John (magistrate)

King Philip's War, 86, 140, 198, 199

King William's War, 4, 86, 140, 197, 198, 199

Lacey, Mary, Jr.: accused, 107; accused Eames, 125; confession of, 108, 120–21

Lacey, Mary, Sr.: accused, 91, 107; confession of, 108

Latner, Richard, 23–24, 180–82

Lawson, Rev. Deodat: on afflicted's behavior, 29, 51–52, 57, 73–74, 97, 185; attacked by Satan, 135; as minister of Salem Village, 17; on number of witches, 184; sermon on satanic plot in Salem, 41–42, 98; visit to Salem, 41; wife and daughter as alleged victims, 41, 61, 100, 135, 136, 141; and witches' meetings, 87–88

legal proceedings: accusations escalated, 89–90; atypical, 72–73; conflict between government and clergy, 78–80; convictions, 77–78; and Goodwin case, 71–72; initial complaints, 71; and *maleficium*, 50, 77, 80; use of spectral evidence, 71, 77, 78–84

Lewis, Mercy: accused Black, 203; accused Burroughs, 137–38; accused Churchill, 121–22; accused Mary Esty, 59–60; accused George Jacobs Sr., 121; afflicted, 53; background of, 44–45, 53; coerced Churchill's confession, 122; description of witches' meeting, 87; description of

Lewis, Mercy (*continued*)
   witches' meetings, 98–99; and Indian
   raids, 199. *See also* afflicted girls
Longfellow, Henry Wadsworth, 201–2

magistrates: on credibility of afflicted,
   64; guided afflicted's performance,
   49–51, 64–65, 73, 200; intimidated
   children, 115; made afflicted a public
   spectacle, 46; reliance on Goodwin
   case, 50; request for Samuel Parris's
   assistance, 152; use of atypical legal
   procedure, 185–86; use of leading
   questions, 38–39, 93, 108, 118; use
   of spectral evidence, 62, 167; use of
   torture to get confessions, 108–9. *See
   also* Corwin, Jonathan (magistrate);
   Gedney, Bartholomew (magistrate);
   Hathorne, John (magistrate);
   Higginson, John (magistrate)
maleficium, 50, 77, 80
maps: geography of accusations in Salem
   Village, 189; proportion of church
   members among individuals accused
   of witchcraft in Salem Village, 191;
   Regional Accusations Map, 183, 185
Martin, Susannah (accused), 83
Mather, Rev. Cotton: accepted testimony
   about witches' meetings, 93; account
   of bewitching, 26, 27; and afflicted
   girls, 29; attended Burroughs's
   execution, 141–42; on Burroughs,
   134, 135, 136, 138, 139, 140–41; on
   confessions, 119–20; on Court of
   Oyer and Terminer fighting satanic
   plot, 160; critical of spectral evidence,
   159; defense of Court of Oyer and
   Terminer, 11, 157–58, 159, 160; defense
   of trials, 65, 160; on executions, 127;
   and Goodwin case, 26–27, 47–48,
   71–72; on own role in trials, 167–68;
   publication of *Wonders of the Invisible
   World* by, 157–58, 159–60, 229n4;

relationship with Stoughton, 76–77;
   on spectral evidence, 78–79, 82–83,
   119, 140–41; on touch test, 79, 112;
   on validity of confessions, 131–32;
   on witch-hunt related to number
   of unbaptized, 190–91; writings on
   witchcraft and demonic possession,
   148
Mather, Rev. Increase: advised on
   charter and governor, 68; on
   Burroughs, 135, 136, 139, 141; on
   coerced confessions, 129–30; on
   confessions, 127–28; criticism of
   Court of Oyer and Terminer, 84,
   130, 156–57, 161; criticism of spectral
   evidence, 10–11, 127–28, 149, 151–
   52, 156–57; criticism of touch test,
   127–28; explanation of witch-hunt,
   155; informed about torture, 123;
   on Margaret Jacobs, 129; on John
   Procter, 129; publication of *Cases
   of Conscience* by, 156–58, 229n4;
   visit to Salem jail, 129–30; writings
   on demonic possession, 148; wrote
   postscript for *Wonders of the Invisible
   World,* 157–58
McCarthy, Joe, 13
meningitis, 4
Milborne, Rev. William, 81, 163
Miller, Arthur, 13, 59, 202
*More Wonders of the Invisible World.
   See under* Calef, Robert
Moulton, John, 175

Newton, Thomas (attorney general):
   on Candy, 205; and Churchill's
   confession, 122; on Sarah Good, 30;
   and Abigail Hobbs, 90; and spectral
   evidence, 80; on Tituba's confession,
   35, 36, 40, 217n12; use of Samuel
   Parris's depositions, 150; use of
   Thomas Putnam's depositions, 100–
   101; and Mary Warren, 90

Nissenbaum, Stephen: on causation of witch-hunt, 2–3; on geography of witch-hunt, 3, 24, 188

Norton, Mary Beth: on connection between witch-hunt and Indian raids, 4, 53, 136–37, 140, 198–99; on court records, 211; on gender, 44, 206; on spread of accusations, 180; on Stoughton, 76

Noyes, Rev. Nicholas: coerced Churchill's confession, 122; day of fasting and prayer in Village, 168; on executions, 195; at Sarah Good's execution, 195; ordination of Samuel Parris by, 19; support of afflicted, 70

Nurse, Rebecca: accused, 42, 51, 53, 55–57, 60, 101; dispute with Putnam family, 55; excommunication of, 169; excommunication cleared, 169; execution of, 13–14, 98; financial compensation of, 177; Nathaniel Putnam's support for, 203; trial of, 63

Nurse family, opposed Parris, 146–48, 152–53

Osborne, Sarah, accused, 29–30, 31–32, 34, 36, 49

Osgood, Mary (accused), coerced confession of, 129

Oxenbridge, Rev. John, 17, 20, 21

Parker, Alice (accused), 104

Parker, Mary (accused), 62, 104

Parris, Betty: accused Tituba, 35; afflicted, 25, 47; and Sarah Good, 30–31; having no standing in court, 70; sent away to Salem Town, 29, 43. *See also* afflicted girls

Parris, Rev. Samuel: and afflicted as public spectacles, 48; aided prosecution, 35, 40, 101, 144–45, 146, 150–53; apology of, 156, 168; arrival in Salem Village, 18; attacked by

Satan, 135; attack on Nurse family, 145–46; attempt to quiet afflicted, 72; background of, 17–18; beat Tituba to confess, 6, 35–36; controversy over parsonage, 18, 24, 86; deposition against Nurse, 150–51; errors in his court documents, 152–53; fueled witch-hunt, 150–53; Halfway Covenant, rejection of, 21, 22, 95, 190–91; on Abigail Hobbs's confession, 116; increased number of witches, 184; left Village, 153–54; official complaint against, 149–52; opposition to, 22, 70, 145, 146–54, 190; ordination of, 18–19; and Betty Parris, 64–65; as persecuted, 10; process of removal of, 146–48; and Putnam family, 95–96; relationship with Williams, 45; response to opponents, 147–49; as sacramentalist, 19–24; satanic attack on Salem, claim of, 5–6, 23, 25, 27, 38, 40, 42, 145, 149–50, 189; sermon of reconciliation, 149; on spectral evidence, 149, 150–52, 153; used afflicted girls to advantage, 29; and Village reprobate, 23; and Williams, 64–65; on witch-hunt as plague, 179

Perkins, Rev. William, 35, 79, 158

Phelps, Sarah, 102, 109

Phillips, Rev. Samuel, 19

Phips, William: arrival in New England, 67, 68, 74–76, 185; attempt to legitimize Salem witch-hunt, 11; ban on publications about witch trials, 158, 163, 229n4; closed Court of Oyer and Terminer, 149, 159–60; on Court of Oyer and Terminer, 162–63; death of, 230n29; denial of authorizing confiscation of property, 175; and end of trials, 2; excused himself from blame, 162–63; explanation of trials to London, 162–64; request for defense

of, 7; historiography of, 2, 3–5, 9, 187–88, 205–7; legacy of, 13–14; legal proceedings atypical, 67–70; as plague, 179–80, 183; reliance on spectral evidence in, 8–9; as Satan's plan to subvert church, 5–6, 7–8, 52, 53, 67, 77, 80–81, 91–92; spread of, 7, 59, 105, 180, 183

Salem Witch Trials Documentary Archive, 9–10, 12–13, 209

Saltonstall, Nathaniel (magistrate), 161–62

Sanderson, Robert, 35

Scott, Margaret (accused), 104

second-generation preachers, 19, 74, 76–77, 112

Second Indian War, 4, 86, 140, 197, 198, 199

Sewall, Samuel (judge), 82; Burroughs's examination of, 139; on death of Giles Cory, 102–3; public apology of, 166–67; support of public fast day, 165; wrote bill for fast day, 165

Sewall, Stephen, as clerk of Court of Oyer and Terminer, 100, 210

Sheldon, Susannah: accusations of, 61–62; Burroughs's examination of, 139–40; and Indian raids, 200

Sibley, Mary, 28, 49

Sibley, Samuel, 57

spectral evidence, 50, 106, 108, 156–57, 181, 186–87; criticism of, 10–11, 81–84; endorsement of magistrates, 62; prominence of, 62–65; questioned, 62; reliance on, 37; and witch-hunt spread, 186–87

Sprague, Martha, 102

Stoughton, Rev. William (judge): attempt to legitimize Salem witch-hunt, 11; Burroughs's examination of, 139; as chief magistrate, 76–78; and escalation of trials, 182; executions rushed by, 131; legal proceedings

rushed by, 84; protected George Corwin, 176; relationship with Cotton Mather, 76–77; reliance on afflicted's testimony, 46; reliance on spectral evidence, 62, 77–78, 79–80; requests defense of Court of Oyer and Terminer, 157, 159; on Samuel Sewall's apology, 167

Superior Court of Judicature, 126; established, 163; rejection of spectral evidence, 125

Tituba, 33–43; accused, 29–30, 32, 49; accused Sarah Good, 36, 37, 38, 39; accused Osborne, 36, 37, 38, 39; announcement of satanic plot, 34, 36, 39, 40, 114–15; beaten by Parris, 35–36; and case dismissal, 43; confession of, 6, 33–34, 71, 114–15, 217n12, 218n25; denial of witchcraft, 34–35; description of leader of plot, 37–38; ethnicity of, 197, 201–2; historiography of, 33; on number of witches, 184; set precedent for confessions, 40–41; and witch cake, 28; and witches' meetings, 86–87, 114–15

Toothaker, Margaret (accused), 106

Toothaker, Mary (accused), 91, 106

touch test, 4, 11, 79, 83, 108, 111–12, 127, 151–52, 157, 200, 210, 224n15

Tyler, Johanna (accused), 208

Tyler, Mary (accused), coerced confession of, 130

Upham, Rev. Charles W., 95, 144, 171, 187, 192–95, 202, 211

Walcott, Jonathan, 138

Walcott, Mary: accused Black, 203; accused Burroughs, 137–38; afflicted, 49, 51–52; background of, 44–45. *See also* afflicted girls